Rapture Culture

Rapture Culture

Left Behind *in Evangelical America*

AMY JOHNSON FRYKHOLM

OXFORD
UNIVERSITY PRESS

OXFORD
UNIVERSITY PRESS

Oxford University Press, Inc., publishes works that further
Oxford University's objective of excellence
in research, scholarship, and education.

Oxford   New York
Auckland   Cape Town   Dar es Salaam   Hong Kong   Karachi
Kuala Lumpur   Madrid   Melbourne   Mexico City   Nairobi
New Delhi   Shanghai   Taipei   Toronto

With offices in
Argentina   Austria   Brazil   Chile   Czech Republic   France   Greece
Guatemala   Hungary   Italy   Japan   Poland   Portugal   Singapore
South Korea   Switzerland   Thailand   Turkey   Ukraine   Vietnam

Copyright © 2004 by Oxford University Press, Inc.

First published in 2004 by Oxford University Press, Inc.
198 Madison Avenue, New York, New York 10016

First issued as an Oxford University Press paperback, 2007

www.oup.com

Oxford is a registered trademark of Oxford University Press, Inc.

Library of Congress Cataloging-in-Publication Data
Frykholm, Amy Johnson, 1971–
Rapture culture : left behind in Evangelical America / Amy Johnson Frykholm.
    p.   cm.
Includes bibliographical references and index.
ISBN 978-0-19-515983-7; 978-0-19-533567-5 (pbk.)
1. LaHaye, Tim F. Left behind series.   2. Christian fiction, American—History and criticism.
3. Protestantism and literature—History—20th century.   4. Antichrist—History of doctrines—
20th century.   5. Apocalyptic literature—History and criticism.   6. Rapture (Christian
eschatology)   7. End of the world in literature.   8. Evangelicalism in literature.   9. Second
Advent in literature.   10. Eschatology in literature.   I. Title.
PS3562.A315 L4434 2004
813'.54—dc22   2003011258
Rev.

9 8 7 6 5 4 3 2 1
Printed in the United States of America

For Peter and Samuel. Né bi fè. I ni tíe.

Acknowledgments

Bakhtin's insistence that "language, for the individual consciousness, lies on the borderline between oneself and the other" seems
particularly appropriate to the act of acknowledgement. There are
many people whose words, thoughts, and ideas are found on these
pages who cannot always be acknowledged within these conventions, but for whose contributions I am grateful nonetheless.

I would like to thank in particular Janice Radway for her insightful reading, well-timed challenges, and for always seeing this project
as more than it was. Her confidence made it possible. Thanks and
admiration also go to Wahneema Lubiano for the depth of her analysis, William D. Hart for his philosophical interventions, Wesley Kort
for his literary imagination and open door, and Susan Willis for her
frank and original assessments of the work as it progressed. All of
my dissertation committee members at Duke University in the literature program and the religion department provided vision and encouragement at critical moments. I would also like to thank the
Charlotte Newcombe Foundation for their institutional and financial
support at the dissertation stage of this manuscript.

I am grateful to Colleen McDannell for her careful reading of
the manuscript and for pushing me to become a better listener of
the readers. Thank you to Cynthia Read at Oxford University Press
for her thoughtful examination of the manuscript. I am also grateful
to Megan Sweeney for her critical insights and generous imagination.

I would like to thank Peter Frykholm for his patience in repeated readings of the manuscript, his committed belief, and for going with me on adventures along the way. For their love and support I am grateful to Jason Johnson, Sarah Hankerson, Kirsten Heidel, the Frykholm clan, and especially my parents, Tom and Michele Johnson.

Finally, I would like to thank Rick and Marian Johnson, whose hospitality, afternoons laughing at the antics of Buster Brown, and willingness to talk about life and faith gave shape and inspiration to this project. All the readers of *Left Behind* who shared their stories and gave their time will, I hope, not be too disappointed.

Contents

Rapture Culture

Introduction

The narrative of the rapture, drawn from the tradition of Christian
fundamentalist apocalypticism, has achieved unprecedented popularity through a recent series of evangelical adventure novels called *Left
Behind*. More than 50 million copies have been sold; the series has
spawned companion comic books, movies, children's books, and au-
dio tapes, as well as a radio drama, a large Internet fan club, and a
revival of controversies within evangelicalism about the particularities of what scholars call dispensationalist premillennialism. Beginning with the fifth book, *Apollyon*, each addition to the series (there
are twelve in all, with two additional series planned) skyrocketed to
the top of every major best-seller list in the United States. The books
have become a publishing phenomenon, surprising their publishers,
their authors, scholars, and industry analysts. Conceived by long-
time evangelical prophecy writer Timothy LaHaye and written by
evangelical fiction writer Jerry Jenkins, *Left Behind* has brought this
religious "subculture" fully into the mainstream.

Left Behind is a series of apocalyptic novels that traces the last
seven years of life on earth. It begins with something called the rapture. In the rapture, Jesus secretly returns to earth and gathers to
him all believers. As they are taken to heaven, the world they leave
behind is plunged into chaos. Cars and airplanes crash; buildings
crumble; people search in vain for loved ones. As the series continues over the seven years that believers in this apocalyptic tradition
call the tribulation, the world suffers plagues and famine. A dictator,

the Antichrist, emerges as world leader and tortures and kills those who oppose him. At last, Christ comes again. This time, he comes in glory, defeats the Antichrist, and reigns over the earth.

The purpose of this book is to examine the audience of *Left Behind*. Using qualitative methods, I examine who the readers are, how they understand the significance of the books, and how they formulate religious beliefs in light of or in contradiction to their fictional reading. I examine the place of dispensa-tional premillennialism in American culture, arguing that it must be under-stood as a fluid part of the broader culture, not as the realm of isolated believers. Readers of *Left Behind* speak of both fear and desire in their relationship to the apocalyptic themes of the series. Only by examining these intertwined themes can we comprehend the complexity of the series and its significance in popular culture.

The origins of this project are, as with most scholarly work, personal. As I write about how the rapture comes to life in texts and audiences, and in the interactions between texts and audiences, I am writing about friends and family for whom the rapture is a tangible hope and a pressing reality. As I write, in my mind's eye I see my grandmother's *Scofield Reference Bible*, a text from which she read every day of her life, a text that told her of the coming of the rapture. I write not only as literary scholar and researcher, but as granddaugh-ter, cousin, and niece. I tell not only the story of strangers, but also the story of my own family. To fail to acknowledge this would be to engage, as Charles Strozier says, in a kind of "false positivism" that remains all too prevalent in our scholarly practices.[1]

My parents both converted to evangelical Christianity as children, but by the time I was born, they had abandoned many facets of their conservative and evangelical upbringing. They no longer believed in literal readings of the Bible and had given up an emphasis on "asking Jesus into your heart" to receive salvation. Even so, evangelicalism had thoroughly shaped their worldviews, and so shaped mine. As a teenager, I became deeply involved in an evangelical church. I served as youth group president and as a counselor at numerous crusades and youth rallies.

This evangelical church, Trinity Baptist in Sioux Falls, South Dakota, was an important place as I forged my identity. I found confirmation and affir-mation there. I built strong friendships and important connections. At the same time, the church provided a context for my questions. I argued passion-ately with leaders about whether or not Jesus drank real wine, about whether it was acceptable to listen to secular music, and whether women should be ordained as ministers. Early on, I was angered by the black-and-white rhetoric of the rapture. At a youth retreat in high school, we watched Don Thompson's film *Thief in the Night,* and rather than being frightened by the possibility of the rapture, I was inflamed by the thought that fear might be used to motivate belief. This was my earliest confrontation with the themes presented in this book, and the anger I felt that day might be the very seed out of which this book grows.

In a way apropos to this project, it might be said that I read my way out of evangelicalism. In high school, feminist reading had the strongest effect on me and provided the context for my break from Trinity Baptist. My father gave me a book written by feminist evangelical Virginia Mollencott called *Women, Men, and the Bible.*[2] I became fascinated with the idea of feminist biblical scholarship. Always outspoken, I became passionate on this subject and quickly found trouble. The first incident occurred at a summer camp when a respected minister came to speak to the youth about vocation. He drew a chart on the board showing the clear, hierarchical, divinely ordained relationship between men and women. He said, "Someday you will be spiritual leaders; someday you will be the wives of spiritual leaders." I walked out. Later I summoned the courage to speak to him about what had so profoundly disturbed me. I remember the coldness in his eyes as he looked past me and refused, in the end, to talk at all. I tried to share my sense of growing alienation with others and found no one to engage me.

The second incident occurred while teaching Sunday school to third graders in my senior year of high school. Fresh from my reading of Mollencott, I told my Sunday school class, "Some people think of God as their mother." A woman walking by our open classroom door heard what I said and came in. "That's blasphemy," she said. The third-graders looked at me wide-eyed. I tried a futile argument before she stormed out and our lesson was over. Afterward, one of the children came up to me. "Is that really in the Bible?" he asked. "Yes," I told him, "it is," even as I felt my own doubts rise.

These two incidents, among others, made me increasingly uncomfortable with my own place in evangelicalism, and although the break was neither easy nor clean, I eventually, predominantly on feminist grounds, distanced myself from it. Evangelicalism and feminism became for me untenable companions, and my commitment to one faded of necessity as my commitment to the other grew. The years following drew me deeper into feminist scholarship—both feminist theology and secular feminist theory. I retained a strong sympathy for religious people and especially for religious language. I was intrigued, and remain intrigued, by religious forms of community and religious visions of social life.

This project in particular was born some years later on a winter day in North Carolina. My fiancé and I drove to Jacksonville to visit an aunt and uncle of mine whom I had not seen in several years. When we moved from Seattle to North Carolina for graduate school, I had long postponed a visit to them mostly out of fear that we would find it impossible to communicate. To my mind, our paths could not have been more different. Mine had led me to secular, feminist, and sometimes Marxist commitments in the academy. Theirs had led them to a conservative and traditional religious faith that coexisted with conservative politics. As we drove through Jacksonville on our way to their rural church, we passed tattoo parlors and pawnshops, and I realized that my sense of alienation was rooted not only in religious faith, but also in social and economic differences. This was a foreign land to me, a place where I was inevitably an outsider, if not an outcast. My fiancé and I coached each other on topics of conversation. We had to avoid both religion and politics, we decided. But what would we say if they asked us where we went to church? Did they know we were living together without being married? Would we find anything to say to each other at all? We censored ourselves, hoping that censorship might prevent conflict and even promote connection.

When we arrived at their church, my aunt and uncle were both inside preparing for the service, and we sat down in a pew toward the back. My uncle was filling in to preach that day. My aunt was singing in the choir. When the service began, my aunt smiled at us, and my uncle introduced us to the congregation. After the service, we lingered a long time so that we could be introduced to nearly every one of the church members.

Later we drove to their mobile home nestled among oak and pine alongside a creek where my uncle spends hours in his boat fishing, dreaming, and reading. Their home sits on land that has been in my aunt's family for generations. We stood outside for several minutes while my aunt showed us the damage Hurricane Fran had done to their trees. Inside, we ate pot roast and, to my surprise and relief, the conversation flowed. We talked honestly about our jobs and frustrations, about stress and money. We laughed at my uncle's description of the new satellite dish he had bought and promptly returned because it had too many channels. "We spent too many evenings pressing the channel button on the remote," he said, "until I thought we were going to lose our minds." I was moved by their hospitality, by how happy and comfortable we felt in their home, by the laughter we were able to share. My fears began to dissipate as we found genuine connection.

After that particular Sunday, we visited my aunt and uncle often. We sat on the beach together, played volleyball, and shared meals. I grew to appreciate their easy hospitality and the strong connection they had to their religious community. The church we had visited on that first Sunday was a second home for them. They often spent more nights a week there than they did in their own home, and their friendships and relationships were vital and strong. I found myself able to look past our political and religious differences to a genuine admiration for the loving way they lived.

I was introduced to *Left Behind* in this context and became interested in the series because of the intense pleasure my aunt and uncle described in reading them. To what extent, I wondered, was the series fiction to them? To what extent was it an expression of religious truth? How did they integrate the reading of the novels into their daily lives and their religious practices? I was introduced to *Left Behind* in 1997, just before the series became nationally popular, while it was still known only to a relatively small group of mostly evangelical readers and sold mostly in Christian bookstores. Over the next five years, I watched the series grow into a national phenomenon; sales shifted into what had been considered a "secular market" and books sold their largest numbers at retailers like Costco, Sam's Club, and national chain bookstores such as Barnes and Noble. In this context, the question of who *Left Behind*'s readers are becomes more pressing. *Left Behind*'s popularity calls into question basic assumptions about the division between religious and secular marketplaces and about American popular culture more broadly.

This book explores the reading and interpretation practices of readers of *Left Behind*. I spent three years interviewing readers and visiting readers' churches, homes, Bible studies, and Sunday school classes. I conducted a qualitative study of thirty-five in-depth personal interviews—each one lasting between one and three hours. If they were part of a religious body, I also attended readers' churches and visited Sunday school classes, often more than once. Because *Left Behind* was an increasingly important part of popular culture during this time, I had no trouble identifying several readers through colleagues and friends with whom to begin my project. Once I had identified a small group of willing participants, I employed what cultural anthropology calls the "snowball method," allowing these readers to lead me to other readers. In this way, I interviewed evangelical and nonevangelical readers, believers in the rapture, and those who did not believe. I interviewed Mormons, Catholics, Baptists, Presbyterians, agnostics, and others with less definable labels. These interviews took place over three years, predominantly in the Southeast, but also in the Northeast and in Colorado.

By using qualitative methods with and against the literary texts, I foreground what Ien Ang describes as "the diverse, the particular and the unpredictable in everyday life." Ang asserts that this kind of academic work is "especially suitable to free us from the desperate search for totalizing accounts of 'the audience.' "[3] Academic accounts of evangelicalism have often been guilty of this kind of totalizing, a process that leads to dismissal on the one hand and demonization on the other.[4] This project attempts to give both a sympathetic and a critical listening to evangelical people and the texts with which they engage.[5]

While I cannot say I became intimate with the participants in the way an ethnographer does who logs hundreds of hours in the field, I did accept hospitality, sip coffee and eat cinnamon rolls, cry when participants told me their stories, and listen through their own tears. Even after only a few hours, I grew to like most of the people I interviewed immensely and to dislike others with similar intensity. In other words, as is inevitable with ethnographic methods, I became personally involved. I feel now a commitment to both accuracy and kindness as I tell their stories. Part of the power of ethnographic methods is the obligation and intimacy that is built through personal encounter. Once I have heard someone's story or received someone's hospitality, my commitment to them, regardless of ideological, political, or religious differences, grows along with my sympathy.

As my work progressed, I felt an increasing disjunction between the interviews I was conducting and the books I was reading. I found the interviews normally insightful, moving, and rich while I found the books narrow, socially and theologically ill conceived, sometimes enraging and sometimes dull. Through the stories people told me I could see the various ways they made sense of the texts in the intricacies of their lives and relationships. I could tangibly sense the way that apocalyptic language and belief in the rapture gave them hope, both cultivated and assuaged fear, and compelled them toward compassion for the world. I was intrigued by the way readers often formed community bonds through reading and used those bonds to support and encourage one another.

Met with the richness of readers' lives, I was repelled by what I saw as the shallowness of the books' characters. Met with the textures of readers' relationships, I was offended by what appeared to me as the pat answers and single-minded political agenda of the novels. While my dislike for the books grew, readers expressed enormous pleasure in them. Readers described their interactions with the books primarily in metaphors of eating. "Reading is like eating a chocolate sundae, or let's say a chocolate-covered cherry. You got to bite into it and go through all the layers before you get to the cherry part," Carissa told me, describing her love of "biting" into the novels.[6] Betty did not savor the novels in the same way Carissa suggested. She "devoured" them, but she also compared them to chocolate. "I couldn't read them fast enough. It was like a chocolate bar that is put in front of you . . . and you just keep eating . . . you know what I mean? And you can't, you can't . . . I was just devouring them. I was really hungry." This description of pleasure, whether savoring or devouring, was nothing like my own experience reading the novels.[7] I read them with a pencil in my hand, making notes in the margins, able to sustain my interest for only a few minutes at a time. I found them painful to read and even more painful to write about.

In the end, I could not resolve the tension between my dislike for the books and my appreciation of their readers. I did, however, consciously try to connect to the concerns, fears, and hopes that readers found expressed in the novels with my own interpretations of the landscape of American culture. In this way, I tried to bridge the gap that our very different orientation to the books opened up. These fictions have become a part of the world readers inhabit and the world they construct for themselves; they have become imbedded in what anthropologist Clifford Geertz calls the "webs of significance" of peoples' lives. To understand why this is so and how it happens is part of understanding the work that pleasure reading does, how it aids people in the project of making meaning.[8]

The question of how reading becomes a part of the process of making meaning is not a scientific one for me, and this book is not a piece of social science. I do not attempt to find the answers in sociological survey data or generalizations about readers and their reading practices. This is a study founded on the particularities of readers and their social networks. As such, it has all of the limits of that kind of study—it cannot see the larger picture, it lacks numbers for proof, its methods are attached to details rather than to broad strokes. But it claims the benefits as well—the richness and detail of "thick description," the sympathy that only particularity can build, and the revelation of complexities often obscured by more generalizing methods. Ethnographic methods, at their best, should disconfirm our assumptions and discomfort us with the complexity with which human beings construct their social worlds. They should detotalize, rather than sum up. Ethnography should allow for readers to speak about real concerns of their everyday lives, and should turn us, at least temporarily and partially, from critics to listeners.

Listening, however, is not a transparent or neutral position, as I quickly discovered. When I began this project, I struggled with how to present myself to readers. I was not sure what of my own history to tell. I was afraid, quite frankly, of shutting down avenues for openness by declaring my own distance from evangelicalism. In my very first interviews, I said little or nothing about my own background and history, leaving readers to fill in this silence however they saw fit. It became rapidly evident, however, that I was creating a problem. As I sat across the table from an interviewee in my very first session and she talked openly and movingly about her life, she said, "When you and I go in the rapture...." I did not stop the flow of the conversation to tell her that I did not think I would go in the rapture, nor did I tell her later about my own religious views. I simply let the comment pass. I quickly learned that saying nothing was a liability and not a strength. It put the interviewee in an awkward and confusing position and often closed off the very openness I was trying to create.

With some hesitation, I decided to try a new approach. At the beginning of the interview, I offered my own story, my own history in evangelicalism and separation from it. I expressed vulnerability and tried to reassure the interviewee that I had no intention or desire to denigrate readers of *Left Behind*. To my surprise, this speech opened up the conversation. Readers variously positioned themselves toward me. Some used my expression of doubt and vulnerability to express their own doubts. Rather than feeling the need to perform the "good Christian" for me, they felt the freedom to tell me stories they might not have told a fellow church member. On the other hand, others used the interview as an opportunity to "witness" to me, to give their testimonies of faith.

Witnessing was perhaps the most difficult aspect of the interview situation for me. To open oneself to evangelism is to be willing to offer one's own views for critique by someone who has already judged them to be inadequate. It is to set aside, at least partially, one's own agenda and the all-knowing position of the scholar. In interviewing situations, where I saw myself as primarily a strong, attentive listener, it meant I had to listen even as I was being told, however gently, that I was damned. I cannot say that this is an easy position to be in, nor that through the course of interviewing I found it particularly pleasant. But, for many of the people I interviewed, witnessing is an essential part of their Christian faith. In order to understand that faith, I had to be willing to persist in listening even when my salvation, beliefs, and life became the uncomfortable object of the conversation. I am using the word *object* here deliberately because, in many ways, I found witnessing to be an objectifying experience. No matter in what way I articulated or failed to articulate a reasonable position for myself, my lack of belief turned me into an object. In Martin Buber's language, I often felt at these moments that I turned from a "Thou" in the conversation into an "It."[9]

Because I found witnessing to be such a frustrating experience, I myself could not walk into the interviewing situation with a strong agenda. This is not to say that there is such a thing as completely disinterested listening or that I was able to practice it. But I found that listening opened up pathways for communication, allowing readers to express doubt and vulnerability and speak from the complexity of their own experience. There is a kind of listening, crucial to the interviewing situation, in which one allows oneself to be changed, becomes vulnerable to the one who is speaking, and opens up a space in which stories can be told, in which the "I" of the interviewer allows the "Thou" of the person being interviewed to speak. This is the kind of listening I tried to practice in the course of the interviews, with varying results.

Readers of *Left Behind* often narrate the rapture and its particular manifestation in the *Left Behind* series as provoking for them thoughts about ultimate meaning and the ultimate nature of reality. It conjures up fears about their own salvation and the salvation of loved ones while providing a lens through which contemporary life can be understood. Often readers narrate their own interaction with the novels as a spiritual turning point where they realize how pressing and significant God's plan for history is, how imminent the end may be. They feel compelled to share this concern with others, with unsaved or religiously marginal people in their lives who need to know that the rapture is imminent and also with fellow believers who need to share the message. Often this powerful desire to share the story of the rapture means giving away and lending the novels themselves; thus the books are passed through networks of friends, families, churches, and coworkers. In this way, the popularity of the novels and the cosmic story they tell has spread to become a cultural force.

As an account of the end of time and the meaning of human history, rapture is rhetoric. It is used to persuade people of their need for faith and to persuade others of the superiority and rightness of that faith. Stephen O'Leary points out that scholars have for too long ignored this aspect of evangelical eschatology. He notes that "even those rhetorical scholars who attempt to account for the appeal of the apocalyptic never seriously entertain the hypothesis that people are actually persuaded by apocalyptic arguments; that is, that the nature of the apocalyptic's appeal should be sought in transactions of texts and audiences."[10] Seeking the rapture's appeal and the rapture's cultural significance in "the transactions of texts and audiences" helps us to see how the rapture functions as a social text and what meanings are contained in its social exchanges. On the other hand, texts and audiences are not enough. The appeal of *Left Behind* and its meaning are created in the connections among readers who develop the significance of the series in relation with one another and with the text. Furthermore, the appeal of *Left Behind* must be sought still more broadly as part of the American apocalyptic, as an integral part of American culture. The prevalence of the rapture narrative in American culture, its broad and even vast appeal, and its persistence now into its third century deserve careful examination. Here I seek the multiple meanings of the rapture in its multiple transactions—between text and reader, between readers and their social networks, and in the fluid realm of text, reader, and culture.

I

The Rapture in America

Rapture—the prophetic belief that Christ will return to earth to take believers with him—has played a significant role in American popular religion for 150 years. In fiction and in doctrine, in public oration and in private devotion, people have expressed longing, hope, and fear through the story of being taken up to heaven to be with God. The rapture has its origins in ancient apocalyptic narratives of the end of time and in human communion with other worlds, and it extends in contemporary popular imagination into stories about alien visitation and capture. The rapture is woven into the fabric of American culture, a part of the culture's hopes, dreams, fears, and mythology. At the same time, rapture as I will discuss it is specific. It has a specific history and emerges out of a specific religious tradition—Christian fundamentalism. It cajoles, teaches, and inspires believers and adherents, and it contributes to very particular beliefs about the nature and structure of social life.

This narrative's most recent popular manifestation is in the bestselling evangelical apocalyptic series *Left Behind*. Like the narrative from which it is drawn, *Left Behind* engages myths and stories gathered from both the specificity of the fundamentalist and dispensationalist history out of which it most immediately arises and the broader popular apocalyptic culture from which it has drawn its reading public. Both of these facets of *Left Behind* warrant examination, and perhaps more importantly, we need to better understand the relationship between the two—between fundamentalism and American popular culture.

Many critics have noted the importance of the apocalyptic in constructing American mythologies. Lee Quinby, for example, has argued that the apocalyptic is a "regime of truth" that shapes political and social discourse.[1] Similarly, Catherine Keller calls American apocalypticism a "historical habit" and a "cultural performance" that provides the material out of which we make the world.[2] Apocalypticism shapes our stories about America itself and about the direction and meaning of the world. This apocalypticism takes various forms—it fills books, comic books, movies, and television and touches nearly every form of popular culture with which Americans engage. Apocalypticism reaches deep into the history of the American nation, emanating from European conceptions of the "New World" and from the preaching of early Puritan ministers.[3]

Left Behind draws from this broader apocalyptic framework in order to create stories that are familiar to readers. For example, the social life presented in *Left Behind* is similar to many American films and books with apocalyptic themes. *Left Behind* depicts a small group of dedicated believers fighting against larger and more powerful forces of evil. In his classic study of apocalypticism, *Disaster and the Millennium*, Michael Barkun argues that the distinction between a righteous microcosm and an evil macrocosm is crucial to the formation of the apocalyptic. Apocalyptic movements create a microcosm, "an insular social world with distinctive norms and goals." The microcosm simultaneously constructs a macrocosm "perceived as evil, decaying, and doomed."[4] A macrocosm provides reason for the microcosm's existence and contributes to a sense of group identity and cohesion.

Barkun's analysis relies on an assertion that apocalypticism thrives in agrarian rather than urban environments and suggests that apocalypticism will fade as the world grows increasingly pluralistic—yet this does not appear to be the case. Apocalypticism flourishes equally well in urban and rural environments and late capitalism has not yet quelled apocalyptic movements or widespread apocalyptic culture.[5] On the other hand, Barkun makes an important point. Apocalypticism may not require physical separation, but it does require imagined separation from the macrocosm and homogeneity within the microcosm. In order for apocalypticism to thrive, boundaries must be constructed— be they the symbolic boundaries of evangelicalism or the physical walls of the Branch Davidian complex in Waco, Texas. The homogeneity that Barkun insists is important need only be imagined, asserted, and then reinforced by physical or symbolic boundaries.

This separation between microcosm and macrocosm is crucial to the apocalyptic mythology employed by *Left Behind* and evident in broader American apocalypticism. It asks readers to identify themselves with a marginalized minority, as "outsiders" to the evil majority. Historian Laurence Moore argues that construction of oneself as "outside" the mainstream has been a significant part of the construction of American identity since the American Revolution.[6] Evangelicals have made frequent use of this mythology of outsiderhood in the twentieth century, constructing their movement as both broadly popular and paradoxically exiled at the same time. But this is part of a national story as well, told and retold with every movie in the *Star Wars* genre. "We" are perennially the underdogs fighting a holy fight against forces of great evil.

While *Left Behind* readily participates in these broader mythological structures, it is also part of a very specific religious tradition, that of dispensationalist premillennialism. Dispensationalist premillennialism provides the immediate context for the series and the gateway through which the majority of readers enter.

Dispensationalist Belief in American Culture

When I note that *Left Behind* emerges from a dispensationalist and fundamentalist framework, I do not mean that the readers of *Left Behind* should be understood primarily as fundamentalists. The question of who the readers are is a complex one that I will treat in this chapter, but for the moment it is enough to note that, for the most part, they would not identify themselves as fundamentalists. The story line that *Left Behind* follows, however, is unique to the American fundamentalist tradition. This apocalyptic story of rapture and tribulation entered American Protestant Christianity with the teachings of a British itinerant preacher who traveled widely in the United States and Canada from 1862 to 1877. John Nelson Darby preached a form of prophecy called dispensationalism that was widespread in Britain and North America in the nineteenth century.[7] Dispensationalism was the belief that human history was divided into eras or "dispensations" that would culminate with the thousand-year reign of Christ on earth. For dispensationalists, the current age was the Church Age and its end would usher in the final dispensation and the end of human history.[8]

To this prophetic structure, Darby added what historian Ernest Sandeen has noted was a unique element. Darby believed that at the end of the Church Age, all true believers would be taken up to heaven in a "secret rapture." Called by Christ, they would rise through the clouds, leaving behind a world soon to be plunged into chaos.[9] Darby's assertion of the secret rapture became a crucial part of apocalyptic belief for many of those who came to call themselves "fundamentalists" in the twentieth century, and it forms the premise of *Left Behind*. The apocalyptic story of rapture followed by a seven-year tribulation became a distinctive narrative with stock characters and a plot outline. Students of biblical prophecy saw the story as truth, but they also readily indulged its dramatic turns and vivid imagery. Meanwhile, they attempted through study of obscure biblical passages to trace the exact events of the period called the tribulation. They charted earthquakes, wars, plagues, the rise of a figure called the Antichrist, and his eventual demise in the battle at Armageddon. The prophetic narrative emerged as a vivid part of fundamentalist imagination filled in by various interpreters with considerable detail. The story was told in sermons, tracts, testimonies, and occasionally in novels.[10] Every time the story was told, it reminded listeners of their special place in human history or their certain destruction. Dispensational premillennialism, as scholars came to call this form of prophetic belief, made order from seeming chaos, put God in charge of human history, and designated a privileged place for believers.[11] But perhaps just as importantly, dispensationalism provided a dramatic and fascinating narrative that captivated listeners and readers and drew them in with its compelling power.

Many recent cultural critics have demonstrated the ability of narrative to convey and confirm identity, structure understandings of the world, and negotiate meaning. Alisdair MacIntyre, for example, writes, "I can only answer the question 'What am I to do?' if I can answer the prior question 'Of what story or stories do I find myself a part?' We enter human society, that is, with one or more imputed characters—roles into which we have been drafted—and we have to learn what they are in order to be able to understand how others respond to us and how our responses to them are apt to be construed."[12] Fundamentalists in the twentieth century found themselves a part of the cosmic story of rapture and tribulation that helped them interpret their place and activity in the world. They discovered their roles through the interpretation of this apocalyptic narrative.

Darby's use of the word *rapture* was derived from the Latin Vulgate translation of the Greek text of 1 Thessalonians 4:16–17: "For the Lord Himself will descend from heaven with a shout, with the voice of the archangel, and with the trumpet of God; and the dead in Christ shall rise first. Then we who are alive and remain shall be caught up together with them in the clouds to meet the Lord in the air, and thus we shall always be with the Lord."[13] In the Vulgate translation, "caught up" was translated *rapiemur*, from the Latin verb *rapio*. In medieval Latin, *rapio* became a noun, *raptura*, which then became in English "rapture."[14] For Darby, rapture designated the event of the "taking up" of the true church to heaven in the Last Days combined with the religious and emotional ecstasy that the word implied.

Darby's use of the rapture in his interpretation of dispensationalism was, in part, social critique. He used it to assert the existence of an invisible church, known only to God, that stood apart from institutional structures. Only with the rapture would the true church be known and the hypocrites left behind. In this way, Darby criticized the institutional structure of the church claiming special knowledge that church leaders and church hierarchies did not have. Confronted with criticism, Darby charged his opponents with the kind of worldly apostasy he saw in the church.[15] The rapture was also, then, a future source of justification, when Darby would be proven right and the apostate church left behind.

Darby's ideas were not immediately embraced by his North American audience. Rather, Sandeen describes a gradual seeping of the story of rapture and tribulation into American life in the latter decades of the nineteenth century and the early decades of the twentieth century. This happened primarily through the work of laypeople and itinerant preachers rather than established clergy, denominations, or biblical scholars. Believers in the rapture saw themselves as marginal to both the church establishment and to American culture more broadly. As the twentieth century approached, dispensational premillennialism became a form of virulent antimodernism that expressed alienation from the institutional structures of modern life. At the same time, dispensationalism achieved astounding and increasing success as a popular movement. Dispensationalists emphasized evangelism over institutionalization and cast their lot with popular belief rather than church leaders.

This success happened in part because of a text called the *Scofield Reference Bible*. Darbyite Cyrus I. Scofield produced a version of the King James Bible that contained detailed footnotes explaining passages of the Bible drawing largely on Darby's understanding of biblical prophecy. Lyman Stewart, a wealthy dispensationalist, contributed $1,000 toward the publication and distribution of this Bible. Stewart had contributed significantly to the distribution of other dispensationalist texts like William Blackstone's *Jesus Is Coming*, and he embraced Scofield's project, urging him to write a "warning and testimony to English-speaking ministers, theological teachers and students."[16]

The successful publication and distribution of this text and its use in the Bible institute movement that began to flourish around the same time gradually made the *Scofield Reference Bible* standard to American fundamentalism during the first half of the twentieth century.[17] Scofield's innovative use of footnotes rather than a separate commentary intimately linked the biblical text with its prophetic interpretation. For many readers of Scofield's Bible, Darbyite interpretation became indistinguishable from the biblical text; it became part of fundamentalists' assertion of a "common sense" understanding of biblical prophecy.[18] Sandeen writes, "The book has thus been subtly but powerfully influential in spreading [pretribulation] views among hundreds of thousands who have regularly read that Bible and who often have been unaware of the distinction between the ancient text and the Scofield interpretation."[19]

While dispensationalism was a distinctive element of fundamentalism in the twentieth century, it was not uniformly embraced by those who claimed the label "fundamentalist." The Princeton Seminary School of fundamentalism, for example, with representative leaders like Gresham Machen, never accepted dispensationalism as a part of their form of fundamentalism. The dispensationalists staked the power of their story with the people. They did not defer to institutions like Princeton or scholars like Machen but instead fostered the story of rapture and tribulation among popular belief. While dispensationalists developed elaborate charts and systems based on biblical study to explain, justify, and detail their beliefs, they scorned the opinion of university biblical scholars, even fundamentalist scholars, and offered their story to laypeople who enthusiastically embraced it. Again, Bible schools, which offered alternatives to secular universities for Christian young people, played a crucial role in the developing history of the dispensationalist narrative. Bible schools grew rapidly in the 1930s and 1940s, and dispensationalism fit these schools' goals by training future missionaries, teachers, and ministers in personal Bible study. Virginia Brereton writes, "Bible schools have served as a primary vehicle for the dissemination of dispensationalism. The system, with its 'facts,' charts, outlines, proved easy to teach large numbers of students possessing varied educational abilities and backgrounds. Though dispensationalism sounds complex to the outsider, it has made a lot of sense to those who have grown up regarding the Bible as a primary text for human history."[20] Dallas Theological Seminary became a center of dispensational theology. Along with Moody Bible Institute and Wheaton College, Dallas Theological Seminary became what Joel Carpenter calls the movement's "institutional core."[21] At Dallas Theological Seminary, Hal Lindsey learned the basics of dispensationalist prophecy that he translated for a broadly popular audience in *The Late Great Planet Earth*, the best-selling book of the 1970s.

Most scholars of American religion agree that the rapture emerged in American Protestant culture at a moment when conservative Protestants felt a decline of cultural power. Two related trajectories of modernity—urbanization and immigration—began to transform an American landscape that had belonged to the powerful Protestant majority for decades.[22] These two forces portended the decline of traditional life and a loss of a sense of cultural security and control. Between 1865 and 1900, 13.5 million people immigrated to the United States. Many of these were Roman Catholics and Jews. While non-Protestant religious communities were certainly intimidated and exploited by the Protestant majority, Protestants also felt threatened. Historian Timothy Weber suggests that evangelicals began to feel that "something solid had gone out of American life" and that their world was in rapid decline.[23]

Simultaneously, the rise of consumer culture destabilized traditional life as well. Mass manufacturing and mass marketing worked to transform and train desires for goods, for pleasure, and for gratification. Protestantism, which Max Weber argues helped to form the capitalist economy, now found itself at war with what it itself had created. With the expansion of visual and material culture, religion became a "marketplace" where faith was a matter of advertisement and promotion as well as of belief.[24]

Rapidly expanding capitalism and consumer culture put pressure on traditional family structures. Betty DeBerg suggests that rapid change in gender roles was probably the most intense and intimate factor to which the fundamentalist movement responded.[25] Growing urban areas gave women increased social freedom and took women outside the home to work. Women gained currency in the culture as consumers who had purchasing power and were often responsible for the buying habits of their families. Middle-class American family life was undergoing a profound transformation.

In the midst of turmoil over the rapid changes in cultural life that were the result of capitalist expansion, new technologies, scientific discoveries, and large-scale immigration, the narrative of the rapture came to hold an important place. In an atmosphere where conservative Protestants sensed a loss of cultural control, the doctrine of the rapture promised an escape. In a complex and confusing social arena, the rapture divided saved from unsaved. As a vivid story of justification, the rapture became a way for these Christians to reject a disorienting new social terrain. The Antichrist, the suffering of the tribulation, and the battle at Armageddon were all the just desserts of a corrupt modern world and the logical end of modernity's godless ways.

While conservative Protestants objected to the social transformations taking place, they often embraced and advanced the technological changes. Preachers like Dwight L. Moody and Billy Sunday urged churches to build on business models and adapt to cultural and social changes. Conservative Protestants developed mass publishing and mass marketing to appeal to a broadly popular audience and quickly understood the power of these tools for religious life. Rather than retreating in defeat, conservative Protestants were adept at drawing on the tools that urbanization and industrialization brought them and transforming these into resources for cultural influence. Even though the Scopes Trial of the 1920s deeply wounded the fundamentalist movement and branded them in the public eye as rural, backward, and unsophisticated, this characterization never did justice to the powerful understanding of popular media fundamentalist leaders had. As inheritors of the revivalist movement of the nineteenth century, conservative Protestants had long used the latest technological developments and a keen sense of popular culture to promote and defend their beliefs. While largely alienated from realms of cultural power in the middle decades of the twentieth century and playing the role of, as Susan Harding puts it, "the quintessential modern American outsiders," they nonetheless skillfully developed both methods of reaching the people and their own alternative institutions.[26] Fundamentalists, as they came to call themselves, not only used the developing structures of mass culture, they were often innovators, especially in radio and publishing. In this way, largely hidden from the view of institutional structures of power, fundamentalism developed into a thriving popular movement of which the story of rapture and tribulation was a central part.

In the late 1940s and early 1950s some fundamentalists appeared to have grown weary of the movement's sharply separatist rhetoric and began to argue for a "softening" of conservative Protestantism toward the larger culture of which it was an uneasy part. In 1947, Carl Henry, soon to be a founder of Fuller Seminary, published *The Uneasy Conscience of Modern Fundamentalism*. The book criticized fundamentalism for its anti-intellectual and separatist stance. It encouraged another form of conservative Protestantism to emerge. Gradually, out of fundamentalism—but with a new openness toward Charismatics, Pentecostals, Holiness, and others—conservative Protestants developed what we now call "evangelicalism."

Henry believed that if conservative Protestants had hope of broadening their appeal, they would need to soften their stance on dispensationalism. Because dispensationalism was fundamentally a rhetoric of alienation, Henry sought to temper it. Carpenter writes,

> Fundamentalist savants were so certain that the present age was the
> final one, Henry charged, that they seemed to "fall all over each
> other in the rush to make it clear that they have no message which
> is relevant" to the modern predicament. Their outlook on the world
> was counsel for temporal despair; all of their hope was pinned on an
> imminent divine rescue. Henry insisted that the "new evangelical-
> ism" would balance the apocalyptic outlook of fundamentalism with

the message that "while the Lord tarries, the gospel is still relevant to every problem."[27]

Henry's urge to make the gospel "relevant" to the contemporary world was a cry that would be taken up by evangelicals in a variety of forms. Some would follow him in founding a new base for an intellectual evangelicalism; others would push for a socially active form of conservative Protestantism that would directly engage social problems beyond evangelization. Still others vigorously pursued a broad appeal to popular culture. At the same time, dispensationalism did not fade in significance as Henry might have hoped. Instead the story of rapture and tribulation was rearticulated for new generations; the outline of the story was colored with new understandings drawn from contemporary political and social realities. It took on new meanings for its adherents, but it maintained a tenacious grasp on Protestant Christian imagination.

The 1970s brought a string of popular prophetic literature, beginning with Hal Lindsey's *The Late Great Planet Earth*. This book became the best-selling publication of the decade, though its sales occurred almost entirely in Christian bookstores and through Christian distribution systems—in part by missionary organizations on college campuses—and so stayed largely off the radar screen of mainstream publishing. Another example of dispensationalists' savvy use of media was a series of movies made by Don Thompson.[28] In a dispensationalist trilogy that drew on the thriller genre, Thompson aimed his story at young teens, warning them of the dangers of failing to embrace the message of Christ's salvation. While never appearing on mainstream theater screens, the films continue, three decades after their making, to be shown in churches and at youth gatherings for Christian young people.[29] While ignored by mainstream media, these films have played a significant role in a large and thriving alternative popular culture that is only now becoming visible to the broader popular culture.

Left Behind needs to be understood as a part of this long-established tradition—a tradition that has used mass publishing and mass culture to its advantage from a very early day. While *Left Behind* is concerned with "truth," it detaches itself from particular church institutions. For example, readers are urged on the books' Web site to attend church, but they are not given specific denominational guidelines. Instead, they are encouraged to seek out a "Bible-believing" church, a code word for what Brenda Brasher calls "second-wave fundamentalism."[30] While this may mean something very specific to the writers and producers of *Left Behind*, it certainly leaves room for a very broad interpretation. On the other hand, *Left Behind* has become successfully connected to institutions of commercial and media culture. It is perhaps the most successful dispensationalist text ever in this regard, building a large network of retail support that includes Wal-Mart, Sam's Club, Costco, and Barnes and Noble—stores that not only sell, but also promote, its literature. Tyndale House, through the success of *Left Behind*, has grown from a $40 million–a-year enterprise to one worth more than $160 million.[31]

Rapture Readers and Cultural Negotiations

Dispensationalism is and has long been a broadly popular movement that has extended its boundaries beyond the labels—such as fundamentalist—that once seemed to contain it. It has seeped into American popular culture and become a part of belief systems through conscious and unconscious means. Its influence is both broad and diffuse. Because apocalypticism and eschatology have been largely ignored by mainline and liberal Protestant clergy, this has left room for a wide spectrum of popular belief. Believers in the rapture may identify with fundamentalism no more than their clergy, but they are likely to have encountered and even embraced dispensationalism without ever learning its origins or ever attaching these labels to their beliefs.

Readers of *Left Behind* in my study largely understand themselves to be "evangelicals." But this label has little meaning for them. Instead, as we will explore in the next chapter, they seek out a church environment that feels like "home" regardless of its moniker. While they share much in common with previous fundamentalists, they do not often identify with this term. Furthermore, they seem, for the most part, little concerned with what label is used to describe them. Unlike their fundamentalist predecessors, they do not need to identify themselves in a way that provides separation from broader American culture. They see their faith as a distinctive testimony in a relatively hostile and needy world, but they are not interested in setting themselves apart in the ways that were crucial to fundamentalists some decades before.

In recent decades, *evangelicalism* has become a broad term for conservative Protestantism. When the American media first embraced the term in the 1970s to describe a religious movement emerging from underground, it was broad enough to encompass both the "born-again" social activism of Jimmy Carter and the growing therapeutic movement of James Dobson. Gradually, the meaning has become increasingly narrow and identified with the religious and political right, leaving politically left-leaning but still theologically conservative Protestants without a name to call themselves. The use of *evangelical*, however, has served the inheritors of fundamentalism well. It has offered a term without the pejorative connotations of *fundamentalist*, giving them a stronger and more visible place in the culture. At the same time, evangelicalism has entered an American religious picture in which labels of any kind have taken on less and less significance. Robert Wuthnow describes the weakening of denominational ties among American Christians,[32] but my study suggests the weakening of even broader labels like "mainline," "evangelical" and "fundamentalist" as well.

Readers come to *Left Behind* from various social and religious positions. How they respond to the texts, what they make of them, and how they integrate them into their own lives is no more contained by the terms *evangelicalism* or *fundamentalism* than the narrative itself. Readers participate in an often fluid relationship between "Christian fiction," which they acknowledge *Left Behind* to be, and American popular culture more generally. While they might make a moral distinction (*Left Behind* is better for them, more enriching, more spiritually beneficial, etc.), in practice readers rarely separate themselves from books, movies, radio, or TV produced by mainstream culture. A reader could likely read *Left Behind* for a few minutes before bed after having spent an evening watching the latest Bruce Willis movie or intersperse the reading of *Left Behind* with John Grisham's thrillers or Peggy Clark's mysteries. Readers occasionally express anxiety about the influence of secular culture and sometimes roundly condemn it, but rarely does this concern inhibit the buying, renting, or consuming of popular culture in its broadest possible sense. So-called secular culture mixes readily—at least in practice—with Christian culture, and *Left Behind* is a significant part of this mix for many.

While a rhetoric of "difference" and separation from mainstream culture is still significant to many readers, it is difficult to see how this rhetoric finds its way into daily life or cultural practice. For a previous generation of fundamentalists, behavior was an extremely important marker for who was inside and who was outside the community of faith. A strict behavioral code that prohibited drinking, dancing, smoking, watching movies, playing cards, and swearing distinguished the fundamentalist way of life from the condemned outside world.[33] Readers of *Left Behind* share the dispensationalist narrative with these earlier fundamentalists, but they do not share the same need for cultural separation. One reader, Sarah, a woman in her late twenties, expresses acute awareness of this shift in practice because she comes directly out of a fundamentalist tradition.

> I have always respected my parents—you know, as you get older and
> are able to look back, my parents always presented what they be-
> lieved to me as the truth, and the complete truth, but they let me

learn and create my own opinions on things differently. My grandmother adamantly believes that drinking any amount of alcohol, you
know it is not going to send you to hell or anything like that, but it
is a sin. It's a good way to get out of line with God. And my parents
pretty much adamantly believe that and for a long time, I also felt
that way. But as I got older and I started seeing other people and
watching how the world was and developing more my own sense of
spirituality, I was like, for me, drinking is wrong. It convicts me. I've
tried it. To me, being drunk at any point in time is wrong. To me,
drinking at all convicts me. I can't do it, but you know, it is not what
goeth into the body, it is what cometh out of the body. I can honestly
say, being at a wedding and people drinking champagne, that
doesn't bother me. It doesn't tear me to pieces like it would my
grandmother. Literally, it would hurt her so bad, she couldn't stay
there. . . .

I guess it goes back to that: does it interfere with your salvation
at all? This is the big deal, Sarah. Don't cause fights, don't push
people, don't upset people on the issues that don't really interfere
with salvation, like drinking, like interracial marriages, issues that I
think a lot of Christians and a lot of Baptists especially nit-pick on.
Whether I think they are right or wrong doesn't have anything to do
with your relationship with God. If I was in an interracial marriage
and that interfered with my ability to—if that to me was wrong, or if
that interfered with my ability to worship or to live a godly life, then
that would be wrong. But if it didn't, then there is no place to nit-
pick, I don't think, about things like that.

Sarah's two examples—drinking and interracial marriage—demonstrate
the tradition of exclusion and separation from which she comes. She certainly
considers herself as devout as her grandparents and part of the same tradition
of faith. But the distinction that her grandmother makes through practice Sarah
is left to make in other ways. She is aware that her position is marginally more
open than that of both her parents and grandparents, and like many readers,
she places the emphasis on "interference with salvation" and personal choice.
Rather than a collective sense of right and wrong that determines communal
boundaries, Sarah relies on an internal "spirituality" and the ability to discern
for herself how she will apply a behavioral code. She leaves the determination
of what constitutes a "godly life" much more open than, in her view, her parents
and grandparents did. While she sees this as largely a function of thinking
through issues for herself and learning more about the world, we can also view

it as a part of a cultural pattern emerging for contemporary conservative Protestants. Few readers are able to trace their history in fundamentalism as Sarah is able to do, but many believe that behavior is not the final marker of salvation. They are willing to defer to diversity of belief and practice in matters of behavior that do not appear to them as crucial.

Sarah's passing mention of interracial marriage as an issue that Baptists "nitpick on" is especially intriguing. Given the history of racial division from which she comes, Sarah's comment indicates a shift in racial thinking. Something has changed in her universe, something that was not true for her parents and grandparents. Race has become for her an issue somewhat separate from religion. "Whether they are right or wrong," she says, "doesn't have anything to do with God." Interracial marriage appears to be something that Sarah relegates to individual choice. Race is still an issue for her, but interracial marriage is no longer a collective wrong. It is something that can be wrong for an individual and prevent that person from seeking a deep relationship with God. She distinguishes the question of personal salvation, always crucial to fundamentalism, from social mores.

Readers involved in this study come from identifiably evangelical, fundamentalist, mainline, liberal Protestant, Catholic, and Mormon religious positions, but many themselves eschew these labels and others simply defy easy definition. Reading *Left Behind* appears to be something equally shared by men and women, crossing class boundaries and racial boundaries.[34] Oddly for an apocalyptic text, *Left Behind* appears to appeal to commonalties among conservative Christians and taps into a broad and vast popular manifestation of contemporary Christianity. When describing readers of *Left Behind* and attending to their unique stories and circumstances, labels become increasingly less helpful and give way to more complex and nuanced histories.[35]

Left Behind is credited with attracting a significant "crossover" audience— an audience outside of evangelicalism. And there is little doubt that it has, perhaps to an unprecedented degree.[36] On the other hand, we also need to recognize that evangelicalism is an increasingly significant part of American popular culture. Since the 1930s, conservative Protestant membership numbers have grown while those in so-called mainline and liberal churches have fallen. But even more subtly, evangelical language and culture have fused with "secular culture." Scholars identify 10 to 15 million Americans who are "doctrinal" believers in dispensational premillennialism and another 10 to 15 million who are what Susan Harding calls "narrative believers."[37] Paul Boyer suggests that there is an even larger group who, while perhaps unclear on the particulars of the doctrine of dispensational premillennialism, nonetheless "believe that the Bible provides clues to future events." Boyer believes that this group is "susceptible to popularizers who confidently weave Bible passages into highly imaginative end-time scenarios or promulgate particular schemes of prophetic interpretation."[38] I would argue, however, that this nebulous group of which Boyer speaks should be understood not as vulnerable to popularizers like Timothy LaHaye and Jerry Jenkins, but rather as active participants in the creation and use of dispensational premillennialism in contemporary life. Their numbers extend far beyond evangelical denominations into mainline churches and even to people who do not attend church and do not consider themselves "saved." Perhaps *Left Behind* forces us to confront evangelicalism as a central part of American culture, not hidden away in a marginalized sub-culture, but fully engaged in creating and sustaining "general" popular culture. In order to understand *Left Behind's* significance, we need to cease thinking of evangelicalism as an isolated and marginalized subculture that occasionally erupts into popular culture with events like *Left Behind*, even when evangeli-calism's own leaders insist on portraying it as such. Instead, we need to rec-ognize how influential conservative Protestantism has been in shaping the American cultural landscape that we all share.

For many scholars of evangelicalism and fundamentalism, separation and distinction from the world have been key to understanding how conservative religious groups develop a sense of identity and continue to thrive in a modern, pluralistic environment.[39] Scholars have frequently argued that religious groups maintain a distinct identity by drawing a sharp boundary between themselves and an outside, perceptibly hostile world. Recently, sociologist Christian Smith has revised this thesis to explain the popular success of con-temporary evangelicalism. Smith argues that the importance of boundaries in evangelicalism explains why this particular kind of Christian faith thrives while others seem to founder. He distinguishes evangelicalism from fundamental-ism on the one hand and mainline Protestantism on the other. Fundamental-ism, he argues, is too closed. It does not thrive in a modern setting because its boundaries are too rigid. Mainline Protestantism and certainly liberal Prot-estantism falter because they are too open. They no longer make a distinction between themselves and "the world." Smith argues that evangelicalism is strong because it manages to retain a distinction between itself and the outside world. It posits clear boundaries of belief and practice that allow its believers to construct their identities soundly on the distinction of religious faith. Fol-lowing from this sense of distinction is also a sense of threat. The world outside evangelicalism is perceived as not merely secular, but as actively hostile. This hostility, or perceived hostility, is also part of what allows evangelicalism to thrive. "Without [distinction, engagement, tension, conflict and threat], evan-gelicalism would lose its identity and purpose and grow languid and aimless,"

Smith argues.[40] It draws strength from this active, if antagonistic, relationship with "the world." Despite this sense of threat, evangelicalism does not close its boundaries entirely. Instead it participates in what Smith calls "engaged orthodoxy," a participation in the world that allows it an active and meaningful role in American culture.

This theory is problematic, however, because it requires locking into stability phenomena that are considerably more fluid. Respondents are required to wear labels that may or may not fit them.[41] They are required to simplify their commitments, desires, and religious beliefs into statements that can be tallied by researchers, but may do little to describe the religious realms that they construct for themselves. For example, Smith's survey data allows him to conclude that 71 percent of all evangelicals "never have doubts about faith."[42] This statistic is more a result of methodology than a reflection of the interior religious lives of evangelicals. By scratching beneath the surface of a statement such as "I never doubt my religious faith," one can find enormous complexities, insecurities, and fears. A statistic like this implies a stability that seems very unlikely to exist.

Smith's theory of boundaries helps us to see how evangelical rhetoric creates the strong sense of distinction from the world that allows evangelicalism to thrive. On the other hand, this very same theory prevents us from seeing how widespread and influential evangelicalism is in American culture. By focusing on the function of symbolic boundaries, he misses the porous nature of these boundaries and how evangelical belief, symbolism, and especially apocalypticism has seeped out into American culture and extended beyond those who claim the label. Smith's theory also prevents us from seeing how even committed evangelicals are enthusiastic participants in popular culture, consuming movies, television, print media, and other cultural forms along with the rest of the population. The cultural influences are tangled, and evangelicals rarely separate themselves from popular culture even as they occasionally complain about its immoral content.

In other words, Smith creates a totalizing map of evangelical identity that cannot see the intricacies of everyday life and practice. He creates an objectifying picture of evangelical life that ignores broader sociocultural and institutional settings in which evangelicals are situated. It posits the "facts" of evangelicalism using the discourse and tools of empirical science without querying the "discursive horizon they construct, as well as what vanishes beyond that horizon."[43] Beyond the horizon are the complexities of belief and social settings in everyday life, the multiple pulls and influences on contemporary religious subjects and the ways that religious subjects work out these subtleties in the textures of their lives.

Sociologist Wade Clark Roof attends to these problems in his research into the religious lives of baby boomers. Rather than focusing on fixed categories, Roof points out the difficulty of pinning down religious subjectivity. "American religion has long been known for its dynamism and fluidity, its responsiveness to grassroots opinions and sentiments, its creative capacity in relation to the cultural environment. It takes on colors drawn from its surroundings, its boundaries always shifting and porous."[44] Roof's emphasis on this fluidity and flexibility allows him to note the differences that emerge between his survey data and his in-person interviews. Roof found that when he moved from the somewhat abstract survey to the concrete interviewing situation, meanings often shifted significantly. In the interviewing situations, respondents had more freedom to express the complex commitments of their religious lives. For example, a man who called himself a Presbyterian in the survey was flustered by Roof's question about whether he considered himself religious. He eventually turned the question back on Roof, "So, you tell me, am I religious?" Roof was struck by how inadequate his categories for placing the man were. Identifying the man as Presbyterian said little or nothing about the man's religious life, but noting "none" under the category of religious preference failed to account for the compelling meanings religion had for the man he was addressing. The man called into question his own label and perhaps the very act of labeling itself.[45]

Roof's study indicates the importance in studies of religious life of listening carefully to how people describe themselves, of allowing religious belief to be flexible even within fairly rigid denominational structures. Roof's discussion of the "dynamism and fluidity" of American religion also helps us conceptualize how dispensational premillennialism exceeds the boundaries of the religious communities in which it was conceived and becomes a part of widespread popular belief. People move in and out of the boundaries of evangelicalism, in and out of its apocalyptic beliefs. Millions of people have come into contact with evangelicalism and been shaped by it in some way. Millions have had "born-again" experiences at some point in their lives. The meaning they make from these experiences and from this contact varies widely and shifts with the passage of time. In order to understand the broad appeal of the rapture, and of its particular manifestation in *Left Behind*, we need to think in fluid and shifting categories. The boundary model may not be the best one for understanding the subjectivity of readers of *Left Behind*, their form and continual re-creation of American evangelicalism, and their participation and influence in American culture.

Evangelicalism's stance toward the wider world changed considerably in the late twentieth century. Rather than maintaining strict boundaries, evangelicals began to use these boundaries strategically and rhetorically. Susan Harding explains, "The cultural walls of separation were torn down but not destroyed in the 1980s. They were miniaturized, multiplied and internalized."[46] Evangelicals became more fully engaged in American culture and American politics, being changed even as they exerted considerable influence. While the rhetoric of leaders often remained distinctly hostile to the general culture, the practice of believers became increasingly integrated.[47] The religious subjectivity of readers of *Left Behind* is constitutive of both rhetoric and practice, at times conjoined and at times disparate. It moves in a dynamic relation with both religious faith and a seemingly secular broader culture.

Negotiated Texts

Like its readers, *Left Behind* must make its way through a complex terrain of culture, positioning itself both in opposition to that culture and in negotiation with it. *Left Behind* is part of a tradition of rapture fiction that dates to the early part of the twentieth century.[48] Since at least 1905, dispensationalists have told the story of rapture and tribulation through novels. They have hoped to depict the "truth" by means of fiction in order to explain this complex eschatology to believers and in order to win converts. The tradition of rapture fiction is virulently antimodern and antiworldly. Its heroes and heroines are largely out of step with the modern world and unable to make their homes in it. In nearly all cases, those who convert to Christianity after the rapture are the victims of the Antichrist and his regime. They suffer passively as the cosmic scheme is played out.

While *Left Behind* shares in this tradition, it also departs from it in many ways. The series opens with a scene of rapture. Pilot Rayford Steele is flying from New York to London when he receives word that passengers have "disappeared" from the plane, leaving behind their clothing and personal possessions. Because of his Christian wife's warnings, Rayford knows immediately that the rapture has taken place. After the rapture, the story follows the lives of several characters who, like Rayford, have been left behind. They convert to Christianity and band together to form a group called the Tribulation Force. The core group consists of Rayford, his daughter Chloe, a newspaper reporter named Buck Williams who eventually marries Chloe, and Rayford's wife's former minister, Pastor Barnes. As the Tribulation Force battles the Antichrist's regime, many characters come in and out of the group, and they face persecution, plagues, earthquakes, and many other disasters.

A significant amount of traditional dispensationalist theology and prophecy has gone into the construction of *Left Behind's* narrative. Timothy LaHaye has long written on prophecy from a dispensationalist perspective and remains traditional in his approach. The story begins with rapture and follows the characters through seven years of tribulation. Like previous dispensationalists, LaHaye has carefully plotted a series of events—earthquakes, plagues, and wars—from biblical texts. The twelfth and final book in the series will depict the battle at Armageddon and the "Glorious Reappearing of Christ." While the series is outlined by LaHaye, the stories are written by evangelical writer Jerry Jenkins. Jenkins is less invested than LaHaye in the meanings of traditional dispensationalism and is more moderate in his approach. In part because of its authorial relationship, *Left Behind* is a divided text. Infused in *Left Behind's* narrative are both traditional concerns that prophecy has addressed—concerns about Christian alienation and modernization—and significant new developments that speak directly to contemporary Christianity. *Left Behind* is a negotiation with contemporary American culture, both amending traditional dispensationalism and continuing to assert a claim of a special place within unfolding world history.

Perhaps one of the most significant locations for these negotiations is gender. Because gender has played a central role in the development of fundamentalism, it has also been a central concern of rapture and tribulation narratives from their inception.[49] Traditional rapture narratives nearly always begin with the rapture of a woman. In rapture fiction, women are often depicted as disappearing at a moment of domestic crisis. They are taken up just as they are about to be beaten by drunken husbands or abandoned by faithless ones. In the midst of these sufferings, the women have preserved their faith and are rewarded by rapture. The husbands face their wives' disappearance with disbelief and then despair, sometimes committing suicide or simply falling deeper into disgrace and sin. In other cases, rapture provides the context for an unbelieving husband to come to Christ. These narratives offer to women the role of the faithful and forgiving victim who disappears into silence rather than name the injustices done to her, who receives otherworldly reward for her suffering rather than this-worldly justification.[50] But in dialectic fashion, the narrative punishes the man who is left behind, perhaps for desiring the woman's disappearance. Her powerlessness and submission to the men who dominate and abuse her in this life become a kind of justification and power in the world beyond. This power has effect, however, only when she disappears, only when she is no longer on earth to receive or act on it.[51]

When the raptured female is not being abused by her husband, she is given another role—that of a mother and devout wife whose purity and faithfulness is the source and wellspring of her family. Women embody the purity of the church and the perfection of piety. While men are corrupted by modernity, women remain, in the dispensational imagination, above it. This gives them a kind of privileged position, but it also means they have no real power to act in and on the world. Instead, they are never truly at home in this world. They are too good, too pure to become embroiled in the political and public difficulties of modern life. By remaining outside the public sphere, they preserve their purity but remain relatively powerless.[52]

Left Behind follows closely in this tradition. Rayford Steele's wife, Irene, is the devout and domestic wife who pleads for Rayford's salvation. She is raptured in the opening scene of the first book and takes on mythological status as the archetypal mother and wife. With roots in the Cult of True Womanhood of the nineteenth century, women within evangelicalism have often been seen as the true keepers of the faith and more "naturally" pious than men. This idealization "permeates evangelical piety," as historian Randall Balmer puts it.[53] In rapture fiction, this ideal woman is embodied in the raptured female who is crucial to structuring the narrative. She is also simultaneously disembodied as a figure who appears only to quickly disappear. In this way, she becomes intensely symbolic—far more powerful as a symbol of faith than she was as a living believer. Irene Steele has no effect on her husband's salvation while she is living. If anything, her commitment to her faith drives him away. But in her disappearance, she comes into full power, and through her example, Rayford is saved.

Left Behind, like previous rapture fiction, initially codes faith as primarily feminine and domestic while worldliness is coded as masculine. Note, for example, how this functions from the very opening lines of the series: "Rayford Steele's mind was on a woman he had never touched. With his fully loaded 747 on autopilot above the Atlantic en route to a 6 A.M. landing at Heathrow, Rayford had pushed from his mind thoughts of his family."[54] This introduction to Rayford identifies him with his "fully loaded 747," an image not so subtly connected to both sexuality and worldly power. The church-world dichotomy on which dispensationalism is built is invoked here as Rayford dismisses thoughts of his family. Domesticity, home, and family are markers for faith. These are the very things that Rayford ignores in order to pursue women, success, and power.

In establishing an apocalyptic narrative, dispensationalism draws clear lines between saved and unsaved, between the raptured and the left behind. In the symbolic and archetypal structures that have emerged from this tradition, this church-world dichotomy has often become a female-male dichotomy as well. Women are pious; men are worldly. Women are raptured and saved;

men are condemned.[55] *Left Behind* seemingly begins with this tradition, but then departs from it. Unlike many men in rapture fiction before him, Rayford is not condemned. Rather he is transformed from a worldly man to a Christian leader. Or is he? Can Rayford Steele retain his worldly savvy, his swaggering masculinity, his rational and unemotional intelligence and become a Christian? This question forms the foundation for many of Rayford's early struggles, and the answer appears to be both yes and no.

After the rapture, Rayford's journey to faith begins as an experiment with domesticity. He finds himself becoming more like his wife emotionally, and he begins to perform domestic tasks that were previously exclusively hers: "Rayford spent an hour at the grocery store and another hour and a half in the kitchen before he had everything cooking in anticipation of [Chloe's] arrival. He found himself identifying with Irene, remembering the hopeful expression on her face almost every night. . . . it wasn't until now that he realized she must have been doing that work for him out of the same love and devotion he felt for Chloe."[56] Gradually, this identification with both home and Irene leads Rayford closer to religious faith. Rayford's masculinity becomes infused with tenderness. On the one hand the Christian men's movement has been alarmed by the "feminization" of American culture—by the increasingly powerful roles played by women to the seeming exclusion of men. On the other hand, this same movement has been concerned with giving men the tools to become more gentle and loving to their families, more expressive emotionally, and more open to religious faith. It has tried to teach ways to be both "tender" and masculine at the same time.[57] *Left Behind* is influenced by this movement and works on some of these very problems in the figure of Rayford. He learns to open himself emotionally to his family and his Christian "brothers." On the Promise Keeper model, Rayford learns to be a "servant-leader."

On the other hand, Rayford retains a worldliness unknown to previous rapture fiction in its depiction of Christian martyrs and heroes. He flaunts his wealth; he flies into ungodly rages; he struggles with sexual temptation. These traits work to create Rayford as a decidedly masculine figure, yet they also seem at times to compromise his religious faith. This negotiation between faithfulness and worldliness constructs a somewhat unstable gender identity for Rayford—not a pure archetype.

Similarly, while Irene remains archetypal through her disappearance, her daughter, Chloe, enters the same cauldron of gender negotiation that transforms her father. Introduced to the reader as a skeptical, Stanford-educated young woman with a feisty personality, Chloe gradually softens into something that looks more like the domestic ideal of Christian motherhood. She marries and has a child. She speaks a rhetoric of submission to her husband that seems inseparable from her newfound religious faith. Despite this apparent surrender to a passive domestic model rooted in evangelicalism, Chloe is an ambiguous figure. She both departs from and conforms to the ideal presented by her mother. In an argument with her husband about an upcoming trip to Israel, Chloe both concedes to and challenges Buck's authority.

> Don't parent me, Buck. Seriously, I don't have a problem submitting to you because I know how much you love me. I'm willing to obey you even when you're wrong. But don't be unreasonable. And don't be wrong when you don't have to be. . . . don't do it out of some old-fashioned, macho sense of protecting the little woman. I'll take this pity and help for just so long, and then I want back in the game full-time. I thought that was one of the things you liked about me. . . . Am I still a member of the Tribulation Force, or have I been de-moted to mascot now?[58]

While it is easy to be distracted in this passage by the rhetoric of absolute submission and Chloe's appeal to Buck's desire, Chloe also strongly articulates herself here. She refuses to become an object and even demands full partici-pation in the work of the Tribulation Force. She both submits and asserts herself, negotiating for a position that will allow her to be Christian mother and Christian warrior. Later Chloe becomes CEO of the underground network of the Christian Cooperative, running the business from the Tribulation Force's bunker. This is a position that allows Chloe to be both a stay-at-home mom and a smart and savvy businesswoman. Even later in the series, Chloe leaves for an adventure in Greece while Buck stays at home with their son.

In other words, the gender identities offered by *Left Behind* seem to be in direct engagement with the concerns of contemporary culture and give cre-dence to James Davidson Hunter's view that feminist ideas are widely dis-persed throughout evangelicalism.[59] The series struggles to pose new mascu-line and feminine identities that are much less archetypal than in previous rapture fiction. While Linda Kintz argues that contemporary evangelicalism relies on the assertion of absolute gender identity, the extraordinary popularity of *Left Behind* seems to offer counterevidence.[60] Absolute gender difference is often asserted in the rhetoric of evangelical leaders, yet *Left Behind* seems to offer, subtly, an alternative. This is not to say that the books are not full of gender stereotypes and scenes of female submission to male authority. They certainly are. This is also not to say that the books are not invested in main-taining a patriarchal order of male leadership, heterosexuality, and female do-cility. Many examples could be offered to demonstrate this. At the same time, we can see evidence of a negotiation in the books and in the lives of readers.

In their everyday lives, men and women work out gender identities in complicated ways, not by pure rules dictated by evangelical authorities. As a work
of fiction, *Left Behind* reflects these more complex realities.[61]

A second site of negotiation with modern life is found in the treatment of
consumer culture and technology in the books. We have noted that the predecessors of contemporary evangelicalism—the revivalists of the nineteenth
century, the religious entrepreneurs of the early twentieth century, and the
fundamentalists of the mid–twentieth century—were skillful users of mass
culture and its accompanying technological advancements. From the early days
of mass publishing to the initiation of radio and television broadcasting, conservative Christians have played a prominent role in the development and use
of these venues for mass consumption.[62] Strikingly, however, rapture fiction
and dispensationalist eschatology have been locations where anxieties about
technology, mass culture, and consumerism flourish. Even when the means
have been very modern indeed, the message, through the narrative of rapture
and tribulation, has often been antimodern.

For much of the history of rapture fiction, technology has been in the
hands of the Antichrist and is used to track, persecute, and destroy Christians.
Mass culture also belongs to the Antichrist. Except for a small band of Christians and orthodox Jews, the world's people follow him unquestioningly. Popular religion and popular culture are the devil's own work. Perhaps the most
striking form of this is the reception of the Mark of the Beast—a scene in
nearly every work of rapture fiction in which people sign up in droves to receive
Satan's mark so that they can participate in the global economy. Receiving the
Mark of the Beast means eternal condemnation, and the Christians who refuse
are persecuted and then martyred.

The Christian heroes of these earlier texts are a small and embattled minority. Christians are depicted as simple, often rural people who do not function well in the modern world. If not exactly backward, they are old-fashioned,
clinging to home and family in the midst of overwhelming social and cultural
change. While the Antichrist and his followers are elites, the Christians are
ordinary people. In this way, authors of rapture fiction have sought to portray
Christians as both marginalized and authentic. They have depicted their own
brand of Christianity as out of step with the modern world, but all the more
sincere and powerful because of this.

Left Behind offers an almost direct reversal of this portrayal of Christianity.
Following the trend of upward mobility among conservative Protestants, *Left
Behind's* Tribulation Force is made up, itself, of elites.[63] Rayford Steele is no
ordinary pilot, but a pilot whose name is known even to the president. Buck

Williams is not an ordinary reporter, but "Ivy League educated, New York head-quartered, at the top of his profession."[64] Rayford is not afraid to flaunt his wealth and his status, but this does not appear to compromise his religious faith. In fact, he uses his money and power to advance Christianity. Soon after his conversion, Rayford arranges to take Hattie, Chloe, and Buck out for dinner at an exclusive hotel restaurant. Rayford plans to present his newfound faith to the other three, especially Hattie, and he wants the waiter to understand why they are lingering beyond dessert.

> "We'd like to spend another hour or so here, if it is all right."
> "Sir, we do have an extensive reservation list—"
> "I wouldn't want this table to be less than profitable for you,"
> Rayford said, pressing a large bill into the waiter's palm, "so boot us
> out whenever it becomes necessary."
> The waiter peeked at the bill and slipped it into his pocket. "I'm
> sure you will not be disturbed," he said. And the water glasses were
> always full.[65]

In this scene, we see Rayford as a man of wealth who is able to clear space for his private business, but this business is explicitly religious, aimed at the conversion of his daughter, Hattie, and Buck. He unabashedly uses worldly means to accomplish this task, something unprecedented in dispensationalist fiction.

Technologically, the Tribulation Force is more advanced even than the Antichrist. They have the most sophisticated machines and the most knowledgeable technicians. They use their technological savvy to infiltrate the Antichrist's network and undermine his purposes. This is strikingly different than earlier rapture fiction in which the Antichrist uses technology to undermine and isolate Christians. The books are full of enamored descriptions of cell phones and computers, and the Tribulation Force is equipped with all the latest technological gadgetry. As Buck prepares the group for its work against the Antichrist, he tells their technician,

> I need five of the absolute best, top-of-the-line computers, as small
> and compact as they can be, but with as much power and memory
> and speed and communications abilities as you can wire into them.
> . . . I want a computer with virtually no limitations. I want to be able
> to take it anywhere, keep it reasonably concealed, store everything I
> want on it, and most of all, be able to connect with anyone any-
> where without the transmission being traced.[66]

In a radical shift from earlier rapture fiction, the technician, a minor character named Donny, answers, "You're talking my language, Mr. Williams." The language of technology is Donny's, an evangelical Christian's. He is at home in this universe of computer technology. Buck's demand for computers with "power and memory and speed," his desire for a computer with "virtually no limitations," is a desire for power expressed through technology. Buck imagines and, within the fiction, provides a way for Christians to extend their power and influence.

Furthermore, the series stages several large stadium gatherings of converted Christians and the Tribulation Force's online ministry boasts converts in the millions. Rather than depicting Christians as isolated martyrs, *Left Behind* portrays a massive, underground, popular movement and pits Christian popularity against the Antichrist's. While the Antichrist has official and institutional control, Christians are building a broad and popular countermovement.

We see then a "new" Christian emerging in this fiction. No longer ostracized, alienated, and old-fashioned, the new Christian is wealthy, technologically savvy, and exerts a powerful cultural influence. Perhaps, given the history of conservative Protestantism, its aggressive engagement with popular culture, its growth among middle and upper classes since World War II, and its participation in emerging technologies throughout the twentieth century, this transformation in rapture fiction should not surprise us. It is a reflection, perhaps, of who evangelical Christians have been all along. On the other hand, *Left Behind* represents such a striking departure from earlier rapture fiction that it deserves more careful attention. The story of rapture and tribulation has long contained an expression of conservative Protestant self-understanding, and the stories evangelicals are telling about themselves are under an important transformation that finds expression in *Left Behind*.[67] With that change comes a change in the guiding mythology and eschatology. What does the story of rapture and tribulation mean if it is no longer an antiworldly and antimodern formula? What does the story signify to its readers if not alienation and isolation? Why does dispensationalism remain persistently popular as an apocalyptic narrative and how has its meaning been transformed?

Interviews with readers of *Left Behind* do not give us easy or straightforward answers to these questions. People use texts to make meaning in a variety of often contradictory ways. But the interviews do offer us insight into a culture that is in the midst of a broad transformation. While retaining some of their original intent and force, rapture and tribulation have become a part of a new set of meanings. While *Left Behind* portrays something that is not exactly the old dispensationalism, it is not entirely new either. The readers of this hybrid dispensationalism do not find in the story the same meaning that their fundamentalist forbears might have, but they still find the story to have compelling, explanatory power. In the following chapters we will explore this power and its effect on the stories readers tell about themselves.

2

Networks of Readers, Networks of Meaning

In order to understand how readers make sense of *Left Behind*, we must first understand the contexts in which the books are read. The assumption that reading is a private act of individual consumption underlies many of the stories the media tells about *Left Behind's* popular success. "Some stumbled on the series by accident," Nancy Gibbs writes in *Time* magazine in an article about the series. "Deborah Vargas, 46, of San Francisco bought her first *Left Behind* book in January at a Target, looking for a good read. She got much more than she had bargained for. . . . Since then, she says, her life has been transformed, and she is now a regular in the *Left Behind* chat rooms."[1] Deborah Vargas is the only reader whose encounter with the books Gibbs tells, and she appears, as in many representations of *Left Behind's* readership, as an isolated individual. We know nothing about her religious background, her motivation to pick up the book, or why she thought *Left Behind* would be a "good read." We know only of an almost magical encounter in a book department that changed her life. From the news media, we gain this picture of readers of *Left Behind*: A customer strolls into a bookstore and sees a display for the latest release of *Left Behind*. Intrigued, she buys a copy and becomes a statistic, one of the 32 million consumers of *Left Behind*. The purchaser is an isolated number, a disconnected wanderer who stumbles onto *Left Behind*, buys, and reads it in the privacy of her free time. Indeed, this is a distinctly modern understanding of reading—an event that takes place in solitude. This view of reading is compounded by consumer culture, which invites us to see the act of consumption as one of individual choice. Just as reading is something a person does in private, the decision to buy a book is one a person makes in isolation.

Reading *Left Behind* is better understood, however, as an act of social connection. It is perhaps as close to ancient practices of "oral, social, and collective" reading as it is to the modern notion of individual and private reading.[2] Readers are tied up in reading networks of family, friends, and church members, and reading is an important part of establishing oneself as a part of a community. Like the Book of Revelation itself, which was meant to be read orally to the congregation for which it was written, *Left Behind* is shared orally by thousands of listeners on hundreds of radio stations—it has become a popular radio drama.[3] Furthermore, purchasing *Left Behind* is also done in networks. One reader is often responsible for buying several copies of *Left Behind* and distributing them to family and friends. Similarly, one copy of *Left Behind* makes rounds through a circle of friends, through a church choir or a Sunday school class. Reading *Left Behind* is a social event, something encouraged by and readily shared with others. Reading of *Left Behind* is often undertaken in order to please someone else and in order to share in someone else's understanding of truth.

Nearly all readers in my study are part of religious communities. They experience various degrees of commitment, and not all religious communities are contained by a church building. Readers do not pick up *Left Behind* in isolation. They engage with the novels as participation in a social network. Readers are often part of two kinds of "families" of readers—a biological family and a church family. *Left Behind* is read and interpreted in the context of these families with their shared worldviews, their tensions, and their disagreements.

The Church Home

On a Sunday morning in rural South Carolina, I visit a small Presbyterian church. Nearly every member of the congregation has read or plans to read *Left Behind*, and the books are passed through the adult Sunday school class and the choir. They are discussed during the social hour after church and in the small group Bible studies that meet during the week. Members of the church have decided to start a Bible study on Revelation, prompted in part by the reading of the novels. Before the church service, the unadorned sanctuary is full of conversation that spills out from the church onto the lawn. Toward eleven o'clock, people gradually come in to the sanctuary and sit down.

The service proceeds along lines that are vaguely familiar to me from my Presbyterian childhood—there are hymns, a Confession of Sin, and a long series of announcements about activities in the church. Before the sermon, the minister asks the congregation for Prayers of the People. There is a brief moment of silence and then hands go up. The minister calls out the names of members, and they offer prayers for sick and dying people of the town and the church, for wayward relatives, for people who are traveling. They offer up joys—new jobs, the decisions of children to go to college or into the military, the visit of relatives. These concerns and joys are given in simple, unpretentious terms, briefly stated and then acknowledged by both the minister and the rest of the congregation. The ritual of the Prayers of the People is repeated every week with new requests, new concerns, but a similar rhythm of offering and acknowledgement. Often a member of the congregation raises her hand and says, "Several unspoken." In this phrase, she signifies that she has prayers and concerns so private that she does not want to say them aloud, yet she desires the support and love of the congregation nonetheless. During this ritual, that love seems tangible. It takes material form in the ritual of speaking and being heard, of being able to speak the ordinary and yet profound events of everyday life and be acknowledged by people who can share those concerns by hearing them. In my return visits to this church, I look forward to the Prayers of the People, and take it to be a key moment in the formation and sustenance of the community that members describe in interviews.

At this particular church, community is profoundly local. It is an insular community, open to visitors like me, but rooted in the connections—often decades and generations long—between individual members and between its locality and the people. Congregants are united by race and class—the majority are white and working class—as well as by religious faith, but it is religious faith that gives the fullest expression of their connection to one another. Without that faith, they might be connected in the less deep and less powerful ways that they are connected to coworkers or other members of the town. Shared religious faith is an important part of what makes them "family" to each other as the members describe, and their connections to one another are often more powerful and more important than their connections to their own biological families.

In another church, I experience an equally profound sense of community, but less local and more global in affiliation. This much larger church is a strip mall unto itself, with offices for its various local and global ministries contained in the same building as the sanctuary. It calls itself an "international" church both because of its world outreach and because of the various nationalities represented in the congregation. As I park my car in the church's vast parking

lot, I am surprised to see a truly diverse crowd gathering for the Sunday morning service. Anglo, Afro, Latino, and Asian people approach the wide front of
the building and stand outside on the steps talking animatedly. I sit on a folding
chair in a room that seats perhaps five hundred people. Around the room are
several screens and at the front is a stage where musicians are warming up
their instruments and setting up a sound system. The room is crowded, nearly
every seat taken, and I take note of the people sitting around me. Next to me
on one side is a young white man, probably a college student, with thick
glasses, neatly dressed in slacks and a tie. On the other side sits an elegantly
dressed African American woman in her thirties and her young daughter. In
front of me are two young men—one black and one white. The white man
wears a dashiki and long hair tied in a ponytail; the black man wears his hair
in dreadlocks and beads around his neck and wrists. Next to them sits a very
conservatively dressed middle-aged white man who engages these two young
men in a warm conversation before the service begins.

Singing spreads across the congregation and an elaborate band with gui-
tars, drums, bass, French horn, trumpet, several singers, and bongos begins
to play. The words to the songs are projected onto screens and people clap and
raise their hands in a charismatic style as they sing. After several songs, each
growing in volume and intensity, the song leader says, "Let's sing a Zulu praise
song. Everyone sing, now, praise God." The words go up on the screen, "Ban
Ba La La. Ban Ba La La. Hold on to Jesus. Hold on to Jesus. I'm holding on.
I'm holding on. Ban Ba La La." The bongos play and people sing with enthusiasm, some moving into the aisles to dance with each other. As I watch the
enthusiastic and emotional singing, I am surprised to find tears in my eyes.
There seems to be, at least in this moment, a genuine desire to embrace the
whole world through singing. I am reminded how diverse evangelicalism is,
how different forms of religious life spring up and take shape in contexts all
over the world.

I went to the church reluctantly. By the time I attended this church, I had
grown tired of churches that advertise "contemporary-style worship followed
by Bible-based preaching," as this one does. I felt I had seen and heard enough
of the suburban smugness, the oppressive self-righteousness that seems to
accompany this particular configuration of evangelicalism. Yet, as the service
unfolds, I am unprepared for the energy, diversity, and ecstatic invocation of
community that this church inspires. I am moved by what appears to be genuine interactions between the people who have gathered and by the spirit of
inclusion that attends the singing. I am reminded of Emile Durkheim's description of religious communities as ecstatically creating the divine through
ritual,[4] yet Durkheim's principle seems inadequate based as it is on the ho-

mogeneity of the community. Here difference—racial, linguistic, and ethnic difference—seems to be ecstatically on display.

These experiences in the churches of readers hint to me that strong social bonds based on religious faith draw readers into evangelicalism and hold them there. Repeatedly, readers describe their churches as "home" and "family." By invoking these domestic images to describe the bonds they feel with other church members, readers suggest that, in Louis Althusser's terms, they are "hailed" by these communities, that the way the community functions feels profoundly right to them. Within these communities, members experience love, support, friendship, and inclusion. At the same time, I wonder at the foundations of such communities. On the one hand, I genuinely accept readers' accounts that these communities are built on a common faith in Jesus Christ, a common salvation. On the other hand, I am struck by the policing of gender roles and sexuality that seems similar in nearly all the churches I visit. I wonder if the sustainability of the community, its very viability, depends on the acceptance of male authority and rigid conceptions of sexuality. Male authority is everywhere in evidence, from the exclusively male clergy to the ushers who collect the offering to the rhetoric of readers in conversation with me. As much as weekly church services work to reinforce profound community relations, they simultaneously seem rituals of patriarchal display. Maintaining the church as a domestic space that can be "family" to its members seems to depend on maintaining it as a rigidly patriarchal space. To what extent, I wonder, could this version of "home" exist without these power structures?

In her study of fundamentalist churches, Brenda Brasher makes a distinction between authority and power. Fundamentalist churches make a point of visually demonstrating male authority. This public display is part of the self-definition of these religious communities. On the other hand, she argues, power is more broadly shared than is evident on the surface. Women in the churches have developed powerful, but less visible, networks that allow them to influence how the churches are run and what decisions are made.[5] Is it precisely this blend of overt authority and covert power that feels right to readers in my study and compels them to call their churches home? Or is it something else altogether?

Evangelical churches extend their communities into many aspects of daily life. Sunday morning worship is only one ritual among many. Readers also participate in Sunday school classes, weeknight Bible Studies, church potlucks and socials, organizational meetings, and volleyball games or other recreational events. For some readers of *Left Behind*, church-related activities extend to several evenings each week. Readers also participate in church communities through activities like personal Bible reading and prayer, where through private acts of devotion they reinforce their connections with the church. All of these activities constitute what readers describe when they say their churches are "home" and "family."

At the same time, "church home" is an ideological category. For many readers of *Left Behind* it becomes a place where "home" can be performed ritually in a way far more satisfying than in their own individual homes. The example of patriarchy, the idealization of devout women, the spectacle of male leadership all make the church home resemble a place that readers find profoundly right. In describing their churches, readers invoke the domestic tradition of religiosity to which evangelicalism has held since the nineteenth century. As "home," the church is a place of protection from the outside world, a place of shelter from the confusion and difficulty of a pluralistic and morally complex society. It is a place where one can become refreshed and prepared for the continual foray into that society. The church has perhaps retained this ideology of the home better than the houses in which believers live. In those houses, very little remains of the celebrated "home" that the Cult of True Womanhood seems to require. Economic and social conditions conspire against this ideology in the everyday lives of believers. In addition, in many readers' homes, unbelievers live alongside believers. This dissonance creates tensions that are less visible in the church where presumably everyone is a believer and shares the same foundational premise of faith.

The church is a place where ideology can take purer form, where believers can palpably sense and experience the peace, order, and harmony that are supposed to emanate from the "home." As Brasher puts it, Bible-believing churches try to function as "utopian families for their adherents."[6] With power structures clearly intact, with male authority acknowledged and acted upon through ritual, with domestic life modeled, evangelicalism retains the ideology of domesticity that it perpetuated throughout the twentieth century. By surrounding themselves with like-minded people who confirm and support their orientation to the world, believers find solace, peace, and a sense of security. When readers express that church is "home," all of this is being articulated and more. Home is a place where burdens are shared and lifted, where love is tangibly felt and experienced, and where the community fosters connection. At the same time, churches function as ritual performances of home where the ideology of domesticity can be acted out and reinforced in a way that is no longer possible in the world outside the church.

Historian Joel Carpenter has noted that for fundamentalists of an earlier era, the church was a place where the boundaries of the community were simply more secure. Like contemporary evangelicals, many came from families where they were perhaps the only person "born again." They came to church with their children, but without their spouses or as young adults without their parents. In any typical congregation there would be those who were single or single parents. "So it was the congregation, one's 'family in the Lord,' where commitment to being a 'Bible-believing Christian' in an increasingly unappreciative world would receive its primary boost."[7] For today's evangelicals, the church plays a similar role. Where families are divided on matters of religious faith, where the world outside church walls makes demands that are not congruent with church ideology, the congregation remains a place where faith can be secured and refreshed.

Not all readers have a church "home," but most acknowledge a desire for such a place. The transience of contemporary life and the constant shifting of communities and populations often prevent readers from becoming invested in a church community long enough that it can feel like home to them, but most are searching for that kind of stability or can remember with nostalgia a church like that from another time in their lives. The contrast between the desire for a church home and the vagaries of contemporary life that prevent such a home from becoming reality increases the power of *Left Behind*, which depicts Christians engaged in a community that most readers strongly desire.

Readers of *Left Behind* feel tied together by common beliefs. Together they share beliefs about the nature of reality, about the rightness of traditional family life, and about the end of time, and these beliefs provide a context for all of the activities that constitute their interactions with one another. In the process of sharing these beliefs and using them as a common foundation, they build community life and often develop long-term commitments to one another. Shared belief takes shape in shared rituals as well as in less formal means of interaction. And from these interactions extend a community that many call family.

The church also provides a structure that gives congregants a strong sense of connection and relation. In the church, they are linked through faith to other believers. From this connection, along with all of the activities that it entails, believers develop strong emotional bonds that feel to them like family bonds. These social connections develop at odds with a culture bent on individualism. In the church, one is a member of a collective; one submits to an authority other than one's own and receives in exchange powerful social rewards. This exchange is satisfying for many of the people I interviewed. When they tell their own stories of faith, they often tell stories of straying from church and then returning "home" to submit themselves to the authority of the church and finding deep bonds of love and acceptance that hold them there.

Left Behind is often read in these extensive social networks of family, friends, church, and work. The books are passed along from parent to child, brother to sister, within a church Bible study group or in other similar social settings. Readers become the books' evangelizers, passing them out to family and friends. One reader might buy several books at once or pick up one copy, lend it out, and never see it again. Books are given to friends and relatives "saved" and "unsaved," borrowed, read, and reloaned. They are also discussed at beauty parlors, on airplanes, and after church on Sunday. Within social networks that support and supplement the reading, readers claim that the books have a powerful effect on their lives. The books give spiritual insight, renewal, and courage. They enable and reinforce certain kinds of communal bonds. At the same time they provide a link to people perceived as "unsaved." The books offer a way to talk about faith in a nonthreatening way and offer subtle invitations to belief. Because the books and their eschatology play such a strong role in articulating community belonging, they give us the opportunity to investigate the foundations of that community, as well as places where tensions and fissures exist. Through the books we can better understand the desires and hopes that foster such a strong sense of connection that readers feel in their church "families."

Left Behind offers a very particular vision of social life that readers find useful in reinforcing their own community life. The books' apocalypticism has a crucial role to play because it is an apocalypticism based on separation and boundary-building. The first line of demarcation occurs with the rapture— who is taken up and who is left behind tells the world who the true believers are. Most readers hope that they will be taken up in the rapture and spared the suffering of the tribulation, and that the rapture will be evidence of the rightness of their worldview. But the books further demarcate believers through the establishment of the Tribulation Force and the "mark" believers receive on their foreheads. With this, the separation of the believer from the nonbeliever, the saved from the unsaved, is clearer than it ever is in actual life. The community can be readily and easily identified, rather than subjected to the endless complexities, doubts, and interventions of everyday life.

The "family of faith" to which readers of *Left Behind* describe belonging often takes tangible form in tightly knit, supportive communities of shared religious faith—the people and routine practices of daily life. This shared religious faith provides the basis for the community, its reason for being. The homogeneity of belief weaves these religious communities together—usually a verbal commitment to "Jesus Christ as personal Lord and Savior" or the act of "accepting Jesus into your heart." At the same time that these communities seem unified by belief and *Left Behind* seems to reinforce these connections, reading also provides opportunities for disagreement. It provides the context for challenges to religious authority, for differences to emerge and be expressed among community members, and for the "church family" to acknowledge and accept these differences. In other words, the church family needs to be understood as itself a dynamic construction of faith embedded in a rhetoric of stability.

The Church Family and Its Discontents

The reading of *Left Behind* and the functioning of the church community are often mutually supportive and constitutive of one another. This should not be misunderstood as saying that church leadership actively encourages the reading of *Left Behind*. In fact, most readers do not think that their clergy read *Left Behind* or that they have ever mentioned it in a church setting. Few clergy with whom I spoke read the series or find it interesting. Reading and passing the books along are activities of the laypeople in the congregation, a way of building connections among themselves, sometimes wholly separate from the clergy. But clergy and the institutional structures of readers' churches support the reading in more subtle ways. In chapter 5, I discuss religious reading practices that are taught both in the books and in churches. These reading practices encourage a particular understanding of reality and the relationship between the text of the Bible and everyday life that is amenable to the apocalypticism of *Left Behind*. Churches also model the patriarchal relations that the books encourage, and readers find the social structures of their churches compatible with those advocated in their reading. And perhaps more important, churches are a tangible form of the community modeled in the books; readers can potentially find or imagine in their congregations a social form of relationship something like the Christian community envisioned in *Left Behind's* Tribulation Force.

On the other hand, many readers find themselves caught in conflicting orientations to the books' theology, value, and even pleasure. By providing a theological argument embedded in narrative, the books open up a space for disagreement. Readers raise questions about the plot and criticize Jenkins's writing skills. Some have theological disagreements; others are suspicious of the authors' motives. Disagreements arise as well among readers about the timing of apocalyptic events, the possibility of redemption after the rapture, and the accuracy of the portrayal according to the Bible. The texts provide the foundation and opportunity for readers to consider and discuss ideas and beliefs that otherwise may have remained latent. This kind of interaction about the text with other readers serves a dual purpose. On the one hand, it strengthens community ties by providing a context for shared belief. On the other hand, it points out theological and social differences over which readers then must grapple. For some readers, *Left Behind* provides an alternative authority that readers use to challenge the authority of their clergy or of other people in positions of power in their church communities.

Sarah faces conflict with her minister over the reading of *Left Behind*. She was raised in a conservative Baptist church in a small mountain town. This church was the center of her religious life and, though she moved away from her hometown, she has not been satisfied in a church since. "I'm just very spoiled by Hillside Baptist [her home church]. Just very spoiled. And I am probably looking for something that I won't find. Not that there aren't other churches, but they aren't family at the same time." Because her connection to her family and her home church is so strong, Sarah often spends weekends at home and always goes to church when she does. The minister of the church there has been influential for Sarah and is someone she deeply respects. Our conversation is speckled with comments about what "Pastor Bill" believes, how he preaches, the kinds of things he has done for the congregation. The bond she feels with him is clearly strong. So I am surprised when Sarah tells me that he disapproves of the reading of the *Left Behind* series. Sarah herself is an avid reader and has shared the books with her entire family and several friends. She has never spoken with him about her reading, but from the pulpit he has addressed the novels. To the congregation, he said, "If you are reading those books that say you can be saved after the rapture, you are just fooling yourself." In other words, her minister disagrees that it is possible for someone to become a Christian after the rapture occurs. The books rely on this premise in order for Christians to witness and respond to end time events and fight back against the Antichrist.

Sarah is somewhat troubled by this disagreement, and as she tries to reason her way through it, she turns to her own reading of the Bible for help.

> Some people believe that after the rapture the only people that will be saved will be Jews. . . . The Bible talks about there will be saints slain at altars praying after the rapture. To me that says there will be, I mean being a saint of God indicates that you have accepted Jesus Christ, right?[8] So there must be some way to be saved after the rapture. . . . My pastor at home deeply disagrees with me. . . . And I respect that, that's fine, but even though I know that God is a just God and a wrathful God, I know those things to be true, I don't think God would turn away an earnest heart. And the characters in the book, whether that was actually how salvation would take place,

I felt like the ones who were saved after the rapture did it with an earnest heart.

Despite the influence of her pastor, Sarah still finds the books' version of salvation after the rapture more persuasive than her pastor's. She uses the narrative depiction of conversion in the novels to support her reasoning: "The characters in the book . . . who were saved after the rapture did it with an earnest heart." While her decision to read the books and even to agree with them theologically is not supported by her pastor, Sarah is supported by other institutional traditions. For example, within Protestantism, there is a long tradition of emphasis on individual reading of the Bible and individual salvation. Protestants generally believe that each soul must work out its own salvation, and for this reason Protestants generally emphasize personal Bible study. Like many Protestants before her, Sarah turns to her own reading of the Bible and her own reasoning to decide this theological question.

While Sarah works out these theological and prophetic complexities, she also readily gives the books to friends and family and encourages their reading in her own social networks. She discusses the books with her mother, friends in the church, her husband, and her coworkers. Sarah uses the books to strengthen her bonds with people who share her faith in this version of the end times. With such an enthusiastic group of coreaders, Sarah's disagreement with her pastor is a fairly minor event. More significant is the pleasure Sarah finds in reading and sharing the books.

At the same time, the strong theological influence that Pastor Bill has had on Sarah's life is challenged by *Left Behind*. Reading provides the context for Sarah to move outside of his influence in order to think through these issues on her own. Her own thinking leads her to a position marginally more inclusive than Pastor Bill's. Sarah concludes that people will be allowed to receive Christ after the rapture, that the opportunity for salvation will not end. By deciding this, she keeps the door open for others whose religious beliefs are different than hers. It will not be too late for them after the rapture. This is a small move for Sarah, but a significant one. She has not yet challenged Pastor Bill's authority in speech, but she has begun to develop an alternative in her thinking that allows her to step outside one of the most significant religious authorities in her life. *Left Behind* facilitates this incrementally more open position and puts a wedge, however small, between Sarah and her "home."

Sarah's boundaries remain very black and white. She is rigidly certain in her own life about who is saved and who is unsaved, about right thinking and wrong thinking, right belief and wrong belief. The apocalypticism of *Left Behind* feeds Sarah's sense of self-assurance and self-righteousness. She has no doubt that she will go in the rapture and is fairly certain she can identify those who will go with her. Yet the reading also facilitates an opening and brings her to question religious authority in her life. Another young woman also uses her reading of *Left Behind* to challenge religious authority. She does so, however, with much less of a sense of the security of these boundaries.

Laura, an art teacher in a private school, was raised as an evangelical and has always been a devout adherent to the faith. Her new husband, Mark, was raised Catholic and is equally devout in his commitments. Laura converted to Catholicism at the time of her marriage. It was an action she took, in part, because of her husband's faith, but as she tells the story, her conversion had significance for her own spirituality. She centers her story around the difference between the Eucharist in the Catholic and Protestant churches.

> The Eucharist, I always felt as though we didn't take communion
> often enough in the Protestant Church . . . and I think just the idea
> of taking it so seriously, "This is the body, this is the blood," was
> more meaningful. I think part of me really wanted to participate in
> that, which I knew I could only do if I became a Catholic. . . . I think
> it came as a shock to Mark when I said I was going to go through
> the first ritual, the anointing of oil.

Laura's desire to participate in this ritual—"which I knew I could only do if I became a Catholic"—was strong enough to lead her into conversion. Through study, she came to accept many of the tenets of Catholicism that had troubled her as a life-long Protestant—the saints, the role of Mary, the Pope—but, even after her conversion, she still struggles with her exact orientation to the faith. Prior to meeting Mark and embarking on an exploration of Catholicism, Laura attended a nondenominational church and was active through Bible study, music, and Sunday school teaching. In the interview, she expressed some ambivalence about her position between the Catholic Church and the evangelical one. At one point, as she discussed the difference between Catholic and Protestant, she stumbled in attempting to label herself. "What is interesting is that I grew up Baptist. I grew up in the Protestant Church where this whole idea of the rapture is much more, well, I think much more into the Protestant way. I don't know why. Even the nondenominational is focused [on the rapture]. The focus is there, for whatever reason. And I was a part of it, or am a part of it." She laughed a little nervously, unsure whether to use the past or present tense.

While Laura is a passionate reader of the novels and a believer in the rapture, her husband Mark disavows both. This disavowal is confusing for

Laura, and she is unsure if her husband will be taken up in the rapture or not. On the one hand, she is certain of his devout faith. On the other hand, by refusing to accept the doctrine of the rapture, he seems in a position to be left behind. At one point, Mark makes a somewhat derisive comment about the rapture, and she teases him that he will be surprised when she is raptured and he is left behind. During the interview, Laura and Mark disagree constantly over labeling. Mark argues that, given the strict rules for what counts as "being a Christian," many people who are Christians are bound to be left behind. In Laura's worldview, this is untenable. If they are left behind, then they are not Christians. The two go around and around on this question, trying many different ways of explaining to the other how the boundaries might be drawn and understood.

Mark's constant questioning of the boundaries that Laura draws has had an important effect on Laura's religious identity. She is no longer wholly evangelical. She is not yet wholly Catholic. Through marriage, she was forced to redefine Christianity and now is in a position to defend Catholic forms of Christianity against evangelical attacks. At the same time, by joining the Catholic Church, she has added a new institutional and religious authority to her life. Whereas her religious beliefs were long formed in the context of evangelicalism, these beliefs are challenged by the authority of the Catholic Church to which she has submitted by becoming a member.

Left Behind provides a context for Laura and Mark to talk about the wide-ranging theological and social issues that divide them across these two religious perspectives. Most of their interview consists of heated arguments, rising to a pitch at times, that Laura then usually tries to quell with a joke. She turns these jokes most often against herself, adding a self-deprecating comment in the heat of the argument to change the tone of their disagreement. In this way, Laura controls the tenor and pace of the conversation, and she seems to feel more obligated than Mark does to keep things civil or to remind me that they do have a good relationship. The reading and discussing of *Left Behind* clearly allows the struggle over religious identity that concerns them both to come to the forefront of their relationship. Laura has read all of the books of the *Left Behind* series and loves them. She rushes to buy the latest installments as soon as they come out. Mark read the first book in the series because Laura asked him to. He hated it and made his dislike evident. Not only does he feel strongly that the books are theologically ill conceived, he also thinks they are cynically motivated by the authors' desire to make money. He teases Laura about becoming "hooked" on the series: "Even like you said, you are going to get the next two [books] because. . . ." Laura interrupts him, not understanding the force of his statement, but trying to answer my earlier question about whether she will buy the next book in hardcover or wait for the paperback, "I'll probably get whichever one I see, if it is paperback or. . . ." This time, Mark interrupts her in order to restate his assertion that Laura is addicted to the books: "But earlier you said you are going to get the next two because you already put in the time." Laura does not quite see his point: "Oh, yeah." Mark makes his statement in harsher terms, "So no matter what drivel falls off the pages. . . ." "No matter what drivel they come out with, I'm going to read it," she laughs. Having won a concession from Laura, Mark backs off on his claim. "Not that it will be drivel," he adds.

Laura uses her reading of the series as grounds to challenge Mark and even critique her newfound Catholicism. Her suggestion that Mark will be left behind is likewise an assertion of power. She holds a special knowledge inherent in the doctrine of the rapture about the end of time and the fate of unbelievers. In order to defend her pleasure in reading the series, Laura has to assert it not only against her husband's disdain, but also against the institution of the Catholic Church and its disbelief.

By dismissing his wife's reading as "drivel," Mark models masculine accusations against feminine reading. As Jane Tompkins argues in *Sensational Designs*, books that attempt to influence readers' lives, as the *Left Behind* series inarguably does, are suspect from a modernist point of view.[9] For Mark, who takes the position of the modernist here, this reading is "drivel"—petty, trivial, poorly constructed. Laura mockingly accepts his disdainful appraisal of the books in order to insist that she will continue to buy and read them regardless. Like readers of nineteenth-century sentimental fiction, she asserts the books' power and significance beyond their literary value.

I find myself torn between sympathy for both of them. Like Mark, I find the books' content unengaging, pedestrian, and even propagandistic. I find his comments about the books' ability to "hook" readers into ever-widening circles of consumption persuasive. But I am also acutely aware of the dynamics of gender playing out in the room. Mark, with the powerful backing of the Catholic Church, belittles the pleasure that Laura enjoys and finds spiritually significant. Laura stands alone in the room in defense of this pleasure, accepting insults in order to persist in reading. She returns his banter, jokingly accepting the designation of the books as "drivel," although she finds the books moving and important in her own life.

Laura is an unusually isolated reader. She put some distance between herself and the evangelical connections in her family by becoming a Catholic and now defends Catholicism against their attacks. On the other hand, she simultaneously defends her very Protestant belief in the rapture against the attacks of her Catholic husband. As a marginal figure from both the Catholic and Protestant perspectives, she herself does not seem to know where she belongs. Neither perspective is securely home. In this configuration of conflicting religious and cultural perspectives, reading *Left Behind* seems to give Laura a connection to her previous Protestantism and grounds to challenge the newest religious authority in her life.

Reading *Left Behind* both secures and destabilizes the dynamics of "home" within church communities. Readers use the books as an authority over and against clerical authority; they use it to defend their faith in hostile environments and also to make their environments more commodious, to claim a greater expanse of the social realm as "home." Reading reinforces the bonds between people already linked by faith, but it does this at times over and against those within the faith who find reason to disagree. If the church is conceived by many readers as a domestic space where they can find refuge from the world outside, this world too is fraught with difference and disagreement that the books seem to both highlight and spark.

The Divided Family

Readers belong not only to church families but also to biological families— networks of brothers, sisters, parents, in-laws, and extended relatives. These families work in various ways to both challenge and confirm the beliefs purported by the *Left Behind* series. These families are at times more heterogeneous in their beliefs than church families, and they present challenges and problems to believers not found within their church networks. As within the church family, the books have the capacity to complicate family connections, to highlight disagreements, and to challenge family structures.

Early on a Saturday morning, I drive to a coastal North Carolina city for several scheduled interviews. I arrive at Margaret's house at 9:00 as we arranged and knock on the door. Margaret answers in a housecoat and slippers. I think I must have come to the wrong place. "Is this the Burns's residence?" I ask a little embarrassed for having intruded on someone's Saturday morning. "Yes, it is. Are you Amy?" Margaret welcomes me into the house with a smoky laugh.

Margaret is a sixty-year-old woman who was raised in the Northeast, but has spent most of her adult life in a coastal, military city in the South. She has the rough voice of a lifelong smoker and a dry sense of humor that makes me feel immediately at home.

"Listen," she says as she pours me a cup of coffee and cuts a cinnamon roll for me. "I've decided you can interview my daughter instead of me. She's a big fan of these books. I'm sure you'd rather talk to her."

Rachel, Margaret's twenty-five-year-old daughter, sits at the kitchen table painting her fingernails.

"Oh, no," I say. "You're not getting out of it that easy. I came to interview you. But I'd love to talk to you both, if you have time."

Margaret laughs. "Oh, so you want to talk to the heathen. Fine. But interview Rachel first."

Margaret and Rachel are obviously close and spend a good deal of time together, but they disagree strongly about religion. As I speak to each of them, the other stays nearby. I sense it is important for each to hear what the other has to say and to be heard, through a third party, by the other. At times, I also sense that they change their responses to accommodate the other's point of view, and that each would have been more adamant in her position if the other was absent. They hover relatively close—in the living room, den, and kitchen— while I conduct separate interviews at the kitchen table, occasionally calling out jokes and corrections to the person at the table, but also staying conspicuously out of the conversation.

Rachel describes herself as "a Christian in the toddler stage."[10] She became a Christian just before her wedding a few years earlier and has only recently become involved in a church and two Bible studies. She sometimes adopts a baby-talk voice to explain her views, as though modeling the religious "toddler" she sees herself as. Rachel reads very little besides the *Left Behind* novels— some religious publications and Bible study materials. She reads the novels with a passion about which she seems to feel almost guilty. "This is not the Word of God," she tells me. "It's based on the Word of God, but it is not the Word of God. I do have struggles with: 'I'm going to do my Bible study, but I really want to read this book.' I should be working on my relationship [with God] instead of worrying about [the characters'] relationships."

Rachel thoroughly embraces the theology and eschatology of the books. She believes in the rapture, the tribulation, and Armageddon without question. When I ask her how accurate she believes the books to be, she answers in a way that shows investment in the books as both a fictional narrative and a revelation of the truth. But she also answers with self-deprecation. "I'm a sucker. I mean, I believe this is exactly what is going to happen. I really do. I mean how else would it happen? Now, if someone else wrote another story, then I'd have to check that out and compare them." By referring to herself as a "sucker," Rachel is mockingly self-aware of being drawn in and persuaded by the narrative. At the same time, she does see the story as reflecting biblical truth and feasible future events. She is caught in a tension between the novels as fiction and the novels as a real representation of prophecy. She does not clearly divide fiction from truth, however, in her response. Instead she suggests that "another story"—not a sermon, a nonfiction book on prophecy, or a reading of the Bible—might convince her to revise the books' version of biblical truth.

Because of her newfound evangelical faith, Rachel is concerned about her mother's salvation. Her mother does not accept her daughter's faith and while she says she believes in God, she rejects the rigid lines between saved and unsaved that her daughter espouses. Rachel's frustration with her mother's refusal to accept the truth of Christian salvation comes out in a discussion about the novel's characters. I ask if anything about the books makes her frustrated or angry.

"Hattie makes me angry. It makes me frustrated, even this Chaim Rosenweig." She struggles to pronounce his name and laughs, "Or however you say it." Rachel seems embarrassed that she cannot pronounce the character's name and acknowledges through her laugh a slight uneasiness.

"These people who won't convert?"

"They won't convert. They are given every . . . they could die tomorrow, locusts could suck the life out of them or whatever. They are being slapped in the face with God and they are going, 'I don't know.' I told my mom, OK, fine, if she is not going to believe, fine. But she has to promise me that if people start disappearing, she has to promise me that she'll believe God did that."

Rachel says this with a slightly joking tone that she means to be entertaining to both me and to her mother. I laugh out loud, as does Margaret from the kitchen sink where she is washing the breakfast dishes. But Rachel is serious as well. She does truly worry that her mother might "die tomorrow" unsaved, but she seems to have had this conversation often enough with her mother that it has taken on this funny and ironic tone. Continuing the performance, Rachel turns to Margaret, "Don't be waiting around until the locusts come and the moon turns to blood and whatever. Just go ahead and admit it." Then she turns back to me, "But she could be killed when all the chaos happens, when all the cars are off the road. She could be killed, so she might as well believe now. That's what is frustrating to me. People who are being hit with it and they still don't see it."

Rachel's return to her initial comment about the books' characters surprises me. She links them directly back to her mother's lack of faith and moves from the book's scenario to her mother without pause. She clearly associates Hattie's and Chaim Rozenweig's stubborn refusal to accept Christianity with her mother's, and she directs her frustration through the books' characters to her mother. Rachel has also tried to get her mother to make that direct association. For Christmas, she gave her mother a copy of the first book in the series. During her interview, Margaret says openly that she read it out of a sense of obligation to her daughter.

"It was a nice story. It was OK. But it reminded me of some of the movies my husband loved where there are good guys and there are bad guys and the fight scenes and all that. . . ."

"So in a book you look for less clear lines between good and evil? More ambiguous characters?"

"Yeah."

"Were you annoyed by it? Bored?"

"I was annoyed that this wonderful God would just come and do this to these nice people. They weren't hurting anybody. That sort of annoyed me. And then, when they see this video and all of the sudden they understand the truth . . . it's annoying because, if God is so good, why would he do that? It's God on a power trip."

Once I suggest the word *annoying*, Margaret uses it several times. Her reading that the books represent "God on a power trip" seems to me a direct critique of evangelicalism. This comment refers directly to evangelicals, perhaps even to her own children, imagining the destruction of the world while only they are saved. Margaret sees in the books a kind of American, Christian, and even southern chauvinism that she finds distasteful. When I ask her why people might be attracted to the novels, her answer contains a lament for what she sees as the narrow perspective of the books and, by implication, her daughter.

> They like the adventure, I'm sure. Talking to Rachel, people like her believe that this is literally going to happen. And I thought, "My beautiful, intelligent daughter could believe something like this?" I mean, maybe 1 percent of the planet's population is Christian or would even be exposed to these ideas. What kind of a God would do that? I mean what about the Buddhists? What about the Jewish people? What about the Indians? What makes you think you little Bible Belt people . . . are chosen? What makes you so special?

Margaret objects to the book's focus on the United States, its condemnation of all other perspectives, and its arrogant refusal to see other points of view. She laments her daughter's adherence to this kind of narrow belief. In response to Rachel's warning that all of her children might disappear and that this should be a signal to Margaret to turn to the faith, Margaret is indignant. She does not respond to Rachel right away, but in the course of her own interview she comments, "If everybody did disappear, I would say to God, 'What the heck did you do that for? It wasn't nice. I'm a nice person and you shouldn't do things to people that aren't nice.'" Then she adds a concession to her daughter's point of view, "Unless you think it will make them better." This last phrase seems odd after her initial scolding of God for thoughtlessness. She indicates that bad things could happen to people through God's will if it strengthened them or built their characters. It seems that Margaret is working out a theory of what theologians call "theodicy" even as we speak to one another. She finds herself suddenly struck with the question of why, if God should be nice, bad things might happen. She answers, "Unless you think it will make them better."

Later, Margaret repeats, somewhat hollowly, her insistence that it is a "good story," but as before, she counters this with another analogy. This time, she defers to her daughter's presence. "It more reminded me . . . Rachel would be upset." From the living room, where Rachel is helping her three-year-old daughter find crayons, she calls, "I don't care."

Margaret finishes her thought. "It was more of a trashy novel-type plot."

"What kept you reading it?"

"My daughter."

Rachel jumps in a little defensively, "Well, I thought you would enjoy reading it, the relationships of the different people."

"I did enjoy the relationships. Father and daughter. But I did not look at it as something that could really happen."

During the course of the interview, Margaret several times tries to temper her harsh judgments of the book's form and content with respect for her daughter's faith and the pleasure she derives from reading the books. She insists that it is a "good story" or that she "enjoyed the relationships," but it is clear to both of them that the book failed to have the impact Rachel desired. Both Rachel and Margaret role-play for each other. Rachel insists that she gave the book to her mother because she thought her mother would "enjoy the relationships." This is partially true, but both know that she also hoped to influence her mother religiously. Margaret pretends to have enjoyed the book at least a little, but again, they both seem to silently acknowledge that she did not. Rachel made no attempt to offer her the second book in the series and Margaret did not request it. When I ask Margaret if she will read the second book, she says, "If my daughter asked me to."

By refusing the apocalyptic belief that Rachel embraces, Margaret is aware of creating a painful split between herself and her daughter. Rachel now belongs to a community that Margaret herself wants no part of. Both mother and daughter try to overcome this rift in various ways—by making concessions to each other's points of view, by arguing for their own view, by proselytizing.

Reading the *Left Behind* series points out to Rachel how stark the difference between her and her mother might become—she will be raptured, her mother will be left behind. The books seem to underline for Rachel that this divide with her mother could be eternal; she will be saved and her mother damned.

Rachel has, she believes, a knowledge that her mother does not possess, a knowledge of how the world will end and what will become of believers and nonbelievers alike. To Margaret this knowledge is arrogant and absurd: "What makes you think you little Bible Belt people . . . are chosen? What makes you so special?" Margaret uses this argument both to try to persuade her daughter and to defend herself against the constant assault of her children on the integrity of her religious beliefs. In this push and pull, Margaret and Rachel strive to maintain their relationship even while other commitments and demands seem to tear them apart. At this particular moment, their intimacy does not seem threatened by Rachel's apocalyptic beliefs; they often seem to relish their disagreement. But the vulnerability of their relationship is also evident in Rachel's irritation over her mother's constant refusals, and in Margaret's lament over her daughter's rigid beliefs.

As another concession to Rachel, Margaret says that she is glad her children have found religion if it makes them happy, but the words ring hollow to me. She has decided that she failed to give her children the foundation in religion that would have made evangelicalism less appealing to them. "If I had to do it over, I would have them in a church, just to give them that background that I had so that they could make intelligent conversation and they could make informed decisions. . . . There are reasons, if you are going to raise your children in the Bible Belt, you need to give them the background. They did not get that and maybe that's how they got sucked in." She laughs at her own harsh language. "I don't know. But it's OK. They are happy; they like their churches. I think they are doing some good things. Still, it bothers me. Rachel is probably the least judgmental."

In Margaret's analysis, her children's engagement with the novels and with evangelicalism is itself a product of growing up in the "Bible Belt." She sees it as constitutive of their desire to unite with the culture in which they were raised, and she blames herself for not preparing them better to face that culture. Giving credence to Margaret's theory is the fact that all of her children became evangelical Christians shortly before their marriages to evangelicals. For Rachel, however, the problem consists of being torn between two very different "families"—her biological family and the family of faith to which she now belongs. These two locations that draw her loyalty and her time are at odds with each other, and she struggles to keep them together. Rachel's newfound apocalyptic faith does not completely give her a sense of security, because her sense of distinction is constantly challenged by her mother's refusal to accept it. In part, this is why Rachel's frustration is so intense and why she keeps continual pressure on her mother to convert. Conversion would resolve this tension and give Rachel a stronger sense of harmony and security. It would overcome the divide that now seems to Rachel eternal.

Readers very often point to divisions in their families—they are acutely aware of family members who remain outside of evangelicalism and who will be unsaved when the rapture comes. I am struck by how often readers question the salvation of their mothers in particular. An unbelieving mother or one whose faith has slipped is the most common representative of a lost family member. As readers repeatedly question their mothers' salvation, I am reminded of Hester Bell Wilson's accusation against unbelieving mothers in Ernest Angley's novel *Raptured*. On the morning after the rapture, Hester confronts one mother who was left behind, "Tears were rolling down Hester's cheeks. She was thinking that if her mother had taken her to church and taught her in the right way, she might not have been left behind either; but she had no encouragement. 'Mothers like you have a lot to think about this morning,' she cried."[11] Because mothers play such a crucial role in evangelical piety, readers seem acutely aware of the failings of their own mothers. Their mothers' rejection of the faith strikes deep at their sense of security and rightness in the faith. Just as the faithful mother is the cornerstone of rapture fiction, the unbelieving mother is a crucial figure in the divided family. Readers very often give *Left Behind* to their mothers as a kind of disciplining gesture, an attempt to draw them into the fold. As far as I can tell, very few find this gesture successful.

The families of readers are not often as divided as Rachel and Margaret. Family structure supports the reading of *Left Behind*, and reading the novels reinforces family identity. While readers like Rachel try to put the books in the hands of unbelievers as a means of conversion, they read the books within already established networks. One reader offers a powerful story of how deeply the reading of *Left Behind* can become embedded in social and family life. Unlike Margaret and Rachel, Katie's immediate family is undivided in its commitment to evangelical Christianity and to the kind of eschatology presented in the books. In fact, the books have come to serve as links between the family members, bonds that grow stronger through reading.

I interview Katie at a coffee shop near the university where she is just finishing a Ph.D. She is young, recently married, and very open to the interview. Though we are meeting for the first time, she suggests we share a bowl of soup and a sandwich. As we begin to talk and Katie begins to tell her story, I keep getting in the way. I interrupt her several times before I understand that

Katie's story has a distinct chronology and that the books are a part of this chronology in a way I cannot understand if I continue to direct the conversation with my interview guide. At last, I interject only with words of encouragement, "Yes," "I understand," "That's interesting," and let Katie tell her story in her own way.

Katie was raised in a religious family. She recounts drifting away from her commitment to her family's faith while in her early twenties, losing the intimate contact with her faith that characterized her years growing up. "I don't know that I ever doubted my faith. I just wasn't as devout basically. I mean, I went to church, but I was more concerned with what I was doing in life, what was going on, my goals, you know, that sort of thing."

Then suddenly, six months before Katie's wedding, her younger sister, Judith, was killed in a car accident. For Katie, that event caused a sudden change in perspective. "We just, my entire family, we all went home to be with my parents, to go through all of the shock together, the funeral and the viewing and everything. That was definitely the hardest time in my life. And our family is pretty strong. We definitely have a very supportive community, so it was very much a bonding time for our family."

Her sister, also a devout Christian, had recently started a Bible study for other college students that, in the weeks following Judith's death, grew from forty people to three hundred people. Katie sees this as God's work through her sister and as something that gives meaning to her death.

> That's just an amazing thing that has come out of her death and that . . . things like that have really kept our family going as far as we can see the fruits of having to suffer that way. And even at her funeral, there were a couple thousand people there, and the pastor gave an amazing invitation, lots of people went forward, even my aunts and uncles who had never accepted the Lord, you know, went forward. . . . It really helped us focus on what's our role here on earth and how can we use that example to really make reaching other people and doing God's will the primary focus of our lives. So that's really for me the changing point.

Katie narrates Judith's death as a transition not only for her own spiritual life, but also for her family's. Death brought them closer together, even drawing unbelieving relatives into her family's religious faith. Judith's death began, as well, to lead them deeper into thoughts about heaven and the end of time. These two things—heaven and the rapture—became inextricably tied to each other through Judith's death. Both heaven and the rapture were eschatological, world-ending possibilities that seemed to link the family to Judith now that she was physically absent. At this crucial moment, the family was introduced to the *Left Behind* series. "[Judith's death] made heaven seem so much more real. . . . My family started studying heaven and really focusing on what it's like, what does the Bible teach about immediately when you die and what heaven is like. Right about that time, we were introduced to this *Left Behind* series. Someone, it may have come out before then, but for some reason, that January [she died in December], my family got a hold of this, the first book."

Katie makes a close connection between her sister's death and the discovery of the series. She also speaks collectively of that discovery. She speaks of "we" and "my family." She does not indicate one individual in the family who began to read the novels but instead suggests that it was a communal discovery: "My family got a hold of this, the first book."

The books had a dramatic effect. They became a part of the family's grieving and instilled in them hope about seeing Judith again soon. "There were these books that talked about the end times, and my family was all like, 'Yeah, bring it on. We want to go to heaven.' My whole family, you know, we are pretty sure we are going to be out with the first batch. When the rapture happens, we're gone."

Katie's family's passion for the rapture is not a desire to escape the complexity of culture so much as it is a longing for reunion. It is founded on a deep desire to see Judith again, a desire that the rapture seems to both answer and incite. Either way, one might accuse Katie and her family of the purest form of escapism. Rather than dealing with the reality of their sister and daughter's death, they choose to imagine that the world will end so that they can see Judith again. Perhaps one might even suggest that for her family, Judith's death was itself a kind of world-ending experience and their subsequent interest in the rapture, facilitated by the fantasy of the books, is simply a metaphorical and narrative extension of a world already diminished by Judith's absence.

On the other hand, we can also see the rapture as a vivid confrontation with the reality of death. Through reading *Left Behind*, Katie's family finds a kind of solace in grief, a hope that they might see Judith again sooner rather than later. For them, the solace of heaven is not quite enough. It is too distant, too many years away. The rapture is something they can hope for at every minute. It might happen at any time; their joyful reunion might be only minutes away. This allows them to live with joyful expectation even in the experience of intense grief. Katie's family does not refuse to grieve nor are they in denial of their grief, but they grasp onto a certain kind of meaning in death and allow death to shape their worldview and change how they live. Belief in the rapture, which until Judith's death was a somewhat passive belief, has become pressing, active, and real.

For Katie, nearly everything in her life is narrated through the before and after of her sister's death. Her family life, her own commitment to God, her reading habits—all of these enter into a particular chronological narrative that hinges on that tragic accident. She describes her reading habits, "I do not read at all. It's really bad. . . . Actually, that's one thing that completely changed when my sister died. I found so much comfort in reading books on grieving. . . . Before she died, I think it's kind of from being left-brained, I like concrete things. Give me a problem to solve or whatever. I never really read. I didn't read the paper; I didn't read books. I didn't read much at all. After she died, I really got comfort from reading, and I got more to where I really enjoy reading. With those books [*Left Behind*], I don't do anything but read."

Reading is a way to manage and confront grief. She seeks out those books that can specifically help her to negotiate this tragedy. The result is comfort. The books have this effect not only for Katie, but also for her family. Katie describes how reading the books draws her family closer. It gives them a common narrative around which to focus their hope and expectation. With her husband, who travels frequently, Katie describes sharing the books over great distance. He might be in a hotel room in Hong Kong, but he is reading the books just as she is at home. They share the stories and have a common experience even though they are separated. With her mother and father, sisters and brothers, this bond seems to be even stronger so that she speaks of a collective discovery and collective reading, "our" reading and what "we" think about the books.

Katie's family not only drew closer together but also tried to draw others into the discovery and the collective sense of meaning they found. Katie's mother went out and bought several copies for friends and family. Katie and her then fiancé did the same. They saw the books not only as comfort for them, but also as hope for others. Again notice how Katie speaks about this experience in a collective voice: "It [reading the books] has just made us more open with the people that aren't saved that we care about. [We can say to them,] 'Here's an example. This might not be the truth. It's someone's story written about the Book of Revelation, but this is a way it could happen, and we want you to. . . . '" Katie leaves this last hoped-for action blank. She may mean simply that they want their listener to know about the rapture, but more likely they hope for more intense action—"we want you to be saved." It may be both of these things at once. Regardless, her family saw the books as opportunities to share this knowledge and belief with other people; the books and Judith's death intensified their concern for the "unsaved."

These attempts to extend networks of faith have not been particularly successful. Katie tells the story of one uncle to whom her mother sent a copy of

Left Behind. This uncle represents an unincorporated figure in Katie's tightly constructed social world. Neither can he accept the way Katie's family gives meaning to Judith's death nor will he read the novels. His refusal to participate in the religious meaning given to Judith's death is troubling for Katie.

> That uncle is an atheist. My aunt, sometimes, the things she says, she might be saved, I'm not sure, but he definitely isn't. He'll tell you, he actually is very hard to argue with because he'll tell you that he used to believe the Bible . . . but now he's enlightened and he knows its just a story and he's into, kind of like, the Indian mythology–type stuff. So he's really hard to argue with because he's kind of . . . degrading. And he thinks we're sort of foolish for believing it. . . . When they came to the funeral, he wouldn't view her body, he wouldn't . . . like before the funeral service, he told—he was talking to some cousins, and he said, "I know what they are going to say. They're going to say she's in heaven and they're going to say this and they're going to say that and don't believe anything they say. There's no heaven and there's no hell. And she's spirit. . . ."

Katie broke off quoting her uncle here as if she were no longer willing or able to imagine how he would finish that sentence. "Just very negative and very offensive. I mean our family is going through this tragedy, the least he can do is keep his mouth shut if he doesn't believe what we believe." Katie speaks this last sentence with a considerable amount of bitterness at her uncle's refusal to accept the family's narrative of hope. She then adds another sentence more gently. "I mean the hope that we have is that she is in heaven."

This uncle's denial that Judith might be in heaven strikes at the heart of the family's hope and causes pain. Katie struggles both with her anger at this uncle's insensitivity and with her family's desire to reach out to him. Katie's mother sent this aunt and uncle a copy of *Left Behind,* and the family received no response. "I'm pretty sure he was offended. They didn't say anything about it. . . . That's one example where we didn't get any feedback and it probably wasn't accepted well." Because this uncle stands outside the faith, he cannot be integrated into their mourning and is not incorporated into Katie's ever-present "we." Like Rachel's attempts to draw her mother in and put an end to the challenge her mother's refusal presents, Katie's family struggles to overcome this challenge by her uncle. By remaining unincorporated, he is a bitter repudiation that, in the circumstances of pain and loss, the family cannot tolerate. At the same time, her uncle's rejection of the faith clarifies the unity her family finds. The division her uncle presents makes the family's own solidarity more visible.

Readers often use *Left Behind* to try to overcome rifts in the religiously divided family. One woman describes what she sees when she looks at her unbelieving mother-in-law (to whom she gave *Left Behind*) with her children: "I watch them and her and when I look at them, in spite of the fun they are having or whatever they are doing, what I see is eternal separation. When I think about them and I think about their family, that is all I see." "Eternal separation" speaks to the deep divide that religious difference introduces into the family structure and perhaps why readers so often seek to overcome this divide using whatever means they can. In church families, readers often find a more stable environment where beliefs can be sustained and nurtured, but there too, divisions and disagreements percolate. "Eternal separation" also hints at a fear of isolation embedded in being left behind or having loved ones left behind. Readers of *Left Behind* often reach out to their churches as an antidote to this fear and use their readings of the novels to try to draw others into this communal meaning and communal identity.

These stories of readers and their various families demonstrate that reading is a social transaction.[12] At the very least, it is a transaction between reader and writer. But beyond that, reading can be an act of social connection, a means through which readers mediate their identity as part of a community or in distinction to it. Readers read to connect themselves to other readers, to distinguish themselves from other readers, and to read themselves into a community. Through reading, they both form social bonds and challenge them.

In many modern understandings of pleasure reading, a reader escapes from the demands of his or her immediate social context. A reader seeks the pleasure of reading as an autoerotic experience indulged away from the judgments of others. Take Alberto Manguel's description of "private reading" in his *A History of Reading* as an example: "Reading in bed is a self-centered act, immobile, free from ordinary social conventions, invisible to the world, and one that, because it takes place between the sheets, in the realm of lust and sinful idleness, has something of the thrill of the forbidden."[13] Reading in bed and the association between reading and sex have become almost commonplace descriptors of modern reading. Reading is done alone, perhaps to the disapproval of others and certainly as a means of escape from them. It is done without thought of practical application or utility. Reading is a route for deep and sensual pleasure and stands outside everyday activity.

Readers of *Left Behind*, like other kinds of pleasure readers, describe reading in bed. They talk about what Victor Nell calls "ludic reading" and Janice Radway refers to as "deep reading"—the intense, absorbing act of reading.[14] Yet this pleasure reading is grounded in a desire for connection with others. The pleasure comes not from avoiding the social, but from engaging with it.

Readers of *Left Behind* seek and find pleasure in the social act of reading—in the way it connects and divides them. And unlike Manguel's bed-reader, readers of *Left Behind* do not so much find "lust, sinful idleness . . . and the thrill of things forbidden" as they do spiritual edification and religious meaning. This does not seem to detract from the pleasure of reading, but to intensify it.

For Sarah, Rachel, and Katie, reading is one way they interpret their place in the social landscape. They find in reading a place of identity and belonging. They consent to the books' narrative of truth. To Sarah's pastor, Mark, Margaret, and Katie's uncle, *Left Behind* articulates difference, a difference that believers fear will be eternal. Yet, in many cases, even unbelievers read *Left Behind* in order to connect themselves with those who love the novels. In the next chapter, I will examine more closely the reading of those who do not find themselves easily hailed by *Left Behind* and the communities to which it presumably connects them.

3

The Margins of *Left Behind*'s Readership

Left Behind's producers make clear their desire to edify readers and even transform them, to "minister to people's spiritual needs," as the president of Tyndale House puts it.[1] Not only are the books written with explicitly ideological intent, they are also, as we have seen, often read in the influential contexts of family and church. In other words, the reading is highly and explicitly structured in a way that may not be true for other kinds of pleasure reading. Producers know what readers ought to think upon reading *Left Behind*, and the contexts in which the books are read also contain strong messages about what the books are and how they should be understood. This powerful ideological context raises important questions about the interpretation of *Left Behind*. Do readers follow the producers' preferred meanings? To what extent do readers use the books for purposes that the producers do not intend? How does reading change when the ideological context changes?[2]

This chapter turns away from the white evangelical mainstream where the books are most often read. Instead, it focuses on the margins of the readership, on those who, because of their different religious orientations, interact with the books in quite different ways. The majority of readers of *Left Behind* are white, evangelical in religious orientation, and committed to belief in the rapture and tribulation before they open the first page. *Left Behind* confirms the rightness of their beliefs and affirms their religious identities. This chapter explores the reading and interpretation practices of people with various religious backgrounds who do not fit into the books' mainstream readership—a liberal Protestant, a Catholic, a Mormon, a woman on the margins of evangelicalism, and an African American woman. While collected here, their stories are, in fact, quite different from each other and resist any easy summation. In each case, however, the ideological context in which the books are read transforms the reading and places readers in various orientations to the fiction.

Resisting the Rapture: Nonevangelical Readers of *Left Behind*

The producers and many readers believe that by passing the books on to unbelievers, they can share and perhaps draw others into their particular kind of religious faith. While the language of *Left Behind* is a conservative Protestant language and its assumptions are both religiously and culturally specific, the series has still exceeded the boundaries of evangelicalism in a way unprecedented in recent Christian fiction. Readers outside the books' immediate religious context, particularly those with another strong religious identity, however, often find the text difficult to interpret, sometimes confusing, and sometimes infuriating. Nonevangelical readers do not read the series with an enthusiasm that matches that of their evangelical counterparts. They often find themselves annoyed, bored, angry, or alienated. Without a connection to evangelicalism, readers often do not find the plot compelling, remember few details about the characters, and rarely read the entire series. This indicates the importance of the context in which the books are read. Readers' "interpretive communities" are not homogenous or sealed, but the books have their most powerful effect within interpretive communities that give credence to the books' premise. Outside of these communities, the books succeed little in engaging readers' imaginations.

Samantha was given the books by a friend with whom she spent significant time talking about religion and matters of faith. The friend found the books spiritually important and gave the first one to Samantha with a high recommendation. Like her friend, Samantha is a Protestant, and she grew up in a Presbyterian church with liberal parents. She is devoutly religious herself, and says with some embarrassment that she attends a Baptist church. "I have a stigma associated with the word *Baptist*," she explains, and then she talks about her own Baptist congregation. Like traditional Baptists, this congregation affirms the "sanctity of the believer" and the "autonomy of the local congregation." For this congregation, however, that means affirming homosexual marriage, opposing the death penalty, and supporting a woman's right to choose abortion. Her church has been targeted for protests by the Kansas-based Westboro Baptist Church opposed to their practice of "holy unions."[3]

Early in the interview, Samantha points to the title at the top of my interview guide, which reads "Christian Apocalyptic Fiction and Its Readers." "You know, it's funny, because I wouldn't think of myself as being grouped as a reader of Christian apocalyptic fiction." She heard an episode on the public radio show *This American Life* in which a woman sees a man reading *Left Behind* on a plane and makes negative assumptions about him. Samantha largely agrees with this woman's assessment of the man, and yet she too read the books. To quell this tension, Samantha says, "I read the novels in the privacy of my own home. You know, this is interesting, I probably would not have read [the book] in public. I have issues with my public persona." She laughs. "I wouldn't want to be known as a person who read the book and believed this as a sort of extension of doctrine."

Samantha's resistance to becoming known as a reader of *Left Behind* raises the question of why she read the novels at all and why, given her opposition, she read more than one. She is very familiar with the kind of religious views and eschatology the books profess and tells me about family members whose views match those in the books. But it was not simple curiosity that led Samantha to read the books. She describes herself as an indiscriminate reader. "I tend to read whatever is handy," she says. It isn't unusual for her to randomly read books given to her by friends. "I was at a time in my life where I just needed to read something that wasn't very. . . ." She pauses a long time as though she is hesitant to fill in the blank, perhaps out of fear of offending me.[4] At last, I attempt to fill in the blank.

"Not very deep? Or very difficult?"

"Yes, it's a very easy read. Like one or two days and then you can knock out a book and go back to your life."

"And what did you think of the first one?"

Samantha speaks very carefully and slowly, choosing her words. "I thought it was a fine, engaging story that sucked you in at the beginning and spit you out at the end and moved along quickly. I . . . I have a . . . I was a little . . . I felt like the interpretation . . . the biblical interpretation was lost on me because I don't subscribe to that. . . ."

"So you felt you could read past that?"

"Yeah, in the first one. I read past that and I thought it was effective in that I thought to myself, 'Wow, if it's like that, that really sucks.'" We both laugh, and I try to signal through my laughter that Samantha need not be concerned about offending me. She continues, "That was really the limit of my reaction. It wasn't strong and it wasn't negative, you know, it was just, that was a good book and now I'm going to . . . you know, sort of like reading John Grisham or something. You read it and probably forget the plot and go on. Except that there was a second book." She says this with a lift to her voice that indicates there is more to the story, that the second book prompted a stronger reaction.

"So I read the second book and I started to get irritated. I think the primary reason was the portrayal of male and female roles. . . . So I think really that was the point where I said, 'OK, enough of this.' "

I urge her to be more specific. "Were there particular moments you remember in the books?"

"I don't remember partly because I don't remember the books very well. I remember of the remaining people who weren't taken up in the rapture, there was a woman who was not a believer, but became a believer and was really dependent on a man for her faith. Her faith was really wrapped up in her relationship with this guy. Then there was a woman who turns out to be really bad. . . . By the time I got tired of it, all the women were either stupid or bad."

Samantha describes ending her relationship with the books because she became "irritated" and then "tired of it." A little later in the interview, however, she describes another response: anger. Anger prompted her to buy the third book.

"Then I started to read the third book. I actually bought the third book. I was mad now and I wanted to see if I was going to stay mad. I didn't know if it was just where we stopped. . . . I was mad and I wanted to know if I was mad for the right reasons."

"Where did you buy the third book?"

"I think it was Wal-Mart or K-Mart. It wasn't even a bookstore. It was on display. It wasn't a completely planned purchase. It was so. . . . OK, it didn't help my irritation . . . it didn't ease it. It remained. This continual portrayal of women and this sort of Cold War approach to [faith]."

After the third book, Samantha could no longer tolerate the political and theological views of the books, and the anger that attracted her to the third book was not enough to prompt her to continue to read what she describes as "propaganda."

"I thought, 'OK, we've lost any reasonable role, connection to the wide variety of faiths that exist and the wide variety of faiths that could be correct. . . . ' This was the first of them that I had bought and when I finished that, I thought, 'No way am I contributing to this.' At that point, I was making a commercial, 'how do I vote with my feet' sort of decision."

Samantha's narrative of interaction with the books is a trajectory from mild pleasure to something that almost resembles disgust. At first she was drawn in by the books. She liked the quickly moving plot, the cliffhanger endings, the kind of story that "sucked you in at the beginning and spit you out at the end." When she began to sense that *Left Behind* contradicted and even offended her own political and religious views, she didn't stop reading, but continued out of anger: "I was mad and I wanted to see if I was going to stay mad." This was enough motivation to lead her to buy the third book in the series, but it was not enough to sustain her interest in the series. Pleasure and anger are not contradictory, in Samantha's case, but feed into one another, so that anger allowed her to continue to find some pleasure in reading the books. By the end, however, she felt morally obligated not to support the books by buying them and now shows no interest in borrowing them from her friend. Anger did not sustain her interest in the books, and she eventually abandoned her reading of the series.

Because she grew up as a Protestant and has relatives whose eschatological views are close to those in the books, Samantha is familiar with the narrative of *Left Behind*—the rapture, Antichrist, and tribulation. She long ago decided that this kind of end-times belief is not persuasive to her. She finds the books familiar, perhaps too familiar—reminding her of her submissive aunt and her domineering uncle who talk a lot about Satan. Unlike other readers whose beliefs and practices are confirmed by reading, Samantha is both alienated and angry. In relation to the books, she finds herself a marginal outsider and is uncomfortable about being associated with them. After the third book, she felt the need to distance herself further from them, so strongly do they contradict positions and beliefs significant to her.

Unlike other, more sympathetic readers, Samantha does not remember the plot or the characters well. She does not remember the characters' names and has only vague, mostly negative associations with them. She remembers that the women are either "stupid or bad," that the male characters seem arrogant. She remembers objecting to the overpersonification of evil in the form of the Antichrist. For the most part, however, she seems to have read the novels as something to distract her, but not something to remember. For other readers more invested in the novels' eschatology and theology, the characters often stand out in sharp relief. These readers remember scenes vividly, and certain scenes bring them to tears while others bring them to their knees to pray. Without a fundamental agreement about the religious premise of the novels, Samantha remains unmoved except to anger.

While Samantha's response stands in sharp contrast to evangelical responses, she is also quite different from Catholic and Mormon readers. For

Samantha, the language of the novels is familiar and offensive. For readers more distant from Protestantism, it is unfamiliar and at times, impenetrable. Laura's husband, Mark, is angered by the books' attempts to scare people into faith and by what he sees as the books' relentless commercialization and marketing, but he also feels put off by what he calls the books' "Protestant-ese."

"I think though that the type of nondenominational Protestant Christians like in the book that I read, there's a whole bunch of Christian-ese built into it, like 'testimonies.' . . ."

Laura encourages him to clarify, "Like vocab that. . . ."

"Yeah, Protestant-ese. There are facets of being a Protestant, characteristics that are built into these books. . . . I don't think it is something you should stay away from, but it is important to note that, in Christian circles, people talk differently. They use phrases, they use sentence constructions, they use words in ways that other people won't understand. . . . We get these things in the mail from Family Life and they are like Mad Libs for Christians, fill in the blank with what you think should go here. 'Dear Brothers and Sisters in Christ,' this whole 'washed in the Blood' thing. . . . As I read through [Left Behind], it was just interesting to watch this whole Protestant-ese or Christian-ese play itself out and try to pretty itself as entertainment."

Mark is clear about the fact that he did not connect with the first Left Behind novel, the only one he read. This can, in part, be explained by the fact that he feels alienated by the religious language of the books. As a devout and lifelong Catholic, he cannot identify with the Protestant language. Instead he finds himself watching, bemused, as the "Protestant-ese . . . played itself out and tried to pretty itself as entertainment." He asks for acknowledgement that "in Christian circles, people talk differently," acknowledgement that the language of the books is not a universal Christian language. Mark is put off by the books' construction of a Protestant worldview that then makes vast universal claims. The books' Christians hold Promise Keeper–like rallies in sports stadiums around the world and assume that the entire world finds this as captivating as Americans do. The leader of the Tribulation Force, a Jewish convert to Christianity named Tsion Ben Judah, speaks like British theologian and evangelical hero C. S. Lewis, sometimes borrowing whole passages from Lewis's books on Christian apologetics. All of the Christian characters, whether they are Middle Eastern, Greek, or from the American Midwest, speak in the idiom of American evangelicalism. In the midst of all of this, Mark wants an acknowledgement that "other people won't understand."

One Mormon reader makes this point even more starkly. A devout woman named Ellen describes her sense of alienation in reading the first book.

The vocabulary is really different between the Mormon Church and other churches. And it always makes me uncomfortable—or *uncomfortable* is the wrong word, but when people talk about these points of having become a believer or accepting Christ or having been born again, those things, they are almost foreign in a way. . . . My experience with evangelism and those kinds of churches has always been awkward. It's something so deep and personal, and so even the first few chapters, you know, "That was the day that Buck became a believer," but his friends wanted him to accept Christ into his life. That vocabulary right there is hard to read. I don't relate to it at all.

Like Mark, Ellen points to the vocabulary of this particular brand of Protestantism that leaves her scratching her head. She is confounded by a sequence in the beginning of the first novel in which Buck Williams claims to have come to believe in God after a miraculous occurrence in Israel, but still is not a Christian. She finds the insistence on "accepting Christ" foreign and does not "relate to it at all." The sense of distance from the language of the text is so strong that she finds it even "hard to read." Like Mark, Ellen did not go on to read the second book, but she does express interest in learning more about Mormon eschatology so that she can compare it with the views of *Left Behind*.

Readers' attempts to evangelize through the books are most effective in supportive contexts where the person to whom they have reached out already has reason to be engaged with their attempts. When a reader is already rooted in another religious context, one foreign to the premise and message of *Left Behind*, the books promote neither pleasure nor persuasion. If a reader is already embedded in dispensationalism or connected in some way through church, family, or other social networks, LaHaye and Jenkins's message of the world's imminent destruction and the need for personal salvation might hit the mark. Without this context, the books' language is usually too culturally specific, though it makes universal claims, to do the work producers and many readers hope it will. For readers on the outside, *Left Behind* can be interesting because, as one Mormon man says, "the language is so far out there, to my mind it is almost wacky." But this does not mean it necessarily has the power to influence or persuade.[5]

On the other hand, *Left Behind* does speak a more broadly cultural language than dispensationalism alone. Readers outside evangelical belief can recognize aspects of apocalypticism that may seem familiar to them, and while Catholic and Mormon readers may feel disoriented by *Left Behind*, they also express an interest in learning more about their own faiths' apocalyptic beliefs. In a pluralistic environment, because boundaries are porous, unstable, and difficult to maintain, reading is shaped by several often contradictory contexts at once. Such is the case for Susan, who reads *Left Behind* in a state of profound uncertainty about its meaning for her.

Susan: "Searching for the Right Way"

The text that Susan creates in her reading of *Left Behind* is one that she uses to speak to, or perhaps even to encourage, the doubts she feels about her own religious life. Susan faces many contradictions within her life experience that position her on the margins of evangelicalism, that cause her to refuse the discipline of the church and yet deeply internalize it at the same time, that cause her to embrace the precepts of her received religious faith and then cast them off when they seem not to work for her.

Susan has been married three times and has two children, both grown and living not far from her. Susan was raised Catholic by a domineering stepfather whom she still regards with significant resentment. When she was in her early twenties, her biological father reentered her life. He had become a fiery, nondenominational preacher. She idolized him and saw him as an alternative to her stepfather—a person with genuine faith as opposed to her stepfather's cultural Catholicism. "Led to Christ" by her father, she had a "bornagain" experience that she still remembers as the time that she was saved. Despite this deeply religious experience, Susan's life took several turns away from the traditional, evangelical church. She married a non-Christian man who was unkind to her and did not like her participation in church. When they divorced, the very church that had provided a sanctuary for her in her troubled marriage rejected her because she was now a divorced woman. She was not allowed to teach Sunday school or have full participation in the congregation. Angry, she left that church only to face a similar sense of rejection at others. Since that time in her early adulthood, she has not participated in an organized church and has chosen to pursue spiritual questions on her own.

Recently, she describes finding these questions more pressing. She finds herself praying more often and turning to various books, including the Bible, for spiritual guidance and help. She talks about religion and faith endlessly with friends and family. Every night, before bed, she has what she calls "my spiritual time," when she talks to God about her life and struggles, her questions and difficulties. This is time that takes her away from her husband and for which she feels guilty and "selfish," but she pursues it nonetheless as some of the most important time of her day. During our interview, she seems to reach out to me for confirmation that these personal religious practices, removed from the institution of the church, are valid. Susan seems both strong in her religious convictions—certain of the presence of demons and angels, for example, and convinced that God is at work in the world and human history—and deeply in doubt about her own salvation and her own religious life. She has constructed her religious practice in such a way that she does not have the constant support of a community of faith; she does not have other people to secure her in religious faith. As a result, she is both more open to challenge and disagreement and more uncertain about where exactly she stands in the cosmic scheme of her belief.

She was introduced to *Left Behind* through the influence of her sister. Her sister, in contrast to Susan, is invested in a religious and evangelical community. Her own religious faith is more traditional, and she is more comfortable in the church, calling it her "home," as is common among readers of *Left Behind*. Susan avoided reading the first book in the series for a long time. She tells me that this was not because she did not want to read it, but because when she reads a novel, she gets too involved in it to the neglect of anything else. "Because when I read, I don't do anything else. I don't cook; I don't clean the house. I hibernate. I don't like to do that because I am not very sociable. When I really read." Susan likes to make the world of the novel she is reading her own. She uses it to shut out the "actual" world of her daily life and become immersed in this alternative world. When she finally picked up the first *Left Behind* novel, this is exactly what happened.

> We went to the mountains a few months ago. It was raining and it was cold, and I couldn't get outside and do anything, so I thought this was a good time to start the book. So I did, and I did not get dressed, after the first day I did not get dressed or get a shower until it was three or four in the afternoon. . . . I'm laying around in my sweats. I'd sneak to the bathroom to read a little bit more, it was one of those books, you know. I hibernated and I read the book. And I loved it.

Susan finished the book in two days, becoming completely absorbed in the lives of the characters. Despite the fact that she has not been to church in many years, the apocalyptic scenario the book presents is entirely familiar and unsurprising to her. She has long believed in the rapture and knows that it is coming. But the novel does more than simply reawaken a long-held belief. It also gives her vivid images for the prophecy that she has embraced all of her adult life. She likes the way it brings obscure biblical prophecy to life, but at the same time, the book piques anxiety about her own salvation.

"I hadn't thought about what was going to happen to the world that was left behind. And hey, what if I'm . . . I am . . . I don't want to be left behind. I mean I know I am saved, but. . . ." She pauses without filling in the blank.

"Do you feel a little doubt, like what if . . . ?"

"Well, you know what if I'm. . . ." Again she leaves off without stating the fear that she might be left behind. "You know in Hal Lindsey it says . . . you'll get a blessing just by reading Revelations. I think it says that. And I'm thinking you know I've never even read Revelations totally through. I want that blessing. I want that. And what if because I haven't gone to church, like today's society says, and I'm not a member, what if . . . and I know my own personal beliefs, but what if these are things I am supposed to do. I don't know. I'm like you, sometimes I'm searching for the right way or what you are supposed to do."

Susan finally locates her anxiety about her salvation in the fact that she is not a member of a church. Without the confirmation of that church body that she is indeed saved and that she is indeed doing what "you are supposed to do," the book raises in her uncertainties that she has in fact been "saved" the right way. Implicit in her response, however, is also a critique. She adds with slight sarcasm the phrase "like today's society says" implying that she feels churchgoing is more a social obligation than a spiritual requirement. The book has not, at least until this point, persuaded her that she needs to secure her faith inside a religious community. She continues to resist that discipline and asserts that she is "searching for the right way" and still at a loss as to what precisely that is.

At the same time, Susan's expression of self-doubt points to another deeply rooted fear—the fear of being "left behind," isolated from family and friends, left alone to face the end of the world rather than participating in the heavenly reunion. She sees herself as someone on the outside looking in, cherishing her independence, angry at the church structure's imposition on her freedom, and yet longing to be included, to be a part of the church "family" rather than "left behind." This fear points to a very powerful effect of the *Left Behind* series. It raises in readers a powerful desire for belonging and inclusion, a desire to be among the elect rather than the rejected. Susan's eloquent "What if . . . ?" seems to summarize this simultaneous fear and longing with precision.

Added to her concern about her own salvation is concern about her husband, as well. "You know I worry about my husband sometimes because . . . my stepdaughter and I talk about things like what you and I are talking about all the time and my husband will come in sometimes while we're talking and he'll come in with this off-the-wall thing and my stepdaughter says, 'Well, Susan, has Jerry been saved? Has Dad been saved?' And I said, 'I don't think he even knows what it means to be saved.' "

Susan makes a distinction between her own problem and that of her husband. At the very least, Susan knows what it means to be saved and feels she has done at least some of what is required. Her husband's "off-the-wall" comments, presumably sarcastic or dismissive about salvation or the rapture, show that he is in a state of denial or ignorance, not even knowing what it means to be saved or why one should want to be. At the same time, she later says that Jerry is a "very religious man," by which she indicates that he has strong ideas about religion and religious life that she respects. Susan is caught in the push and pull of the assurance of salvation. She feels confident neither in her own salvation nor in that of her husband, but she is also entirely unsure how to go about securing this. *Left Behind* seems to reinforce doubt rather than certainty and doubt seems to propel her reading of the series, the way that anger propels Samantha's.

Susan's doubt is tied to her lack of a religious community, but at the same time, she is well aware of the demands, restrictions, and beliefs of evangelicalism, to which she nominally belongs. In discussing the novels, she very often takes up orthodox positions that she also later, in another context, undermines. Susan expresses her belief, common to many evangelical readers, that the rapture and tribulation are coming soon. When I ask her what makes her think this is so, she answers without hesitation. First, the way our children are being treated. Second, the prevalence of homosexuality. By raising the issue of homosexuality, Susan reiterates a position that is common among readers and common to the books—that homosexuality is a sign of the depravity that leads to the end of the world. This repetition of the "sign" of homosexuality is significant to understanding the kind of disciplining work the narrative attempts. Homosexuality disrupts, challenges, and presents a profound threat to the patriarchal boundaries on which the narrative is constructed. It threatens the masculinity of the novel's male characters, and it threatens the structures of the community that are grounded on female desire for a male object, first for the husband, then for God.

Homosexual characters frequently arise in the books, especially as enemies of the Christians or lackeys of the Antichrist. Early in the series, Buck has several conflicts with a woman named Verna, who readers eventually learn is a lesbian. Her lesbian identity explains her power struggle with Buck and why she always gave Buck the "willies."[6] She is repeatedly contrasted with Chloe, whose femininity is obvious in her deference to Buck, her "selfless and loving" nature, and the fact that she is never "catty or a nag."[7] Later the authors introduce another homosexual character, this time an artist who works for the Antichrist. As with Verna, Guy Blod is meant to be funny, a character at whom we should laugh. Guy giggles and prances through his scenes. His sexual identity is set up in contrast with the authentic masculinity and heterosexuality of the Christians. We last see Guy worshipping the statue of the Antichrist that he himself has made.[8]

By picking up and vocalizing the antihomosexual themes in *Left Behind*, Susan shows a strong investment in the discipline of the community that she both rejects and has felt rejected by. She seems to agree with the books' premise that homosexuality—considered inauthentic masculinity and femininity—undoes societal structures and causes the swift apocalyptic end the books imagine. In fact, homosexuality and "what's happening to our children" both speak to the same anxiety: that the social structures that define and defend the "family" are unraveling.

As happened often in my conversation with Susan, this forceful statement of orthodox belief is later undermined by a story that she tells me. Her strong support of the church's position becomes complicated through her life experience. Toward the end of the interview, Susan tells the story of the death of her husband's sister. This woman lived an openly lesbian life in a town a few hours away from where Susan and her husband live. Jerry and Karen had been close growing up and her gay life troubled him. At the same time, Karen was the only family that Jerry had. Their parents had died many years ago, and Jerry wanted to stay in touch with her, so Susan and her husband visited frequently. On one visit, a few months before my interview with Susan, Karen died. Susan and Jerry had arrived the night before. They had all gone out for supper and celebrated Karen's birthday with a few drinks. They came home, said goodnight, and went to bed. Overnight, Karen suffered a heart attack and was dead in the morning.

Karen's death was a terrible shock to both of them. They were completely unprepared for it, and since Jerry had to return home for work, Susan was left to take care of the details of the funeral and Karen's possessions. Susan relates how during the days that she spent in Karen's house alone, Karen's community gathered around her. "The gals" as she called them, including a Unitarian minister, came over, brought food, told stories, and helped her plan a beautiful memorial service in Karen's backyard. Remembering how her sister-in-law was loved by these women and how both she and her husband were easily encircled by this love moves Susan to tears as she relates the story to me.

This community seems to raise a challenge to the evangelical community reinforced by *Left Behind*. Susan does not know what to make of the warmth, kindness, and generosity of the lesbian women. She seems genuinely baffled by it. She struggles to reconcile these two communities, but has made little progress. She concludes to me, "I feel totally different about . . . I still don't agree with the lifestyle, I don't understand it, but I have to say they are very compassionate and very caring people." She tries to stake her ground by not agreeing with the "lifestyle," but then feels that position challenged by a tangible experience of compassion and care. Perhaps Susan's own refusal of the discipline of institutional evangelicalism, her own marginal status as a believer unsure of her salvation makes possible her ability to see and experience the alternative community provided by Karen's friends. In fact, as she muses about Karen's friends, she comes back over and over again to the sense of community she experienced. "They were wonderful people! They were wonderful! And they have a network you wouldn't believe." This "network" is what enables Susan to experience the love and support her sister-in-law had while she was living and to come to an acknowledgement of this alternative love.

At the same time, Susan worries about Karen's salvation in much the same way she worries about her own. Can she possibly be in heaven? Didn't her "lifestyle" prevent that? Doesn't the fact that she didn't know Jesus as her personal Lord and Savior ensure that she was now in hell, "unsaved" and eternally damned? Just as she is unable to reconcile Karen's loving community with the certainty in evangelicalism that homosexuality is wrong and bad, she is unable to reconcile her love of Karen with the church's condemnation of her. She continues to struggle over this, praying during her nightly devotions for Karen's soul. One night while she was still staying at Karen's house, she had a powerful dream.

> That night, I don't know if I was dreaming or if it really happened, but I fell asleep and Karen was running around the house and she was singing, "I wish I was in Dixie." And she was happy. In the next scene, she came by the bed where we were sleeping, and it was like vapory, and she crawled in the bed between us and she put her arms out like this and she put his head here on her arm and she put my head on her other arm and she pulled us to her and she said, "Everything is going to be OK." And the next morning, it was like I was at peace.

Susan sets up this experience as a mystical one—she is not sure if it was a dream or if she experienced Karen's spiritual presence. In this way, Karen exceeded the boundaries of physical existence, became spirit, and was able to speak from the other side of death. This gave an authenticity and a truth to what Karen said. The message she brought to Susan was one of peace and reassurance—"Everything is going to be OK." This message was lovingly erotic—it was delivered in bed, where Karen physically entered between Susan and her husband and reached out to include both of them. The dream offers Susan peace and hope for Karen's salvation, though after she awakened, she was no longer certain on what grounds that salvation might be offered. Rather than resolving the question for Susan, it continues to pursue her in her prayers and dreams: "I think about her all the time now. Probably because I am so worried. I know what I feel is right, and I worry that her soul isn't in heaven. That really concerns me." This worry that so profoundly troubles Susan is the worry of standing on the margins of two communities—of allowing one community to challenge and disrupt the assumptions of the other. Susan's worry remains unreconciled as she turns back and forth from the love she experienced among Karen's friends to her certainty that homosexuality brings God's wrath and judgment.

Susan's construction of religious faith from the assorted material of her life forms an eclectic composition. Through conversion, a religious cultural environment, and the influences of her father and sister, Susan is positioned within an evangelical worldview. In her search for the "right way," she often speaks the language of evangelicalism and turns to it for a stronger sense of what she is "supposed to do" to be saved. At the same time, divorce, a lifetime of anger and a sense of rejection, and, more recently, experiences with her husband's sister pull Susan toward a different "right way." This right way is made out of the eclectic experiences of everyday life; it turns to solitude, mystical experience, and an intimate God for guidance and offers, because of its difference from the institutional church, self-doubt instead of assurance.

Left Behind has recently played an important role for Susan in raising the question of salvation and offering her answers that seem to turn her toward the discipline of the church. She uses the books to strengthen her visual images of biblical prophecy and therefore to reinforce for her a version of the "truth." At the same time, other experiences question and challenge that decision. In her search, Susan finds herself caught between competing knowledge and fear, which place her on the boundaries of evangelicalism, and yet longing for a community that will accept her unconditionally. Evangelicalism offers one model, Karen's friends another. Susan uses *Left Behind* to teach herself about these fears, to question her own place in evangelicalism's religious universe, and to express her profound desire not to be left behind.

Carissa: The Rapture as "Fuel for the Soul"

Like Susan, Carissa also expresses a terrible fear of being left behind. This is a fear that captivates her throughout her reading of the *Left Behind* series and powerfully influences her spiritual life. At the same time, Carissa's engagement with the series comes out of a very different historical trajectory. As an

African American raised in African American churches, she comes to the idea of the rapture with a different understanding that many white readers do not share. While Carissa appears to have received no formal training in dispensational premillennialism, she ties *Left Behind's* teaching about the rapture to a broader form of social critique than most white readers, who are more concerned with individual salvation. She weaves the stories into a distinctly African American apocalypticism that imagines a transformation of society in the "end of the world."[9]

I meet Carissa in a women's prison where she is serving a five-year sentence. We speak in the small back room of the prison's Academic Center, where Carissa is a dedicated student. She has been working on an associate's degree and hopes to go on to finish her bachelor's degree when she leaves the prison. I am immediately impressed by Carissa. She has come from a long day of classes and agreed to an interview with me that precludes dinner. She tactfully, but powerfully, convinces the administrator in charge to let her get her dinner before our interview. In fact, she does not ask his permission, but simply lets him know what she has planned and that she will return in a few minutes. She does not give him an opportunity to object.

Carissa is an attractive young woman in her twenties. She somehow manages to give the institutional uniform—a blue button-down shirt and jeans—a sense of style. She is forcefully articulate during the interview, controlling the tempo and preempting my questions with her thoughts, opinions, and ideas. She clearly relishes the opportunity to talk with someone outside the prison, and our interview stretches on for more than two hours.

A member of Carissa's home church puts money every month in a book club account, and Carissa discovered the *Left Behind* series through this book club. She reads everything "from Alex Haley to Mary Higgins Clark to Dean Koontz to W. E. B. DuBois." She saw the fifth book in the series advertised in the book club catalog, ordered it, and found herself confused about the plot and the characters. Another inmate, with whom Carissa has extensive discussions about the books, saw her reading it and introduced her to the rest of the series. Since then, Carissa has been an enthusiastic reader, soaking up each book in the series as it comes out.

Carissa accepts the eschatology of the books without question, but she describes her religious life and her religious faith in complicated ways. She tells the story of her religious life in cycles of faith and doubt, commitment and failure. "I grew up Baptist until I was about eighteen or nineteen. Then I went to a nondenominational church. My whole family went. The main reason we switched was that my mom said that religion is being too commercialized. Baptists do it this way. Catholics do it this way. Muslims do it another way.

There is too much categorization. In the nondenominational church, we have ex-Protestants. Well, I guess I shouldn't say they are ex-Protestants, and ex-Catholics, ex-Muslims."

"Are they still practicing Muslims?"

"They have the head things. They say you have to take the Holy Koran in one hand and the Bible in the other. At first I was pissed that we switched churches. I got baptized in the other church, I had friends in the other church, I had a Bible study leader that I'd known since forever and amen. But my mom was mad at that church, and she was like, 'We have to change.' We did what she said."

"Why was she mad?"

"Our pastor at United International [the Baptist church] took money, you know, for the stained glass windows and then spent it on himself. He threatened old women in the church. It's hard to explain. Her best friends of thirty-one years—I mean her best friend, he's a man. He went to divinity school and he wanted to start a church. So we left immediately. She didn't ask us. She just said, 'I made a decision. Pack your bags.' And I loved that other church. The pastor there, he had his faults. He had a lot of faults, but he was an amazing teacher. Just a great teacher. Our new pastor is a great teacher too. He really focuses on the youth. At the other church, we were just ignored. But this pastor, he calls the kids up and asks them to say a Bible verse and if they get it right then the whole church is like cheering for them. He does a lot with the homeless. He says you can't cast out the homeless because you never know what form an angel will take. . . ."

The church has continued to be supportive while Carissa has been in prison. The congregation paid for her most recent appeal. Many people have come to visit and many have sent cards.

"At first it bothered me. I mean I should be cast out. They shouldn't be calling and writing to me. They should say, 'She was a drug dealer.' Whether I am or not, that doesn't matter. I can't even get mad and tell them to stop calling and writing. I just get more letters and more calls."

"Did you try that? Telling them to stop calling and writing?"

"Yes. When I first got in here, I was really aggravated. A lot of things went wrong. Like one lawyer I had took the money and just split. I got upset. They just sent more letters, pictures, cards. It lets me know they're thinking about me. They remember me. My mom is an activist. She always has been one. She used to be one of the radicals of the radical. Now she's more on this peaceful God-type activism. But when I was younger, I was the one going to church. On Sunday, she'd be planning her next move against the state; I'd be in church. When I was about fifteen or sixteen, I was really religious—Bible study, prayer, everything. Instead of going out, I'd be looking for a Bible study. The kids in the school called me weird. Then when I was about seventeen or eighteen, I had sex and that was it. It all went away."

"What do you mean, 'That was it'?"

"I mean I had read 'no fornication' in the Bible. Then I had done it, so I thought I was just out of it. The pastor said you never fall out of grace. He said you are always forgiven. I said, 'Why? I wouldn't forgive somebody if they said, "Don't do this" and I went ahead and did it.' He said, 'Isn't it great that you're not God?' Then again when I was pregnant, I got deep into it. You know a lot of seeds get planted when you are carrying a child, so I wanted to plant all the good seeds that I could. I got to reading more books; I got back into Bible study. The people at the church wouldn't let me fast, but I did everything else I could. When I was twenty-two or twenty-three, I got married. Here I was so in love with this man and he started beating me. I would ask him to go to church with me and he would say, 'I'm not going to church!' After I had my son, I left. I left my husband. I got really mad then. I started hanging out with the wrong people and that landed me here.

"When I was going through the trial and everything, I thought, 'Here's this spirit-God person. God knows everything. He's not going to let this happen.' But it is like he felt that I deserved this. Even though he knows I didn't do it, maybe it was more of a saving grace. But he pissed me off. It had to be done. Even though I was not a drug dealer, I was hanging out with drug dealers, and it could have escalated to that point. What kind of a parent would I be then? What kind of a daughter, sister, parent would I be? At first when I was in here, I would think, 'When I get out, I'm going to go hang out with Carrie. I can't wait to see her. She's got such a cool car and cool friends.' Now I don't even know where they are, my friends from those days. They don't come see me, they don't write. There's no way I'd go back there."

"Do you go to church here in the prison?"

"No. They use the pulpit here for too many things. There's a time and a place for everything. They just do moralizing. This one minister just gets up and she says, 'I know there are a lot of you out there bulldagging (that's like what we call lesbian sex). And you have that bracelet: What Would Jesus Do? And I know a lot of you play cards.' It's all don't do this, don't do that. I just don't care about that. I mean, could I have some scripture, please? Could I have some fuel for the soul? And I don't do the Catholic thing. I mean, it's up and down, up and down. I guess some people say that about Baptists too, but I am just not into it. And then there's the Muslims, but I am not into the submission thing. And I can't exactly have church by myself. I mean I pray and read the Bible, not like I should. I used to fast on

Wednesdays, but I've been thinking so much about my appeal, I can't focus on anything else."

"Why do you fast?"

"Well, you know, the Bible says, 'Fast and pray all day.' I mean it makes things happen. Things get done. On those days when I used to fast, I had no problems. Like once, I didn't have any money to break my fast in the evening. I was just going to have sleep for dinner. And someone woke me up to offer me something. You know that he (God) is there, but to actually get that special shout-out right to you, that's something. I don't fast now. I'm lost for the moment. For one thing I am in a culinary arts class. One time, I was fasting and she made ribs. I had to eat the ribs. Maybe I need to get back to it. I'm just obsessed with my appeal. I sleep, eat, and think that appeal. My grades are starting to fall. I got all As last semester and I'll be a lucky girl to get one A this semester. I'm trying to stay focused. My mom says, 'Girl, you've got to focus.' I say, 'Mom, do you know what it's like to be in here?' She has to say no to that. They've got you locked up away from anything normal and then they open the door just a little so you can see the sun coming in and you've got your running shoes on ready to sprint out the door. I could know any minute on the appeal. They post it on the Internet. I'm constantly calling my friends asking them to look it up on [the Web]. I can't get the Internet here, so I'm always calling them until they are like, 'No,' click."

Our discussion of Carissa's religious background ends here, as abruptly as the hanging up of the telephone in her story. Carissa's religious faith, strong in her youth, reappears in various circumstances in her life—at times when she is most self-forgiving or when, as in the case of her pregnancy, she is trying to do well for the sake of someone else. She talks of self-doubt and even of something close to self-condemnation, as in her discussion with her pastor when she insisted she would refuse grace to someone like herself. Even so, she has a strong sense of what matters in religious life.

Carissa struggles to reconcile the concrete experiences of her life—her decision to have sex when she was young, her abusive marriage, incarceration, and her expectation of an appeal—with the abstract beliefs about the judgment and/or goodness of God. Were Christian Smith to include Carissa in his study of American evangelicalism, it is not at all clear that she would fit among the categories that he provides, nor does it seem that questions of doctrinal belief, community boundaries, and categorization are the most fundamental questions about religion that Carissa raises.

The prison ministry's rule-bound faith is frustrating and dissatisfying for her. The emphasis on behavior, on "moralizing" against "bulldagging" and card playing strike her as out of place and unhelpful. "Could I have some scripture, please? Could I have some fuel for the soul?" she asks emphatically. This "fuel for the soul" is perhaps what Carissa finds in the *Left Behind* series in a more powerful way than she does in church. The narrative of the novels provides Carissa with a number of things that she is unable to find in other places in her life. For one thing, the series offers her a reason to do what she believes is necessary for the welfare of her child and relationships with her family, a reason to "make things right." Carissa describes the reaction she has from reading the first book in the series: "I read it and I thought, 'Oh my God, I'm not doing anything right!' I used to joke with my friends that when the horn blows and all the people start to go up, I'll just follow them. But reading these books, I saw that I might not hear the horn blow. Maybe only the people who are going will hear it. I got scared. I said, 'I don't want to be left behind. I've got to make things right.'"

Carissa's description of her revelation is revealing. How or where Carissa was introduced to the rapture, it is difficult to say. As a former Baptist, she may have been taught a version of dispensational premillennialism in her church. But dispensational premillennialism is not a standard teaching among black Baptists, and Carissa does not appear to have received any formal training.[10] Instead, she had a vague idea that she would jump on the bandwagon when she heard "the horn blow." *Left Behind* convinced her that her former understanding of the rapture is not sufficient. She sees that she "might not hear the horn blow" and will miss her last chance to go to heaven. This frightens her into a desire to "make things right."

Carissa does not appear to mean by this that she needs to have a conversion experience of the kind common in evangelical circles. This never comes up, in part because Carissa already sees herself as a believer. Instead, Carissa uses this language to describe a realignment of her life with her family, renewed intimacy with her mother and with her son. This is tied to her earlier questions, "What kind of a parent would I be then? What kind of a daughter, sister, parent would I be?" She sees herself as "hard-headed" and needing repeated chances to learn life lessons. This realignment takes place within a sense of threat. Later in the interview, Carissa approaches the same subject, but in another, even more emphatic way. "God is not playing. The end is the end. You get one more chance and then you are going to burn, burn, burn. It made me realize more of what I need to do. I may only have another day, another year, another week." This is the significant disciplining role that the rapture narrative plays. It uses the threat of being "left behind" as a way to realign believers with religious life and religious demands. These demands often combine, as in Carissa's case, with the demands of family so that it becomes difficult to distinguish between religious duty and family duty.

Still Carissa leaves "what I need to do" as significantly vague. She does not attach this lesson to specific duties or specific actions. The narrative creates an urgency—"I may only have another day, another year, another week"—but what this is an urgency for or toward, she does not say. Part of this lack of specificity has to do with Carissa's position within the prison. Until her appeal comes through and she is able to leave the prison, she feels that her whole life is on hold. Her sentence in the prison robs her of the very short time she may have, and whatever action she needs to take has to wait until she is free.

Carissa specifies why she believes time is short. "A six-year-old killing another six-year-old. Kids are all into such violence. God has such a spiritual connection with kids. Satanism, drugs, kids selling drugs. To me, kids are the chosen people. They say the Jews, but to me, it is children. There is so much crap going on. I don't think God is going to let it go on much longer."

The conditions of the world—particularly those pertaining to children—lead Carissa to the conclusion that time is short. Again this may be tied up with Carissa's direct concerns with her family. She has a four-year-old son, and the time she has to spend with him is limited. As he gets older, violence and drugs may be pressing realities in his life. Carissa's sense of urgency is part of her belief that "time is short" in more ways than one.

While the narrative of the rapture ties Carissa to the world outside the prison through this sense of urgency, it also helps her to escape from her everyday life in the prison. "I read all the time. . . . I can read eight hours a day. I've been known to stay up all night if I am trying to finish a book and put it down when the sun starts coming up. . . . I've always loved reading, but in here, it is the great escape. The worst thing is when I finish a book before I am sleepy. Then I will immediately pick up another one and start reading."

Carissa's sense that reading is a "great escape" is figured by the narrative itself in which believers escape the conditions of the present by being taken up to heaven. Other books that Carissa tried as "the great escape" were not as successful as the *Left Behind* series. She read a true crime novel that she found disturbing and enraging. Rather than allowing her out of her current conditions, it trapped her even further inside. She also read John Saul's novel *The Right Hand of Evil*, but rather than comforting her enough to allow her to sleep, it terrified her with descriptions of demons and Satan worshipers.

Left Behind is ideal not only because it figures an escape in content as well as form, but also because one story flows immediately into the next. Carissa can finish one book and immediately pick up the next. The fantasy remains in place without rude interruption. Also the narrative is itself a promise of escape. It not only lifts Carissa out of her present circumstances, but it promises a more permanent resolution to her problems. When I ask her how the series will end, she laughs, "You know, everybody goes to heaven and you have a big party. All the angels and people. I guess the first time, that's the first busload up to heaven and then Christ comes again. I don't know. God wins. The Glorious Reappearing of Christ. John was, like, drinking when he wrote Revelations. I see this glorious being coming down. We don't know worry, we don't know pain, sadness. Only happiness."

Carissa's rendition of the utopian impulse at work in rapture fiction is told with a touch of irony. She both celebrates this vision and makes fun of it: "I don't know. God wins. . . . John was, like, drinking when he wrote Revelations." Carissa strikes a note of incredulity, but as she speaks she becomes increasingly invested in the vision, echoing Revelation directly, "We don't know worry, we don't know pain, sadness. Only happiness."

The rapture plays out on many metaphoric planes in Carissa's life. It provides a sense of moral urgency that convinces her of the need to "make things right," to strengthen ties with her family, and, in particular, it urges her to be a good mother to her son. It also offers comfort in the midst of the trying circumstances of the present by offering escape both in the practice of reading itself and in the promise that the narrative offers an end to suffering. Carissa clearly articulates the utopian impulse in the narrative—the moment when sadness passes away and only joy remains. Because of these metaphoric riches found in reading about the rapture, Carissa finds that the narrative is "fuel for the soul" in a way that the prison's institutions of religion and other types of reading simply are not.

Carissa's reading of *Left Behind* does not eclipse the ideological demands of the narrative. Like other readers, she uses the narrative to remind her of the duties of family and the need to "make things right." She uses it to give herself a place within a worldview that includes divine judgment and retribution. She reads *Left Behind* as a way of fulfilling very personal and specific desires and needs and finds the books instrumental in her cause. She also peers beyond this disciplining function of the rapture to the utopian dreams of resolution and peace on the other side. She sees in the narrative a way to imagine herself beyond her present circumstances and fuel her soul for the road she will take once she steps outside the prison's doors.

While *Left Behind*'s immediate ideological context is structured by a particular message about individual salvation, readers draw from broader social contexts to "create the message" of the texts for themselves. While some, like Susan and Carissa, feel deeply and even painfully the power of the producer's message, they also reform that message to suit the life lessons they are already teaching themselves. For those not predisposed to learn from *Left Behind*, suspicious of its producers and their motives, the books contain messages that are confusing and difficult to read, spoken as they are in "Protestant-ese." With all of these readers, we can see the variability of the moment of decoding, the dynamic and multiple purposes it serves within each given reader's circum- stances. In the midst of an act of reading shaped by social circumstances, readers are still "poachers" who take what meaning they can, shape it to their liking, and use it to teach themselves.[11] For readers like Samantha, Mark, and Ellen, pleasure is found in the rejection of the text, for the compelling identi- fying power of saying, "This is not me." For Susan and Carissa, pleasure is located in the edification, in the ability of the text to instruct and guide them. Yet for both of them, that reading takes place in an environment that the producer's text of *Left Behind* is not adequate to explain. They must incorporate it into uncertain and contested terrain, where its meaning remains malleable and unstable.

4

"I'm a Survivor and He's a Survivor"

For those at a distance from Christian evangelicalism and to some degree at a distance from popular culture, reading *Left Behind* can be an exercise in modernist disdain. The characters seem flimsy and ill developed, the plot contrived, and the writing thin. Perhaps even more disturbing is the overt political bent to the novels: a strong conservative agenda, a hostile antifeminist perspective, hints of anti-Semitism, and an overt homophobia. All of these can easily lead one to what Eve Sedgwick has called a "paranoid" reading of the texts. In a paranoid reading practice, we learn what we already know: that Christian evangelicalism is engaged in right-wing politics, that it is a religion, at least publicly, of male domination and female submission, that systemic oppression hides itself effectively in narrative. Sedgwick asks, "What does knowledge do—the pursuit of it, the having and exposing of it, the receiving again of what one already knows?"[1] If the knowledge produced in a paranoid reading of *Left Behind* merely leads us to a smug sense of superiority over evangelical men and women and opens up a wider chasm between the secular academy and those who embrace traditional religion, then I would argue that we have accomplished very little.

Sedgwick counters a paranoid reading practice—one that she argues is still necessary—with what she calls a "reparative reading practice." In reparative reading, one stays open to good and bad surprises that can emerge from the text; one does not imagine that one already knows what the text is or how it is interpreted by others. In reading *Left Behind* and engaging with its readers, a reparative reading practice, and perhaps more precisely, a reparative *listening* practice, is crucial for understanding how the text behaves and what effects it has. Remaining open to surprises—both good and bad—teaches us not what we already know, but what we may be unprepared to learn.

For me, as a researcher and reader of *Left Behind*, Sedgwick's distinction between paranoid and reparative readings was never more real than when I discussed gender with readers. Though often disagreeing about the details, scholars generally agree that gender is central to the history and development of evangelicalism.[2] While evangelicalism relies theologically on the belief that each individual believer, regardless of gender, must accept Christ to be saved, the state of being saved involves a social contract in which gender plays a central role. For evangelicals, gender roles are part of a God-ordained order for human life, and accepting and participating in this order is part of the joy of Christian living. Brenda Brasher writes, "One of the more significant fruits a believer can show is a life aligned with biblically based order. . . . the cornerstone of this order is heterosexual marriage headed by an adult male: a family."[3] The harsh rhetoric of evangelical leaders on the subject of male headship and female submission often dominates the public image of evangelicalism and leaves little room for multiple interpretations.[4]

On the other hand, readers of *Left Behind* do not appear to read the novels through the categories of gender that this history and the rhetoric of contemporary leaders would suggest. Instead, they read the novels to strengthen their own faith in a way that makes gender part of a much more complex story. Reconciling the interpretations of readers with both the patriarchal history and my own reading of the novels involves listening beyond my expectations toward complex transpositions of the text.

The Relevant Irrelevance of Gender

For many scholars of evangelicalism, gender is a central issue in the history and construction of the religious movement. In particular, gender is, in my view, central to *Left Behind*. For example, the books struggle with creating a viable Christian masculine identity. Buck uses computers and indestructible SUVs to consolidate his masculinity. Rayford rages in anger and lusts after Hattie Durham to demonstrate his. Strong women are a problem for the novels as well. Chloe is silenced through marriage and family; Hattie is excluded as a "bad" woman who refuses to concede Rayford's authority. The series is both consciously and unconsciously a largely negative response to feminism.

This is my view. It is not the view of *Left Behind's* reading public or of the people that I interviewed. Most readers have little interest in engaging with me on the question of gender. They see the characters not as gender types, but as personality types. Hattie is not the "bad woman," the "whore of Babylon," as I peg her, but a "tragic" and "proud" person whom readers use to identify unsaved people in their own lives. Chloe is not a domesticated woman, but "hard-headed" and "spunky." Buck is a "survivor," Rayford "impulsive." Readers often say, "My mother is like Hattie" or "I am like Rayford," but these identifications do not necessarily follow gender lines. Overwhelmingly, male and female readers alike identify themselves with Buck. Readers find Buck "brave," "fearless," and "adventurous." Some identify with his life circumstances, or with him as a new convert and a worldly person who needs to "humble himself to the Lord."

Through identification with Buck readers teach themselves spiritual lessons: how to strengthen their faith or tell their own stories. This appreciation for Buck steps outside the rigid gender categories that I construct and suggests that gender needs to be understood in a more subtle way. Readers use the characters, particularly Buck, to nurture aspects in themselves such as strength, spontaneity, and faith.

In an early interview with Carolyn, I ask about the portrayal of the female characters. "What do you think about the way women are portrayed in the novels? Do you like the way they are portrayed or does it bother you?" As I learned more about readers and gained interview skills, I came to see this as a very poorly constructed interview question. First of all, it fails to take into account the kind of reading that most of the readers do—a reading practice that does not abstract to the level of "portrayal." Carolyn, like many readers, wants to experience the characters, their lives, and adventures without the level of abstraction that I introduce here. Second of all, rather than asking Carolyn what she thinks of Chloe or Hattie, I ask her to respond in general to the "female characters," a category grouping she is uninterested in making. Third, I give her an either/or choice—does she like the portrayal or does it bother her? By the look on her face I see that I have asked a question that closes doors for her rather than opens them. She looks at me rather blankly as though trying to discern the meaning behind my question before she answers. "They are strong women. It doesn't bother me. They are strong."

Now it is my turn to be surprised. "Strong" is not the word I would choose to describe either Hattie or Chloe, the books' two main female characters. I press a little further, feeling awkward. "Do you like to read books with strong women characters?" Carolyn responds in a way that seems intended to shut off this line of questioning. "I do," she says, "but I also like strong men characters."

This exchange with Carolyn illustrates the way I often miscommunicated with readers on the question of gender. While I am highly interested in the function of gender as a category of analysis in the novels and how readers interpret it, they have little or no reciprocal interest. In Carolyn's case, her introduction of the word *strong* is a way of interpreting and generically dismissing my question. When I continue to single out women for special scrutiny, she hastens to introduce men. For her, "strength" is far more significant than gender. Carolyn finds my questions irrelevant to her interest in the books. Perhaps she is surprised because she has not considered separating the women from the men for special attention, and she finds little reason to do so.

On the other hand, Carolyn expresses that the most interesting book in the series is *The Tribulation Force.* She enjoys reading about the development of the relationships between the characters as the community of Christians draws together. When the tightly knit group of believers dissolves into a wider network of believers, she finds herself bored and distracted. Her interest in the Tribulation Force as a community of interwoven relationships and people sharing a common faith reflects her own reason for reading the novels. She often reads books recommended to her in her circle of church friends, and she likewise recommends them. Even though she has become somewhat bored by the series, she persists in reading it because "other people had read it. They were talking about it and I thought, there really is something here that I need to go ahead and—not really force myself to read it, but find out what everybody is talking about." She reads the series in order to participate more fully in her own community, a network of church friends and acquaintances that she describes matter-of-factly as "family."

Further, she uses the books to examine her own Christian faith. In this context, Carolyn again raises the question of strength—as an element not of gender, but instead of faith. "Sometimes I wonder what else these guys can endure. . . . Then you think, it could happen to me. They are strong and you wonder, 'What would I do in a similar circumstance? How strong would I be?'" Gender has very little to do with Carolyn's meditation on strength. She places the characters—male and female—onto a different map, one in which the primary division is not male/female, but Christian/non-Christian. And within Christianity, Carolyn thinks strength of faith and the ability to endure through trying times essential. Thus, she admires Buck as the "hero," but perhaps even more, she admires the Tribulation Force as a community of faith bonded together to endure the difficulties of the tribulation.

In other interviews, the word *strong* repeatedly appears to express readers' interest in, identification with, and admiration for the books' characters. Like Carolyn, Susan insists that she likes Buck best, but rather than wondering at her own capacity for strength, Susan identifies herself with Buck. "I could just see myself in his situation. . . . It's like when something has to be done, I know that I am a strong woman and I can do it. . . . I'm a survivor and he's a survivor." Susan turns to Buck as an example of her own strength, a way to identify herself as a "strong woman" and a "survivor." Identification with Buck is an important function of the pleasure in reading the series for Susan, although as we saw in the last chapter, she also, and perhaps more importantly, uses the books as an opportunity to explore her religious doubts and the question of her own salvation. She sees herself in Buck and likes what she sees. Reading gives her the opportunity to name herself and claim a powerful identity.

On the other hand, being a "strong woman" does not have wholly positive connotations for Susan. Later in the same conversation, as she begins to discuss other characters, primarily the female ones, Susan expresses a distaste for strong women in general. I ask Susan what she thinks will become of Hattie and she answers confusedly that Hattie will become the wife of Rayford, not of the Antichrist.

"Well, I know from reading the back cover that she becomes his wife. I kind of knew that anyway. I think she was probably tempting him. He was probably trying to be a good husband and she was being flirtatious. She used a lot of her womanly skills to lead him astray. In other words, if the rapture hadn't happened, she would've eventually gotten him into bed."

"And you would've put a lot of the blame on her?"

"Women have a lot of control, I think, and I also think—and my husband and I talk about this a lot—that women have become the stronger sex. Men are not strong like they used to be. Men used to be the head of the house; they made the decisions. Women have become in today's world the stronger sex. We pay the bills; we work outside the home; we take care of the family and work and pay the bills."

"Why do you think that happened?"

"I don't know. It's scary. And look at the women in politics now. I'm old-fashioned. I think the men should be the leaders. I don't think women should be barefoot and pregnant, but I think that the women have become the men and the men have become the women. The men are just wimpy."

In Susan's interview, gender and strength play two very different roles. In the first case, Susan circumvents gender binaries by thoroughly identifying herself with Buck—a man who, like her, can handle any situation. Then, she reintroduces gender to insist on separate social roles for men and women and the transgression of those roles as "scary." Feminism becomes the subtext of the conversation. Women have become too strong—they pay the bills, work, and take care of the family, presumably leaving men to do nothing. Is Susan contradicting herself or is "strength" being employed to do different kinds of work? When Susan describes herself as strong, she refers to an inner fortitude that allows her to handle personal trials and personal struggles. This is not a question of social power. The binary is introduced when Susan makes reference to social roles and politics. There she finds reason for less strong women and more powerful men. Here she replicates what scholars have found to be the gender structure of evangelicalism—equality at the level of spiritual things, but a powerful public voice for men and not for women. At the same time, even as she discusses the need for stronger men and more submissive women (though she never uses this word), she constructs herself as a "strong" woman, in this case a woman of strong opinions. Despite her complicated past, her abusive stepfather and first husband, and her rejection of the institutional church, she refuses the role of victim, constructing herself instead as a survivor and identifying herself with the worldly, savvy, and sophisticated Buck Williams as a model of what that means.

Perhaps as counterevidence to readers' regular insistence that gender does not matter to them is a persistent response from readers to Hattie. For the first seven novels Hattie is a significant figure for her unwillingness to convert and her penchant for placing at risk the lives of Tribulation Force members who are trying to save her. She is not the only unconverted person with whom the Tribulation Force interacts, but she is the only unconverted woman. In my "paranoid" reading of *Left Behind*, it seems obvious that Rayford's obsession with Hattie has to do with his extreme discomfort with a woman who refuses to submit to his authority, who routinely breaks the rules, and whom he finds attractive at the same time. Readers frequently reject this understanding, arguing that Hattie is treated poorly in the novels not because she is a woman, but because she is an unbeliever. If she would accept Christ, she would be spared the suffering that she endures. Yet readers themselves treat Hattie differently in their responses than they treat other unbelieving characters.

Nearly every reader has a strong reaction to Hattie, whether it is a response of compassion or aversion. A few readers find themselves drawn to Hattie and name her among their favorite characters in the books. One woman puts her feeling for Hattie this way: "I see her as a little girl and she just wants to be loved. I pray she will receive Christ and be OK." Another reader, a man, feels deeply for Hattie's fate, which he sees affected by the sins of the Christians who are striving for her conversion.

> Hattie was probably the most tragic person in the book to me, because of her relationships to the other people, she repelled the message that they had. A sorrow comes over me, because it's like, wow, she won't listen to them because of what happened between her and [them]. . . . That to me was very much like when I became a Christian . . . my message was probably repelled, even though I didn't even know what my message was at that point. It is real sad to see.

A more common reaction to Hattie, however, is one of disgust and annoyance. Jill, a new convert to evangelical Christianity, forcefully expresses her dislike. "Hattie, she just gave me the chills. And the amazing thing is that they [the Tribulation Force] have taken her in and I'm like, I know God wants us to take care of these people, but I can't believe you are doing that! Put her out in the cold! She's jeopardizing their lives and it just amazes me. I do read it and think, 'Oh, she is making me ill.'" Jill expresses a physical revulsion to Hattie brought on by her refusal to become a Christian. She turns this frustration into a sense of amazement at the Tribulation Force's compassion despite the fact that Hattie jeopardizes the existence of the group itself. For Jill, "these people" are, as one character puts it, "unlovable" and she cannot imagine herself expressing compassion for them.

Carissa agrees. "Besides the Antichrist, Hattie got on my nerves. She's just stupid. All that glitter and glamour, she doesn't know it is not gold. When the stuff hits the fan, she is just out in the cold. She puts the Tribulation Force in jeopardy. . . . Just put her out. Slap her first, then put her out. . . . I'd like Hattie to say, 'I was such a butthole.' She just got on my nerves. I don't like reading those parts."

A feeling of disgust for Hattie arises much more often among female readers than male readers. Male readers rarely single Hattie out for attention— and when they do, it is with sympathy—but female readers regularly express their dislike. Perhaps this dislike, even disgust, indicates an identification in reverse. Female readers feel a persistent need to define themselves against Hattie, to say, "I am not like her." Hattie's rebellion raises a desire to articulate their alignment with orthodoxy and their rejection of her alternative.

At the same time, the other role that Hattie consistently plays for readers is that of a quintessential nonbeliever who stands in for the nonbelievers in their own lives. If Buck is the representative of faith with whom readers readily identify, then Hattie is the representative of those who reject the faith. Jay puts it this way: "You can see her in a lot of people . . . I can see in her the way I was before, before I started to live my life for Christ. I felt like if I did this or if I did that then I would be worthy. Or if I did something that was horrible, I would beat myself up with guilt. Guilt's not from God; it is from the Devil. I feel like she is constantly in turmoil from all this guilt and remorse. She just can't accept that it is so easy."

Readers do not so much discount the importance of gender in the novels as act bewildered by my insistence at its significance. This does not mean that gender is unimportant in an analysis of either the novels or the readers. For example, in Susan's comment that she is a survivor like Buck, identification with a male character becomes a vehicle for female agency. Susan more readily finds the possibility for her own activity in the world, her own persistence through difficult times embodied in a strong, male character. She appropriates male agency in order to buttress her own strength. Even so, readers resist understandings drawn through gender categories preferring instead to think in personality types and in representations of people in their own lives. Given the central importance of gender in the history of the dispensationalist narrative and in the religious traditions from which many readers come, this dismissal of gender is a difficult one to read.

The Gender Dynamics of Dispensationalism

What these readers say about their reading of the novels, their resistance to reading gender as central either to religious faith or to *Left Behind*, stands in contrast to the patriarchal history of evangelicalism. In the standard history formulated by scholars, fundamentalism, a precursor to today's broader evangelical movement, emerged as a response to the dramatic social changes in the United States in the late decades of the nineteenth century and the early twentieth century, in particular to the transformation in the social roles of women. Betty DeBerg, Margaret Bendroth, Brenda Brasher, and others have demonstrated how crucial gender was to formulating the vision of the church that anchored fundamentalism.

Early fundamentalist leaders claimed that mainline and liberal Protestant churches had become effeminate, and they called for a more virile interpretation of Christianity.[5] Preachers like Billy Sunday drew on masculine images of Christ and denouncements of a feminine church to draw men to their ranks. Historian Margaret Bendroth argues that fundamentalists reversed the Victorian formula of pious women and worldly men. "By the 1920s, fundamentalists had adopted the belief that it was men, not women, who had the true aptitude

for religion. . . . In fundamentalist culture, women became the more psycho-
logically vulnerable sex, never to be trusted with matters of doctrine, and men
stronger both rationally and spiritually, divinely equipped to defend Christian
orthodoxy from its enemies within and without."[6] By reversing the Victorian
formula for the religious aptitude of each gender, fundamentalism provided a
context for the domination of men in positions of leadership, a domination
that has continued to the present.

Gender was similarly crucial to the development of dispensationalism.
Fundamentalist leaders described the "Church Age" that would be ended by
the rapture as inherently effeminate. The critique of the Protestant church that
gave rise to dispensationalism was a highly gendered critique that cast contemporary Christianity as "womanish" and weak and in need of masculine reform.
As dispensationalism took root in American culture, the stories it told were
stories in which gender played a critical role.[7] Yet in contradiction to Bendroth's
assertion that the formula for piety was reversed, narratives of the rapture
retained a devout woman and a worldly man at their center.

The central event of dispensational premillennialism is the rapture—the
event in which Christ appears on earth to take only true believers with him.
The word *rapture* came into English in the early seventeenth century from
Latin, not to denote the taking of the church to heaven, but rather to designate
the "carrying off of a woman." In this way, rapture was very early on associated
with rape—a woman was seized and carried off presumably for rape and potentially for marriage. *Rapture* also came to mean the carrying off of anything
"as prey or plunder" and, within a few decades, took on meanings of both
emotional ecstasy and the act of being taken to heaven.[8] In the late decades of
the nineteenth century, when *rapture* was used in dispensational premillennialism to describe the carrying off of believers to heaven, it subtly retained
the original sense of the word, that rapture was the "carrying off of a woman"—
in this case, the woman symbolically embodied in the church.

The ancient text on which the rapture narrative relies for confirmation is
the first-century Book of Revelation. Here the church is figured as the Bride
of Christ with whom Christ unites at the end of time. Conservative Protestants
added rapture to this story by finding evidence in other books of the Bible.
Christ, they said, would first "take up" the church through rapture and then
unite with "her" in heaven. Fictional narratives of the rapture played with this
theme. In the stories that began to appear in the early years of the twentieth
century, the "raptured" were nearly always female. In fact, the classic form of
the rapture narrative is one in which a devout wife and mother is raptured
from her own home leaving behind her worldly and ungodly husband. This
essentially domestic image of the rapture weaves together the "carrying off of

a woman" with images of female piety. The "raptured" woman becomes Christ's bride in heaven.

At the same time, a prominent figure in both the biblical narrative and rapture fiction is the Bride of Christ's symbolic opposite—the Whore of Babylon. In the biblical text, the Whore of Babylon, a key figure representing the decadence of the pagan world, is destroyed—consumed by her own demons—and a voice from heaven calls the faithful to celebration. The voice praises God and invites the listener to a wedding banquet: "Let us rejoice and be glad and give glory to Him, for the marriage of the Lamb has come and His Bride has made herself ready."[9] It is no accident that the wedding banquet of the "Lamb" and "His Bride" takes place following the destruction of the Whore of Babylon. This contrast is crucial to establishing the Church as "pure" as opposed to the impurity of the Whore. In rapture fiction, the role of the Whore of Babylon belongs to women who refuse their God-ordained positions as wives and mothers. These are women who go off to seek their fortunes and end up as prostitutes in lives of faithlessness and decadence. They are women who leave the home, refuse domesticity, and pay a price with their souls.

While condemning the increasingly free place of women in the social structure, rapture fiction retained the pious, Victorian woman maintaining religious faith in her home as the dominant image of female identity. This woman is immediately raptured while her husband or son, who fails to heed her warnings, is left behind when the rapture comes. Even as fundamentalist leadership recast Victorian understandings of gender, popular fundamentalism kept the archetypes of the pious woman and the worldly man, particularly in dispensationalist fiction. At the same time, dispensationalist fiction challenged these images by suggesting that it was no longer sufficient to be a worldly man who relied on women to maintain the "private" sphere of religion and family. Fundamentalism insisted that these men become the spiritual leaders of their homes and families. Early rapture fiction punished the worldly man and exalted, but rendered irrelevant, the pious woman.

Dispensationalism offered a means to an ordered world. Even the seeming social chaos of the historical moment was contained within a God-ordained story that explained the state of the world and made clear its future. Men and women alike were attracted to the movement's explanatory power and, perhaps, its narrative drama that gave them a specific and exciting role in human history. Margaret Bendroth argues that the gender roles offered by dispensationalism were more attractive than secular alternatives. Particularly, men were offered a masculine identity with a cosmic role that contained a "more nuanced expression of manliness than the tireless virility demanded by the secular world. It opposed the feminizing forces in religion and society, yet allowed men a romantic, passionate outlet."[10] For both men and women, dispensation-alism offered a provocative story—a story of human history and its conse-quences—that made order out of chaos and simplicity out of complexity. And gender was a crucial part of order.

The role of women within fundamentalism and, more recently, contem-porary evangelicalism has always been more complex than the rhetorical stance of leaders has indicated. Historically, women found fundamentalism an ap-pealing alternative to mainline religion and even first-wave feminism. Ben-droth notes that it was difficult to maintain fundamentalism as a "masculine enterprise" when many women "responded so readily to its call."[11] From the beginning, fundamentalism had to balance a fiery, masculine rhetoric with a willing and able female following that could not be excluded entirely or the movement would fail. While women accepted a reduced public role within fundamentalism, they never relinquished a significant role in the popular for-mation of the movement. Women were a central part of the movement and remained active through teaching Bible classes, embarking on missionary work, and providing the labor and attendance at local churches.

Women often converted before their male partners and brought men into the movement with them. Women were attracted to fundamentalism for many reasons, reasons perhaps as individual as each woman who entered the fold. Women may have been drawn by the focus on family life. Men were given a significant role to play in the family, and fundamentalism demanded of them moral behavior and loyalty. Furthermore, fundamentalism offered a clear set of standards in an increasingly complex world. Fundamentalism provided clar-ity, simplicity, and order out of the confusion of the secular world. It gave men and women alike a vision to follow. Fundamentalism placed a value on family life that many women shared, and they were willing to trade public authority for the willing participation of men.

Despite the hard-line antifeminist position of fundamentalist leaders throughout the twentieth century, feminism began to have an important, if subtle, effect on the movement. Like first-wave feminism, second-wave femi-nism of the 1960s and 1970s produced a crisis in gender roles and, to some degree, a hardening of the rhetoric of religious leaders. Also like first-wave feminism, second-wave feminism helped to produce a turn toward the apoc-alyptic documented by a sudden rise in interest in the end times. At the same time, a more subtle transformation was under way. The Christian therapeutic movement emerged to instruct Christian families on how better to live their lives, raise their children, and build their marriages. This movement was, and continues to be, deeply influenced by the concerns and the language of femi-nism. On the surface, the Christian therapeutic movement has counseled

Christian couples in a God-ordained model of marriage with male headship and female subordination. It has urged women to embrace this role as a gift from God and not to question male authority.[12] At the same time, the very same movement has promoted an increasingly "tender" Christian man, one much more able to express his emotions, engage in relationships, and openly communicate with his wife.[13]

In her study of women in two contemporary fundamentalist congregations, Brasher found the appeal of these congregations rooted in something far more complex than an interest in female submission and male domination. Women were drawn to these congregations during times of social crisis, and they found there a network of female support unavailable in other cultural locations. The churches offered female-led Bible studies and female-only activities that provided women with social, emotional, and spiritual inspiration and a context in which their fears and anxieties could be expressed.[14]

Furthermore, contemporary evangelicalism makes significant demands on men, perhaps greater demands than it does on women. It insists that they be involved in their families' lives, take responsibility for family problems, and work within the family unit to resolve them. It prohibits adultery and looks down on alcohol. In other words, women involved in "Christian" relationships can make significant demands on the men in their lives to support the family. They can make emotional demands as well because the contemporary Christian men's movement urges men to be more emotionally available and open to their wives. In exchange for this kind of familial devotion and responsibility, women must only acknowledge men to be the spiritual leaders in the household. Judith Stacey has called this the "patriarchy of the last gasp" that always waits to be asserted in a moment that never comes.[15] Successful evangelical marriages, she and Brasher both argue, work in far more flexible realities than the absolutist rhetoric would imply. Robert Cole, who conducted interviews with men involved with the Promise Keeper's movement, found a similar "flexible absolutism":[16] "While they speak of needing to act as stronger leaders in their families, churches, and communities, no allusion is made to aggressively wresting control back from feminists, and they resist the hard-edged rhetoric of natural hierarchies. For the most part, the men seemed to respect women as their friends and partners, and they often report that the conference heightens their sensitivity of how they treat their wives and girlfriends."[17] The absolutist rhetoric works in conjunction with a much more flexible reality to create a sense of distinctiveness among evangelicals. Unlike the "unsaved," they live according to a divinely established order, but like the "unsaved" they too make up their lives from the cultural material available to them, strategically employing hard-line rhetoric when it works and discarding it when it fails.

Even given this complexity, the history and contemporary practice I have outlined here cannot quite explain the indifference toward gender I perceive from readers. Nearly all of the women I interviewed are college-educated and professionals. All except two—those with very small children—work outside their homes and make a significant contribution to their families' financial well-being. None of them mentions the submission model of family life that so dominates both the scholarly view of evangelicalism and, often, the rhetoric of leaders, and as far as I could tell, none of them find this model particularly useful in family life. These women do not belong to women's organizations in their churches, and they do not attend women-only Bible studies like the women in Brasher's study.

Even in the limited scope of this study, women's disinterest in gender as an interpretive category perhaps allows us to see that evangelicalism is undergoing dramatic changes and that formulations of gender are a crucial part of these changes. In the social context of *Left Behind* and its intense negotiations with contemporary culture, what is common sense to readers about family life and gender is transforming. Women and men alike find the possibility of conservative faith, of definitive right and wrong answers, and of a special place in the drama of world history attractive. But the model of family life that once accompanied this particular manifestation of contemporary Christianity no longer has as much relevance. This is not to say that if pressed about gender roles, the readers in my study would not fall back on the rhetoric so prominent elsewhere. Perhaps they would. But in the structure of their own lives, their relationships, and their reading practices, this rhetoric is increasingly less relevant.

Gender and Reading Practices

There is another possibility, however. In interpreting readers' responses to gender in the novels, we might suggest that female readers of *Left Behind* are simply unaware of their own function within a system of oppressive patriarchy. We might even argue that women participate in their own oppression through the reading of the novels, absorbing the symbolic and semiotic messages of the text into their everyday lives. To do so, however, would be to fail, in Judith Stacey's words, to "take women at their word."[18] To do so would be to keep the meaning of *Left Behind* stable and securely in my hands, as the "expert" reader, and to fail to acknowledge the strategic ways that readers put the text to work for themselves. Instead of attributing the deep gap between readers and myself on the question of gender to my enlightenment and their failure to grasp the internal messages of the text, we might instead turn to the very different reading practices that readers and I employ to come to our conflicting transpositions of the text.[19]

As a literary critic, I bring to the text both historical and ideological reading practices that differ greatly from the practices of those I interviewed. First of all, I read *Left Behind* in order to place it within an historical framework. I try to understand how it coheres to American religious history and the social transformations of the twentieth century, how it remains within the tradition of dispensational premillennialism and how it departs from this tradition. Without this historical interest, what appears on the pages of *Left Behind* may seem a timeless representation of biblical texts. Because I am reading through a historical lens, the text is confined by history and limited by its historical moment. I ask, "What can *Left Behind* tell me about this contemporary moment in evangelicalism?" Readers often ask, "What can *Left Behind* tell me about God's plan for humanity and about the Bible as God's Word?"

Second, and perhaps most important for the question of gender, I have employed a practice of close reading. I have read the text for its semiological significations, for what it says about American culture and American evangelicalism on various levels of social consciousness and unconsciousness. In other words, I have engaged in a kind of ideology critique that tries to understand meanings the texts evokes, perhaps even against its own intentions. This kind of reading practice leads me to a very specific understanding of *Left Behind* in which gender—in particular the control and exclusion of women—plays a central role. Reading semiotically, the rapture of a domestic woman and the redemption of a bad woman are crucial to the ideological underpinnings of *Left Behind* and rapture fiction more generally. The characters in *Left Behind* have very specific ideological roles to play.

Most of the readers with whom I spoke could hardly care less. Readers engage with *Left Behind* using far different methods, questions and, not surprisingly, outcomes. For the most part, readers engage with *Left Behind* for two primary and intertwined purposes—entertainment and edification. While this is an oversimplification, we might say that where I want to deconstruct the text, they want to use it. For their purpose, gender appears to play a very small role. Instead readers put the text to work in their lives, drawing on it for inspiration, courage, guilt, strength, and understanding. In using the text, they divide the world into those saved and those unsaved and evaluate themselves and their environments accordingly. This is not to say that gender is unimportant, but to ascribe to readers an unconscious interest in gender, to decide that they are mere victims in a system of oppression, hardly does justice to their subtle, sophisticated, and strategic readings of the text.

Readers use the *Left Behind* series to teach themselves about the Bible, to encourage themselves to be more open about their faith, to castigate themselves for failures of courage, to fantasize about a life of adventure, to secure themselves in their evangelical faith, and to teach themselves how to handle various struggles in their own lives. This engagement with the novels arises from desires and intentions so different from those I employ that we should not be surprised at the bafflement of many readers when I approach the subject of gender. What is primary for me is something they barely register, and their use of the text defies the very ideological content that I claim to find.

This does not mean that my understanding of the *Left Behind* series is wrong and theirs is right, or vice versa. Instead we need to understand the text as a dynamic object, alive in their minds and in mine. The text is not just one thing, but instead is written anew with each reader. Each of us brings to the text a set of patterns, rules, expectations, and methods with which we make sense of what is written on the page. Our experiences intersect with the text in various ways to create interpretations and understandings.

We should not overemphasize the difference between my reading and that of many readers. All of us participate, using James Kavanaugh's terms, in a "'rich system of representations' worked up in specific material practices, which helps form individuals into social subjects."[20] We draw on this "system of representations" to make sense of our own reading and put it to use in our formation as "social subjects." Furthermore, at times, I apply the text to my own life—though often in opposition to its intentions—and readers critique the text, questioning the authors' motives or the texts' biblical reliability and undermining the text's authority.

Still the practices that readers and I bring to the text separate us and produce a gap that I did not find easy to overcome in interviews. While I draw my methods from literary traditions of close reading and the Marxist tradition of ideology critique, readers draw their methods from Calvinist reading practices that aim to weave the texts into their daily experiences, to live along with the text and use it to shape their religious practices and experience.[21] Interestingly, both reading practices have their origin in biblical hermeneutics—in close and intimate readings of biblical texts that were meant to transform and direct readers' lives. These two practices—close reading and application—have become increasingly disparate and even antagonistic. I seek to take apart the text so that its ideological underpinnings can be exposed. Readers desire the text's unity so that it can be put to use in their lives.

Reading is, as de Certeau put it, a wandering. Readers move in and out of texts, stopping when they please, going on when they are interested. Readers use the act of reading to serve their own purposes and often reinvent the text to make this possible.[22] We cannot recreate individual moments of reading. In the interview process, I receive from readers only a reconstruction of their reading, something already far removed from the impressions and desires of the momentary interaction with the text. To say, as de Certeau does, that readers "escape from the law of each text in particular" is to say that reading is a process that allows for relative freedom of interaction.[23] Readers still nod their heads in agreement when the authors chastise Hattie for contemplating an abortion or offer a rhetoric of male domination to explain God's plan for humankind. At the same time, the uses to which readers put the text cannot be automatically anticipated, nor can their reactions—a complex array of gestures, desires, and momentary visions—be completely documented. They are as intricate, unusual, and tactical as the uses to which readers put evangelicalism itself.

5

Reading the Signs
of the Times

On an October night in 1844, thousands of people gathered on hill-tops all over the United States and waited to welcome the end of the world. Many had not planted crops that summer and consequently had no harvest for the winter, so certain were they that this particular night would bring an end to the world as they knew it. They came to be called the "Millerites" because they followed the teachings of William Miller, a New York farmer and Baptist who had spent the better part of the 1830s expounding his apocalyptic biblical interpretation. Miller developed his view of the end of the world through a systematic and, he believed, logical reading of biblical texts. Using a numerical study of biblical texts, he mapped the year for the end of the world as around 1843. When 1843 came and went without event, one follower set a precise date—October 22, 1844. Followers of Miller accepted this new date with fervor, and while Miller himself resisted the new date, he too finally embraced it, compelled by the force of his following. The result of Millerism was what historians have called "The Great Disappointment," but the teachings of William Miller were so influential in their time that nearly all other theories of human destiny had to take up argument with his.[1]

According to Ernest Sandeen, the failure of the Millerites to accurately predict the end of the world thwarted premillennialism for a generation.[2] When it arose again in American Protestantism, its most popular forms did not claim to know the day and time when

Christ would return. Instead, premillennialists turned their attention to the "secret rapture" and emphasized Jesus' words that no one would know the day and the hour. Stephen O'Leary points out that this position had several rhetorical advantages. First of all, if the rapture could appear at any moment, believers could insist on the urgency of salvation and thus the need to accept the gospel immediately and live purely in the moment. Second, believers could avoid the sufferings of the tribulation period because they would be gone before it began. Third, belief in the rapture allowed believers to imagine that they could avoid their own deaths. And finally, belief in the secret rapture could not be falsified because it did not rely on any event happening before it.[3] Whether for these reasons or for others, the validity of the rapture was persuasive to many Protestants, and this version of premillennialism grew in popularity.

Despite the brief and unsuccessful rise of his theory, Miller made one very significant contribution to American premillennialism that affected its later forms. Miller believed that anyone could interpret biblical prophecies and, as Paul Boyer suggests, "Millerism heralded the full democratization of prophetic belief in the United States."[4] Using mass communication to spread their message, Millerites helped to make prophectic prediction an ordinary person's game. Long after Miller, dispensational premillennialists continued the ancient practice of reading the signs of the times to predict the nearness of the end.[5] The work of interpretation now belonged to every believer, not to scholars with specialized training or to preachers with a particular message from God.

Readers of *Left Behind* inherit from Miller a practice of reading the contemporary moment through the lens of its apocalyptic end. They read the morning newspaper and watch the evening news as if current events reveal clues to human destiny. In *Tribulation Force*, one character puts it this way: "This millenniums old account reads as fresh to me as tomorrow's newspaper."[6] Political events, diplomatic missions, wars, earthquakes, floods, and other natural disasters are not random, but woven into a complex narrative about the world's approaching end. This method of interpretation highly structures readers' understanding of the world they live in. It offers coherence to what might otherwise appear random and secures for them a very specific and special place in world history.

Dispensational premillennialism tends historically to read all of the world's signs as negative. The world progresses in a way decidedly hostile to the interest of these Christians, and within the narrative, true Christianity must become increasingly isolated and marginalized. Christians must face discrimination and persecution, the world must become increasingly dominated by evil, and true believers must seem increasingly scarce. The political and economic success of evangelicalism in recent decades—the rise of membership in evangelical churches, the strong media presence in radio and television, and the prosperity of the Christian Right in politics—has done little to transform this rhetoric of marginalization, but as we shall see, it has had some effect on how believers interpret the rapture narrative.

The End Is Near?

Unlike what one might expect, readers of *Left Behind* are not unanimously convinced that the end will be soon, nor are they convinced that Timothy LaHaye and Jerry Jenkins's version of the end is correct. For many readers, believing that the end will come soon is an edifying practice, whether it comes soon or not. Carolyn, for example, notes, "We might get too complacent if we think it might come in another generation. It could come tomorrow. You just have to be ready. And even if the end doesn't come for everybody, it might come for you." Sarah's answer is a little slyer, a very practiced response accompanied by a mischievous laugh. "I think the rapture is just as imminent as Paul thought it was imminent." The point, many readers stress, is that whenever the end comes, we should be ready. The possibility of the rapture gives readers a sense of urgency to prepare themselves and those around them. It provides a moment, imminent and elusive as death, we have no choice but to prepare for now.

Readers are quick to point out that Jesus said no one would know the day or the hour, and they strongly resist theories like those that accompanied Y2K. Despite this resistance, readers still use the signs of the times as evidence of the need for readiness. Carolyn speculates, "I know God must get tired of the way we do things, the mess we've made of the world. I think people are becoming more and more evil every day and they don't care about their fellow man. That's kind of scary."

"What kinds of things make you think that?"

"The drug problem we have now, the violence, the way that our television and media—they are just not like they used to be. Anything goes, just about. Even on prime time. After a while you just think, where is it all going to end? Sometimes it is just like a repeat of history. Sometimes I think our world is getting just as evil as Sodom and Gomorrah was."

Carolyn focuses on the media for her explanation of the moral decline that presages the rapture. She watches television almost every evening after work and frequently goes with her husband to movies. Her sense that the moral standards of the media are changing is based on this commonplace interaction with it, and her judgment is also influenced by Christian radio, to which she listens every night on the way home from work. For her, reading the signs of the times in light of their decline is a daily habit, something she does as a part of her regular engagement with the world.

Bobbi, a first-grade teacher, agrees with Carolyn that the world is in decline and, like Carolyn, focuses on American society for her evidence. She emphasizes the plight of children. "I just see the world getting so away from God, such bad things happening. I see so many things happening to children. God, I think, might allow some things to happen to adults, but when it starts happening to the children, I feel like he'll say, 'Enough is enough.' Children killing children, being brought up in homes that are not Christian-oriented, getting farther away from God and closer to the world."

Carolyn and Bobbi both use eschatology to critique the culture in which they live. Both use dispensationalism to explain and judge what they see and hear everyday. Carolyn's daily interaction with the media and Bobbi's daily interaction with children help to convince them that the dispensationalist account is correct. Perhaps we should put that another way. The dispensationalist account, in which they have both been believers since childhood, provides a lens through which they interpret the events of daily life and gives them the material to read the signs of the times.

Unlike Carolyn, who hesitates to offer a time frame for the return of Christ in the rapture, Bobbi thinks that it will happen soon.

"I think it is going to happen within the next thirty years."

"Why that amount of time?"

"I guess, just seeing from the time I was born, being forty-five and seeing how things were, and how they are progressively getting worse. And putting that in a time frame. If it is this bad in this amount of time and it gets this much worse in this amount of time, I just think. . . ."

The next thirty years places the rapture toward the end of Bobbi's expected life span. For her, the rapture is an event contained within the story of her life, her own life's expected end. Another reader, an older man named Jackson, tells me, "I don't expect to die before the rapture happens. . . . I expect to be here when the rapture comes." I ask Jackson if he hopes for that. "No, I don't particularly hope for it," he tells me. "That's just what I feel. I think that things in the world and in the Bible are all pointing toward. . . ." His voice trails off just as Bobbi's does on the same subject. Then he adds, "There is no way to know." Both of these comments raise a point about the rapture that many scholars of dispensationalism have noted.[7] Belief in the rapture allows readers to imagine an "end" that does not include their own deaths. They can, in a sense, escape death through the rapture. O'Leary notes this desire in some early adherents to rapture eschatology; we can perhaps see its emergence here.

Yet both Bobbi and Jackson deny that there is anything in their personal lives that makes this end desirable. They do not personally wish for the rapture to save them from death. Instead it is a condition of the world, something "pointed to" rather than something they consciously desire. While it would not be fair to say that Bobbi and Jackson believe in the rapture because they want to escape their own deaths, we might say that the rapture is a means they use to interpret not only the world's end, but also their own ends. And not surprisingly, they both place the timing of the rapture close to the likely end of their own lives.

Bobbi and Jackson, however, are atypical in their response to the timing of the rapture and the coming of the end. More commonly, readers place the rapture outside of their own lifetime or insist that they have no way of knowing when these events will transpire. Jay points to biblical and historical figures who all thought the end would come in their lifetime. He does not want to make the same mistake. At the same time, he says with a chuckle, he hopes for it.

"I'd like for it to happen because I wouldn't like to see some things happen. Having a little girl, I worry about her dating."

"You want the rapture to happen so you don't have to see your daughter go out on a date?"

He laughs. "One of my friends, he has a little girl and we joke about it. 'Hopefully, the Lord will come back before we have to worry about dating.'"

Jay's joke about his daughter's future love life points to the irony and light-heartedness with which many evangelicals approach dispensationalism. While it is serious business on which human destiny and individual salvation rest, it is also rich ground for humor. Readers frequently make jokes about the rapture—its timing, their desire or lack of desire for it, their own fate. Jay's particular joke, which also contains an element of seriousness, also points out the intertwining of the rapture with personal history. Like Bobbi and Jackson, Jay enfolds the universal story about the rapture into his own particular life circumstances. If the world ends, he reasons, at least he will not have to worry about whom his daughter dates.

Readers' approach to the timing of the end is a subtle blend of personal desire, evaluation of human history, interpretation of an inherited tradition, and a process of self-instruction. Nearly all believe that the imminent possibility of the rapture gives a special shape to their lives and urges them to live in a particular way, but they resist any simple suggestion that the end is near. Instead they use the rapture as a means of interpretation, a way to read scripture and human destiny.

The Take-Home Message

Left Behind, as many readers remind me, is not the Word of God. It is not itself scripture, but they believe it is based on scripture and inspired by scripture. *Left Behind's* particular connection to the Bible is significant because it helps to give *Left Behind* an authority that in turn produces a script for the direction of the world. *Left Behind's* connection to the Bible provides evidence for the Gnostic view toward which readers already tend—that there is indeed an alternative plot behind the seeming chaos of the world that is driving it toward a particular end. The script of history that *Left Behind* illuminates and the Bible confirms also provides a script for believers and advocates for specific modes of behavior and configurations of social life. It secures for readers a particular place in the cosmic plan but demands the participation of body and soul.

Readers link *Left Behind* and the prophetic texts to which it refers. This is not the same thing as saying that *Left Behind* becomes scripture for readers or takes the place of scripture. Most readers, even those most invested in *Left Behind's* "truth," reserve a different place for the Bible than they do for the novels. This is a line drawn not only by rhetoric, but also by reading practices. Readers read the Bible in a significantly different way from the way they read *Left Behind*. Popular among readers I interviewed are texts like the *One Year Bible* and *Daily Bread*. These texts organize the Bible into short passages that provide structure for the significant Protestant practice of "daily devotions." Many readers of *Left Behind* spend some time each day in private reading of the Bible usually combined with prayer. By reading the Bible day after day, year after year, readers strive to intertwine the Bible with their everyday lives. They memorize certain verses or passages that they can repeat to themselves as forms of prayer in times of crisis or need. Biblical words take root in thought and speech.

This practice of formal repetition and discipline is sharply contrasted by the reading of *Left Behind*. Readers describe long, absorbed hours of reading, where dishes go undone and social responsibilities are left unattended while the book entirely controls the reader's attention. In contrast to the discipline of daily devotions, this reading is undisciplined, all-consuming, and even produces guilt. During the time that readers are engaged with a certain book in the series, that book demands large amounts of time and attention. Rather than reading *Left Behind* on a daily basis in small doses, readers tend to read intensely and then lapse into a period without reading while they wait for the next novel in the series to be issued. Also in contrast to biblical reading, the exact words of the narrative have little significance to readers. When reading the Bible, readers often scrutinize individual words for layers of meaning. Passages are read in very small sections so that this kind of careful reading can take place. When reading *Left Behind*, however, readers read for plot outlines and character development; they read to find out what will happen next. They are unconcerned with the individual words used to express these dynamics of the narrative.

Both kinds of reading have a commanding effect on readers. In the disciplined method, the words of the Bible become ingrained in readers' minds and very often sprinkled into speech. Readers use biblical texts to frame and understand their everyday lives and to guide particular actions. The undisciplined reading of *Left Behind* is also powerful. It draws readers entirely into its world, suspending everyday reality and shaping, if only for a short time, how the world looks.

While *Left Behind* is significantly different from the Bible, it does engage with the Bible in particular ways. It offers readers a model for Bible reading that carries over from the reading of scripture to the reading of the world in which readers live. I will call this method for scripture reading the life-application method. It insists that scripture must be directly and immediately applied to one's daily life. The life-application method encourages readers to seek connections and messages in scripture for action in the world. Readers are called to self-scrutiny and then to apply a biblical message to the world in which they live. When scholars talk about literal readings of the Bible as a hallmark of prophecy belief, they often refer not to an actual literal understanding of the words of the biblical text, but instead to this process of directly applying the Bible to the reader's life and world. The text becomes alive through the process of interpretation. Readers of both the Bible and *Left Behind* constantly ask, "How does this apply to my life?" One of the key roles of *Left Behind* is to help readers see the application of obscure prophecies.

Prophecy does, however, present a problem for life application. Prophecy, by definition, is that which has not yet happened. While other biblical passages often seem straightforward in the actions they demand from readers—"forgive your enemies," "do not cease in prayer," "do not commit adultery"—prophecy is often concealed in strange symbols, unclear meanings, and images that border on the bizarre. In order to directly apply these passages of scripture they must first be transformed into something usable. The end-times narrative does this work. It takes a set of unincorporated images and places them into a narrative framework where their meaning becomes transparent. Through this process of translation and incorporation, readers receive a framework through which to read the world, and perhaps more importantly, to understand their own place in the cosmic scheme.

The *Left Behind* series is effective in this act of translation. In the first book in the series, Rayford brings home a videotape that had been prepared by Christians before the rapture to explain to people who were left behind what happened. In the videotape, the pastor reads a biblical passage from First Corinthians about the victory of Christ over death. "Behold, I tell you a mystery: We shall not all sleep, but we shall all be changed—in a moment, in the twinkling of an eye, at the last trumpet." After reading the passage, the minister says, "Let me paraphrase some of that so that you'll understand it clearly." He then explains that this passage refers to the rapture of the church, that believers will be "changed" from corruptible beings into incorruptible ones as they are taken up to heaven. By directly translating the passage, the pastor is able to give believers its true and applicable meaning. "Changed" means "raptured"; "we all" means "all true Christians"; "at the last trumpet" indicates the beginning of the end times. Rayford models the reader's response. He sees that this explanation makes perfect sense, that it is the most logical understanding of the biblical text. He, of course, has evidence that readers do not. His wife and son have disappeared; he has seen the chaos the rapture caused. For readers who can see no tangible form of the rapture in their own world, Rayford serves as a surrogate through which they can receive the direct application of this passage. The action that the reading demands from Rayford is that he must become a believer. The pastor says, "This is God's final effort to get the attention of every person who has ignored or rejected him." He then leads the viewer in a prayer asking for salvation and forgiveness. Rayford kneels down in front of the television and prays with the minister. This is the moment when Rayford is "born again."[8]

Rayford stands in to demonstrate how the message should be applied and participates in the ritual of invitation and acceptance. This ritual, the ritual of conversion that attends much of evangelicalism, is one repeated in many churches every Sunday.[9] At the end of the sermon, the minister offers a call to unbelievers to come forward and accept Christ as their Savior. This is done in churches where every person in the congregation has been a member for years as well as in large gatherings of strangers. It is a ritual that affirms the believer in her identity. It reminds the believer of her own conversion and acts as confirmation of that decision. Repeated week after week, year after year, the ritual of invitation is directed at both the believer and the unbeliever. It is the one aspect of the life-application method that always and everywhere applies.

The practice of life application has ancient roots. It is related to *lectio divina*, a monastic practice of scriptural reading originating in the Middle Ages that involves intimate relationship with the biblical text. Jean Leclerq suggests that the practice of *lectio divina* was derived from images of eating and digestion so that the body of the reader becomes one with the text. Through the consumption of the text, the reader is transformed in both body and spirit.[10] Anselm of Canterbury describes Scripture reading: "Taste the goodness of your Redeemer, burn with love for your Savior. Chew the honeycomb of his words, suck their flavor, which is more pleasing than honey, swallow their health-giving sweetness."[11] *Lectio divina* involves a very slow and attentive reading of biblical texts that does not rely on other commentaries or writings. The reader becomes absorbed by the biblical text alone, consuming it until one is transformed.

While the *lectio divina* provides a method for solitary reading and a way that scripture becomes absorbed into the life of a reader, *application* is perhaps not the right word for what the reader does with the text. In fact, the crucial point is not what the reader does, but what the text does. The reader aims to become passive before the text so that it can do its work of transformation through the Holy Spirit. For contemporary Protestants, the practice of life application comes more directly out of Calvinist reading practices that emphasize the authority of the ordinary reader in interpreting scripture and in Calvin's insistence that scripture could be applied to all of human life.

In the sixteenth century, John Calvin drew on the *lectio divina* to develop a doctrine of scripture from which much of contemporary Protestant reading practices are derived. Wesley Kort points out that Calvin took the practice of *lectio divina* "out of its monastic setting and inserted it into the life of every Christian."[12] Calvin encouraged lay Christians to be active readers of scripture, and his doctrine of scripture was instrumental in spreading literacy across Europe. By taking the Bible out of the exclusive domain of the clergy and putting it into the hands of lay believers, Calvin opened up the possibility that ordinary people could be able interpreters of scripture. In extending the practice of reading scripture to laypeople, Calvin also extended how scripture should be integrated into Christian life. Kort writes that for Calvin, "the Christian life is marked by a diligent application of Scripture to the whole of life. Scripture has consequences for and can be extended and applied to everything."[13] Reading the Bible became a way of reading the world, a way of extending scripture out into every facet of a Christian's life, and a lens through which the world could be interpreted and understood as well as to which it could be applied.

Kort distinguishes between two related reading practices in Calvin—practices he calls centripetal and centrifugal. Centripetal reading is a solitary practice that involves the reader's divestment of self and open reception to the Word of God. In centripetal reading, the reader puts aside all desire to extract something from reading and merely allows the scripture to move in the reader's

spirit. Centrifugal reading carries this solitary practice outward into the world.
Once one's life has been transformed by the practice of centripetal reading,
one can read outward into the world, applying the lessons of the Holy Spirit
to the world.

Kort would not argue that contemporary Protestants actually practice centripetal and centrifugal reading as Calvin advocated. He argues that contemporary Protestants are more likely to come to Scripture already certain of what
they will find there, not with the radical openness of centripetal reading. Even
so we can see the outlines of these practices in contemporary evangelicalism.
The frame of centripetal reading is found in the practice of personal devotions
when a reader engages in solitary reading of the Bible. For many evangelicals,
this has become a highly structured practice, guided by study guides, "study
Bibles," and devotional materials. These additions to the biblical texts tell readers what they are likely to find through reading and therefore undermine the
possibility of an open centripetal reading, but personal devotions contain the
seed of it nonetheless. Centrifugal reading is found in the life-application
method that evangelicals practice in almost every encounter with the Bible. At
the end of nearly every study guide for devotions, as well as sermons, Sunday
school, and Bible study materials, the reader is asked to apply what she has
read in some direct and immediate way.

In evangelicalism, the life-application method has become so powerful, it
has eclipsed almost any other way of reading the Bible. Rather than, as Calvin
indicated, receiving the Bible openly without intention or certainty, contemporary Protestants often come to the Bible seeking very specific answers and
knowing ahead of time what kind of answers they are likely to receive. We
might look at one Sunday school lesson at a small rural church to see how this
kind of Bible reading plays out. Following a published study guide that they
use every week, the Sunday school teachers ask a group of about twenty-five
adults, "What are you afraid of?" The group offers a variety of answers: being
a bad parent, crime, disease, failure. Once the group has offered several responses and established the theme of the lesson—fear—the leaders then ask
participants to read aloud a story from the Old Testament. They frame the story
as one that will show how the Israelites were afraid to move into the land of
Canaan and how God helped them to overcome their fear. After reading the
story, the group answers some basic reading-comprehension questions and
quickly moves on to the application: how to move from fear to faith. Participants are asked to think about specific areas of fear in their lives and how they
might overcome these.

The Sunday school lesson is an extremely structured environment in
which the drive toward using and applying the Bible story is the focus for the

entire lesson. Participants know, as soon as the theme is announced, the direction in which they will be asked to think about the Bible story, and the leaders provide a frame and context for incorporating the story of the Israelites. The purpose of the Bible study then is not to explore the Bible, nor to contemplate various meanings or to look into the historical context of the passage, as it might be in liberal or mainline churches. Rather, the purpose is to focus the reading through the lens of one's own life and then determine how the reading can be directly and somewhat immediately applied.

In much of evangelical Bible reading, including Bible study guides, personal devotional materials, and sermon illustrations, materials emphasize what is often called a "take-home" message; in other words, how can what has been read be integrated into one's life? *Left Behind* draws on this method to take the narrative of biblical prophecy derived from dispensationalism and transform it into something that readers can apply to their lives. This method is employed in *Left Behind* in two ways. First, *Left Behind* itself has a "take-home" message, and second, as we have seen, *Left Behind* models this form of Bible reading. Under the Frequently Asked Questions section of *Left Behind's* official Web site, the books' producers write, "What is the take-away message of the *Left Behind* series? Nothing is more important than making a decision now where you stand with Jesus Christ. Don't wait until it is too late. Read the Gospel of John from the Bible and consider your life in the light of God's love."[14] As a "take-away message," this fulfills a purpose very similar to the invitation offered by the minister in Rayford's videotape. On the one hand, producers genuinely want to reach people who have not made that fundamentally important decision. On the other hand, perhaps more importantly, the message is directed at people who have already committed themselves to an evangelical worldview. Through it, they offer confirmation. They reassure believing readers that they have indeed done the right thing and have received the correct "take-away message." At the same time that reassurance is offered, a threat is also elicited. If one receives the wrong message or does not seek out the right message, one is sure to be "left behind." "Don't wait until it is too late" is a warning issued to believers and unbelievers alike.

"Setting It Up for the End Times"

The ideological demands the narrative makes on readers go far beyond this message. *Left Behind* offers a script for the reading of the political and social world. It imposes a specific set of meanings through which both global and local events can be interpreted. Then it securely places believers in this world giving them the privileged position of knowing how to read the signs of the end. Within the schema that *Left Behind* creates, fiction becomes an important means of conveying the truth of prophecy. It translates the Book of Revelation, giving readers a code for interpretation, which then is placed back onto the biblical text as its most obvious meaning.

This process of translating the Bible into a prophetic code and then calling on readers to recognize the "plain meaning" of the text has a long history in rapture fiction. Nearly all rapture novelists rely on a dispensationalist understanding of the Bible that develops fairly complicated means of understanding prophecy and then declares these things "obvious." In *Fundamentalism and American Culture*, George Marsden argues that this kind of "literal" reading of the Bible is rooted in Scottish Common Sense Realism of the eighteenth century, in which the relationship between language and reality was understood to be direct and transparent. Beginning in the nineteenth century, evangelicals believed that the Bible was a collection of facts, that its meaning was clearly articulated on its surface, and that its plainest meaning was the right one. Dispensationalists were "absolutely convinced that all they were doing was taking the hard facts of Scripture, carefully arranging and classifying them, and thus discovering the clear patterns which Scripture revealed."[15] Rapture novelists, while translating the biblical prophecy into narrative, retained the sense that they were merely presenting the "facts" of the Bible in a "pleasing" form. Rapture novels often contain long, convoluted preaching sections where a minister or the narrator lays out these facts and the Bible can be seen, as rapture novelist Ernest Angley puts it, to mean "just what it says."[16] In order for readers to reach this plain meaning, they often need the narrative that the rapture scenario provides and the kind of translating work that the pastor in Rayford's video does.

Readers of *Left Behind* repeatedly express their faith in this kind of Bible reading. Jason notes that while not everything in prophetic texts can be taken literally and much is left open for interpretation, "when the Bible mentions something like earthquakes, I think we can take that literally. An earthquake is an earthquake." By limiting the symbolic meanings of the text, Jason is able to fit the biblical text into a cosmic plan that has been outlined for him by prophecy writers and dispensationalist preachers. While this reading makes the Bible seem transparent, Jason has been given a narrative through which it makes sense that an "earthquake is an earthquake." He uses that to set the biblical texts into place.

Jason sets up a one-to-one correspondence between the Bible read through the lens of dispensationalism and the world in which he lives. He not only moves from the narrative that *Left Behind* provides back to the biblical text, he also moves from this narrative out into the world. He uses both the narrative and the Bible to interpret the world in which he lives. He reads "earthquakes" not only on the pages of the biblical texts, but also in the newspaper. In this way, dispensationalism is not only a way of reading the Bible, but also a way of reading the world. The narrative of rapture and tribulation gives readers a fantastical scenario through which they can imagine future events and read the signs of the times. When Revelation mentions the Mark of the Beast or the coming of a plague of locusts or the turning of water into blood, these images are woven into a scenario that many evangelicals take to be actual— these things will actually take place on Earth after the Christians have been raptured. Prophecy writers like Timothy LaHaye often claim to know at exactly what point in the seven-year tribulation these things will take place. The pastor in Rayford's videotape says, "Bible prophecy is history written in advance."[17] Written there are reports from the future of exact events.

Even so, within this narrative, a literal reading is not always the most compelling and not always possible. Susan Harding points out that while the "interpretive tradition" of fundamentalism presumes a literalist reading of the text, "the Bible is read within a complex, multidimensional, shifting field of fundamental Baptist (becoming evangelical) folk-narrative practices. . . . The Bible is at once a closed canon and an open book, still alive, a living Word."[18] Rapture novelists have often taken liberty with the texts in order to devise vivid and provocative scenarios. Readers often derive considerable pleasure from these fantastical possibilities that draw on images from the biblical texts but are not bound by them. One example is the plague of locusts that dispensationalists believe will torment unbelievers during the tribulation. The passage from Revelation 9 that describes the locusts reads:

> And the appearance of the locusts was like horses prepared for bat-
> tle; and on their heads, as it were, crowns like gold and their faces
> were like the faces of men. And they had hair like the hair of
> women, and their teeth were like the teeth of lions. And they had
> breastplates like breastplates of iron; and the sound of their wings
> was like the sound of chariots, of many horses rushing to battle.
> And they have tails like scorpions, and stings; and in their tails is
> their power to hurt men for five months.[19]

Left Behind takes this passage very literally. It depicts insectlike creatures with human faces and long hair, riding horses. But other prophecy writers and prophecy imaginers have gone a bit farther. Hal Lindsey, for example, suggests that the locusts of Revelation could be a first-century attempt to describe and understand the modern invention of an attack helicopter.[20] He suggests that the "locusts" are not literal insects, but modern technology described through a first-century imagination. This obviously requires a leap of imagination that takes the reader far beyond a "literal" understanding of the text. Like the literal interpretation, however, it does the work of correspondence and translation, taking something from the biblical text, coding it within a particular narrative, and then giving it a correspondence to the real world.

One reader, influenced by Hal Lindsey, expresses disappointment in the *Left Behind* books' portrayal of the locusts. When I ask Cindy if she has any disagreements with the books, she responds that her only disagreement so far has been with the depiction of the locusts: "The only time was when the locusts came. They took the Bible literally, literally locusts. Who knows? But when John [the presumed author of Revelation] was on the island getting the stuff, he had no way of, he didn't understand modern machines, so why couldn't it have been a helicopter with a stun-ray gun or something?" Cindy finds the image of Lindsey's helicopter more compelling than the image of actual insects because it does a better job of translating the biblical image into her contemporary imagination. The correspondence between the locusts and instruments of modern war technology gives Cindy a richer translation that she can use to think about the influence of technology in the modern world and in her own life. She can use the image of the locusts to offer a broader interpretation of contemporary life.

When I ask Cindy about whether or not the *Left Behind* books have changed her religious practice in any way, she says no, but she then immediately points out that her TV-watching practices have been influenced. "Whenever I see things on TV, I'm like, 'Setting it up.' Jay and I are always saying to each other, 'Setting it up for the end times.'" Drawing on the dispensationalist narrative and the alternative plot of the end-times scenario, Cindy integrates what she sees on television into props on a cosmic stage. I ask her to be more specific about what especially gives her that impression.

"Let's see . . . things like the United Nations. Things like relationships with China and Russia. They are getting so extremely mad at us for . . . what was it . . . oh, yeah, for bombing their embassy."

I laugh. "Just a little thing like that."

"Yeah, they are getting so mad at us and that's just the start of it. Clinton and corruption in the higher levels that we all know is there, but is now starting to come to a head. Faith in the government is not what it really was before. Things happening in the Middle East, the peace talks, them not following through."

In her answer, Cindy identifies all of the key players of the apocalyptic scenario of rapture and tribulation, almost as if she is reading the chapter titles from Hal Lindsey's *The Late Great Planet Earth*. China and Russia, the Middle East, the United Nations—these signify special roles within the global and cosmic plan laid out by dispensationalism. No matter what is conveyed about these locations through the media, prophecy believers integrate that information into the end-times scenario. World events gain coherence, information is disciplined into a specific schema, and the "signs" provided by the world are coded and properly stored.

Prophecy makes strong claims about the course of human history. Because *Left Behind* is a conduit to this meaning-producing narrative, readers often make a correlation between the books and what they read in the newspaper or see on TV. Katie says that she never reads the newspaper and rarely watches the television news. She relies on her husband, David, to keep her informed of world events if there is anything she needs to know. Even so, Katie gets pleasure from working out the rapture narrative on the events of the world. During the interview, she finds herself trying to recount the details of King Hussein's death in Jordan and his son's ascent to the throne. She laughs at her inability to remember names and places, and yet the point of her story is to give this event cosmological significance.

"The son got complete power and he was pretty young. David was like, 'Hmmm . . . he could be the Antichrist.'" She laughs as she finishes this speculation.

I try to probe a little into the meaning of her laughter. "Was he kidding?"

"He was kidding. But just the circumstances, his being so young and all, it all happening so fast and reading the books, just kind of made him. . . ." She raises her eyebrows and gestures to indicate David connecting these events with prophecy.

David's speculation, reported by Katie, is playful. It is not entirely a serious means of speculation on the greater significance of world events. He uses the rapture narrative he has received largely from the *Left Behind* books to interpret an event like the rise to power of King Hussein's son. Without the prophetic narrative, this event would be just another random world event, one that has little meaning in David or Katie's world. But through this narrative, they are able to lend to this event some significance, however speculative.

Making the kind of connections that David playfully makes is not at all unusual among prophecy believers, whether they are readers of *Left Behind* or not. Paul Boyer catalogues the post–World War II identifications of the Antichrist, including Moshe Dayan, Anwar el-Sadat, King Juan Carlos of Spain,

Sun Myung Moon, John Kennedy, Henry Kissinger, Ronald Reagan, Mikhail Gorbachev, and Saddam Hussein, among others.[21] For outside observers of dispensationalism, there is something almost comical about the rapidly changing identification of the Antichrist.

Rather than seeing this kind of eschatological guessing as random, however, we need to see this way of reading the world as arising out of a coherent mythological structure. So coherent is it, in fact, that it stifles and represses other kinds of scripts that might be imposed on the world and forces everything that happens into a place within its boundaries. In a sense, we might compare this kind of mythological structure to formula fiction. In *Adventure, Mystery, Romance*, John Cawelti defines formula fiction as the "synthesis of cultural mythology with archetypal story pattern."[22] A formula fiction takes cultural myths and weaves them into familiar story patterns so that readers can engage the familiar as they read. By presenting deeply rooted cultural myth in a formula story, formula fiction works to confirm readers' worldviews and resolve tensions and ambiguities in the culture. At the same time, it provides a means of fantasy that readers can use to explore the realm of the forbidden within very safe boundaries.[23]

The prophetic narrative applied to the world of politics and social life does much the same thing. The narrative lays out a formulaic series of events and characters. Believers do the work of filling in the blanks in order to understand and give shape to the world they live in. The Antichrist shifts in identity so often because he is an archetypal figure mapped onto the world at any given moment. Evangelicals seek to "read" the contemporary world through this mythological structure, variously interpreting the scene at different historical moments. What looks erratic is actually a very coherent application of cultural myth. Morning newspapers and evening news broadcasts present the opportunity for this "fiction" to be read and understood anew. Readers engage with biblical prophecy as a form of what Susan Harding calls "narrative belief." It is a living story that repeats itself over and over. Biblical prophecy is a "specific narrative mode of reading history."[24] Yet within this mode there is a considerable amount of free play. Readers like David engage in the "folk practice" of prophecy belief by speculating themselves on the various meanings of world events. While the structure within which this speculation happens is determined by a particular narrative, individual readers and believers rewrite and reconstruct this narrative within a complex and shifting framework.

Readers of *Left Behind* often use this myth to speak to anxieties about the swiftly changing world of late capitalism. No matter what new information they receive—and that information appears to be more and greater every day—

it can be sifted and sorted into myth. Disorienting and potentially frightening events begin to make sense. For example, "globalization" has long been translated through the rapture narrative into the "One World Government." Since the early twentieth century, rapture narratives have described the consolidation of the world's economic, political, and religious diversity into one totalitarian force. Through the figure of the One World Government with the Antichrist as its head, the rapture narrative has spoken to fears about globalization and the advancement of capitalism. It has expressed concerns about the possibility of totalitarianism inherent in the vast homogenization of capital.

For contemporary readers, these remain partially articulated fears that find some expression in the rapture narrative. Disorientation and fear are answered by the narrative as it clarifies and codes the meanings of world events. One reader addresses globalization specifically. He mentions a friend who worked for the World Trade Organization and who is an evangelical also. After reading *Left Behind*, he asked her about the possibility of a One World Government of the kind that the books describe. "She said it depends on the way you look at it because economics, in and of itself, we are already a one-world economy. We don't have government sitting at the top of that, but the reality is we are much more controlled as a country by what goes on in the world. We don't have a lot of control over the econ—if something happens over in Asia, that is going to effect our finances."

Darren's fear focuses on a loss of control. With interconnected economies, disaster for one means disaster for all. By invoking the World Trade Organization, Darren points at one of the quintessential symbols of globalization. He then mentions that his friend had been in Seattle when the riots occurred and that all of this made him ponder the question more. While on the one hand, globalization hints at the end-times scenario, the political instability in Seattle that sought to protest and disrupt the process of globalization likewise feeds into Darren's apocalyptic view. Reading *Left Behind* causes Darren to seek out conversations on the possibility of the end times and, as he says, *Left Behind* "brought it into my visual consciousness." Darren's thoughts on the end-times remain speculative and conversational. He insists that he does not "dwell" on these scenarios and is not at all sure the end is coming. He is merely intrigued by the narrative that offers so much coherence to potentially frightening world conditions that portend instability.

The script that Scripture provides is a flexible one within which readers find ample room for maneuvering. It is also a strongly influential one that guides nearly every encounter with world events and the world's future. Opportunities to participate in this kind of reading present themselves at every turn and allow readers flights of imagination and speculation. As readers extend their readings of *Left Behind* and the Bible itself into the world, they become active participants in interpretation of modern life.

Reading Commodities

The most famous image from the *Left Behind* series is the opening one. On a plane across the Atlantic, dozens of passengers disappear. They leave behind all their worldly artifacts—clothes, contact lenses, wedding rings—for those who have been "left behind" to find. For many readers of *Left Behind*, no scene exemplifies their fascination with the series so much as this one. Matt is particularly enthusiastic. He ascribes this scene to what "hooked" him about the series: "Just thinking about sitting on a plane talking to someone, just like I'm talking to you and all of the sudden your contact lenses and your earrings, your sweater and your shoes and stockings and your wedding ring are just sitting there. It's like, Wow! I think they actually said somebody's contacts. I never thought about that." Matt finds this image forcefully expressive of the rapture in a way he never imagined before. He is amazed that personal effects could remain behind while the physical body disappears. The remnants fascinate him—contact lenses, stockings, wedding rings. For Matt, this is an intense moment of visualization. He imagines commodities suddenly empty, lying on the ground useless, unanimated, and lifeless. This picture of consumer culture undone draws him into the narrative so that the books' images seem to become inseparable from the truth.

Matt's response needs to be understood in light of the conflicting relationship to consumer culture that dispensationalism and fundamentalism provide. On the one hand, commodities are interwoven with the work of God. They are not inherently evil, but perfectly capable of being part of a life of faith. In fact, they may even be necessary. Colleen McDannell points out, for example, that "Christian retailing reflects the positive intersection of faith, profit, and goods." Consumers buy Christian products, including the *Left Behind* series, to mark themselves as Christian, to link themselves to other Christians, and to invite nonbelievers into the fold. "The stress that is placed on critically *thinking* about religion in liberal traditions holds less importance in conservative Christianity than *doing* religious activities and *identifying* oneself as Christian."[25] The work of "doing" and "identifying" is tied up with the act of purchasing. Purchasing is something that one can do to identify oneself as Christian. *Left Behind* itself has spawned a flood of products that can be purchased in order to identify oneself as a reader. Hats, mugs, t-shirts, videos, and compact discs can all be part of the experience of reading *Left Behind* and participating in a broader community of readers. In this sense, commodities are the expression of one's Christian identity, not an expression of crass consumerism.

At the same time, these items have little value for readers in my study. A few visited the *Left Behind* Web site, but none purchased any item other than a book or audiotapes of the book. They express little interest in buying anything else. The majority of readers purchase their own books and do not wait for the books to come out in paperback. They splurge and spend their money on the hardcover as soon as the most recent book appears. But this act of consumption is also carefully monitored. Readers seek out the best deal on books and advise me to go to Sam's Club or Costco rather than buying the books from a local Christian bookstore.[26] Also, one book is often sufficient for several readers. They are passed from hand to hand unless a reader becomes "hooked" and must have her own copy right away. A few readers express an interest in owning the entire series and keeping it on their bookshelves at home as a display. But most lend the books out immediately after reading them and pay no attention to whether they see their copy again or not. They read the books in public places in order to be seen and identified as Christians and readers. As we will see in chapter 7, they often do this as a subtle act of witnessing to strangers. But on the whole, readers are far more interested in reading than in owning and far more invested in the story's plot than in the object in which it is contained.

The tradition of dispensational premillennialism has long expressed concern with consumer culture and its role in bringing about the ruination of the world. Consumer culture promotes homogeneity; it distracts from the work of God; it promotes greed. Perhaps the quintessential image for this concern about consumer culture within dispensationalism is the Mark of the Beast. Dispensationalists have long believed that during the tribulation, the Antichrist will require everyone to receive his "mark."[27] With this mark that proves their loyalty to him, people will be able to continue to participate in the economy. Without it, they will be permanently excluded. In rapture fiction, the introduction of the Mark of Beast always produces a dramatic crisis. Those who would be loyal to God cannot take the mark. They can no longer go to the grocery store for food. They cannot even be seen in public without the mark. Refusing to take the mark means that they must stay hidden or be persecuted and martyred.

In the image of the Mark of the Beast, concerns about consumer culture come vividly alive. Those who take the mark conform to the world. They become zombielike followers of the Antichrist and can no longer think for themselves. They are slaves to an evil economy. Those who refuse show themselves to be true followers of Christ. This scenario has been one of great fascination for dispensationalists and is played out over and over again in rapture fiction. The interviews I conducted took place before the Mark of Beast was introduced in the *Left Behind* series, but readers eagerly anticipated this turn of events.

Like her reformulation of the locusts into a stun-ray helicopter, Cindy wants to see a less literal translation of the Mark of the Beast. "I'll be interested to see what they do with the Mark of the Beast, because if they say it is the numbers *666*, I'd be like, well you know, that's not practical. Anyone could . . . I don't know." Cindy thinks if the Mark is actually *666*, people will too easily identify it with the biblical text. The mystery will be removed. And, once again, the literal *666* will not be as effective in expressing the antimodern nature of the narrative as another fantasy that Cindy substitutes. "I envision more of a microchip. . . ." She points to her forehead and her hand. "Where it is like a scanner. Everything is with a scanner now. So some people say that every scanner code is a number you add in a certain way to get *666*."

Cindy's vision of the mark as a microchip and scanner translates the apocalyptic image into contemporary parlance. She invokes the mark as if to point to the homogeneity and standardization of contemporary capitalism as a sign of the approaching end. Of course, Cindy would never put her interest in the mark into these terms. Instead she merely conjures an image—one that appeals to her imagination—and like generations of fundamentalists before her, she expresses a profound concern about modern life.

Reading Technology

Like commodities, dispensationalists have seen technology as an ambiguous sign of the times. On the one hand, they have embraced modern technology as the primary means to spread their message. On the other hand, rapture fiction has long portrayed technology as the devil's work. Readers of the *Left Behind* series pick up and articulate both strains of dispensational orientation to technology.

One reader, a forty-five-year-old white housewife named Betty, offers her continuing fear of technology, particularly computer technology, as a tool of the Antichrist. *Left Behind* is one of the few books she has read in recent years. After graduating from high school a few miles from where she now lives, Betty worked for several years as a government employee and now stays at home with her children. A few years before reading *Left Behind*, Betty experienced a powerful religious revival. She began to see religious faith as more than living a good life and being a good person. She felt that faith demanded more from her and began to read the Bible and attend church in earnest. Both she and her husband began to attend an evangelical church that she describes as "home" and "homecoming." She sums up her church for me in one word, *family*. These close social bonds are crucial for Betty. They support her in difficult emotional times; they provide a safe space for self-expression and strong friendships. Within this church, Betty feels loved and needed.

Betty raises the issue of technology in a conversation about what makes the books seem "real" to her. "I look at all the computer . . . see I'm . . . all the computer technology, all the things that I think could be pretty true to life today, I think the Antichrist is going to have those powers and probably more. And I think he is going to be very alluring for awhile, as portrayed." Betty readily identifies computer technology with the Antichrist and suggests that the books confirm one of her firmly held beliefs that computers are a means the Antichrist will use to be "alluring." Betty hints at this belief with her aborted statement, "See, I'm. . . ." Later she fills in this blank, "See, I have been so scared of computers, so scared of the Internet."

Betty's fear of computers seems distinctly at odds with the books' portrayal of computer technology in the hands of Christians. I ask her if the books have had any influence on this fear. Betty answers by making her fear more precise, "I think it is all in how you use them. I guess I was afraid the Antichrist was going to be using the computers to find out what he needed to know. I don't know [now] that he is going to have to do so." Betty's fear echoes a long tradition in rapture fiction that envisions computer technology as a way of depriving people of privacy and of "finding out what he needed to know." For Betty, computers seem a perfect way for the Antichrist to obtain information that could be used to hurt her. Betty suggests that she is growing toward a more neutral view of technology, that it is "all in how you use it." At the same time, Betty is invested in keeping the Antichrist as a figure of supreme power. She underlines this power in her next statement: "He has power, power beyond what I thought. He's really going to have a lot of power. I think the Lord is allowing him to have such great power until He decides it is over. It's amazing." By emphasizing the power of the Antichrist, Betty keeps the traditional eschatology intact. The world is still ruled by the Antichrist and will eventually be judged by God. Within this eschatology, Betty can keep a position of special privilege and special knowledge; she can be sure the "alternative plot" of apocalypticism from which she constructs meaning in the world is in place.

Betty's need for special knowledge is important, in part because of her social position as well as her religious orientation. As a working-class woman without significant exposure to computer technology, this fear of technology, and the association between technology and the supreme worldly power of the

Antichrist is, in part, a class-based fear. Computer technology always belongs to someone else, people who do not have her best interest at heart—employers, wealthy people, "jet-setters" as she calls them. Betty does not articulate class resentment in our interview. Instead, she is adamant that she would not want that "lifestyle." Even so, she lives in a world in which her own interaction with computers is significantly limited. Fear of technology, linked to this religious narrative, seems natural and goes largely unchallenged.

Left Behind has given Betty some reason to think otherwise. For example, she proposes an alternative understanding of the Internet. She suggests that rather than being used by the Antichrist to glean information, she could see the Internet being used "for the good of the Lord." "It's important to get those messages [of salvation] across to people. That's an important message that is being transported, you know, on the computer." By ascribing an alternative use to the Internet, she suggests that her views about computers have the potential to change. She concludes, "I still have the fear, but not like I did." Betty tries to balance her fear of the Internet and the Antichrist's power with these new possible uses for computer technology. She struggles for a new orientation to computers but still does not find herself entirely comfortable.

While Betty is experiencing a small shift in her own orientation to technology, the *Left Behind* novels represent a more significant shift. Modernity, always the enemy in rapture fiction, has not meant the same thing at every historical moment. Likewise, rapture fiction has not targeted the same mode of modernity for condemnation at every turn. For Forrest Loman Oilar in 1937, chain stores represented the modern world's turn to evil. For Salem Kirban in 1970, computer surveillance technology was the greatest threat.[28] *Left Behind* redeems computer surveillance technology, placing it in the hands of the Christians, but presents global politics, global culture, and a global economy as the most present dangers.

Readers with more orientation to computer technology than Betty readily accept the Tribulation Force's use of computers to carry out their mission. Jason and his wife have been particularly active in international mission movements, and they attend a church with an international focus. Jason is well educated and works in a field that requires him to use computers almost constantly. During our interview, Jason raises the issue of technology in the context of signs that the end of the world might be coming. For Jason, the end of the world is a positive event. It denotes reunion with Christ in heaven and an end to worldly trouble. The end is something that all Christians should anticipate with pleasure. But it is preceded by disaster. Jason notes this: "I think that it is not just coincidental that there have been a lot of natural disasters lately."

He rattles off the names of places where there had been recent earthquakes and floods with a studied precision.

> I think the Bible is clear in certain passages that there will be those kinds of signs when the end is near. But the Bible also says that the Great Commission needs to be carried out before the return of Christ. That means that the Gospel needs to go out into all the world. That doesn't mean that everyone becomes a Christian, but just that everyone gets a chance to hear. I get a lot of e-mail from mission organizations that are trying to accomplish that goal in our generation. With the advent of technology like the Internet and broadcast technology and satellites, they are able to reach people much faster and makes that an achievable goal.

Jason sees computer technology as providing the means to "spread the Gospel." His viewpoint is not at all new to evangelicalism. Historian Joel Carpenter points out that "faith in technological signs and wonders to evangelize the world and usher in the end of the age has been a character trait of modern missions over the past two centuries, and American evangelicals in particular have been charmed by such visions."[29] Internet technology is merely the latest in a long series of technological innovations that evangelicals have seen with the potential to evangelize the entire world. When that goal is accomplished, the end of the age can come. Jason's succinct restatement of this century-old belief demonstrates the flexibility and adaptability of dispensational thinking to the developments of the modern world. For him, unlike for Betty, technology is not associated with the Antichrist, but rests firmly with the work that Christians are already doing in the world. Jason feels comfortable with computer technology and secure that it is working not against him, as Betty fears, but for his benefit.

On the Front Lines

Despite the work of mission organizations and the possibility that the entire world might be reached with the gospel "in our generation," Jason says he does not anticipate the rapture is coming any day. In fact, he says, "I'm not even sure which theory of the rapture is true." By this, Jason refers to a disagreement among believers about the precise timing of the rapture. The dominant view of evangelical Christians has been that the rapture will come at the beginning of the tribulation period, sparing Christians all the suffering that it entails. This was Darby's view and has dominated conservative Protestant eschatology ever since. It is the view offered by the *Left Behind* series. A less dominant view is that the rapture will not come until midway through the tribulation. Christians will witness the rise of the Antichrist and have the opportunity to be deceived by him or resist him. In evangelical jargon, this position is called "mid-trib" while the former is called "pre-trib."[30] Another possibility is that Christians will not be taken to heaven until after the tribulation. This is called the "post-trib" position. As a well-studied evangelical, Jason is aware of these various positions and is not an adamant proponent of any. In *Left Behind* Web site chat groups, pre-, mid-, and post-tribulation views are among the topics most heatedly discussed. Noting this, Timothy LaHaye and Jerry Jenkins recently released a defense of the pre-tribulation position espoused by the novels.[31] Even so, alternatives to the traditional pre-tribulation rapture are growing in currency and popularity.

Jason's openness to these alternatives is clarified by comments he makes later in the interview. As I ask him about characters he identifies with, he says he does not really identify with any of them. "I see [the action] more in my mind's eye, like on a movie screen, just kind of unfolding in front of me. I don't see myself participating in that. Although sometimes, I wonder if it is more of a post-trib scenario, I sometimes wonder if I would be involved in something as adventurous and dramatic as all of that."

I have heard other readers express this interest in being present during the tribulation, so I press Jason further to see if I understand him, "Do you feel any sort of desire for that? I've had some people say, 'You know, I'd kind of like to stay around.'"

Jason responds by both affirming and, in his carefully rational way, denying my suggestion, "Yes. Yes. I don't know if I would go so far as to say that. We're not going to have any choice in the matter, but I still kind of wonder. . . ." Jason pauses and smiles slightly, a rare smile in the interview. "I guess in that way I can identify. I wonder if I would be on the front lines, part of this secretive organization."

Jason's smile signals a recognition that this desire is part of a fantasy. He expresses his identification not with an individual character, but with being part of a secretive and special organization. This identification shows that, as for Betty, the rapture narrative gives Jason the sense that he holds privileged knowledge about the world. He is already, in a sense, part of an organization that sees itself "on the front lines," as it were, battling against those forces that undermine religious faith. Desiring to stay around during the tribulation and fight it out with the Antichrist hints at the call to arms *Left Behind* attempts and some readers accept. There is still a battle to be fought and won, a battle for power in both the church and the world.

Like Jason, many readers identify with the Tribulation Force as a group. By identifying with the group, these readers express a genuine longing for community relations, for a community that will overcome the isolation, competition, and fearful complexity of the modern world, a place they can call "home." Jason imagines himself not as an individual hero, but instead as "part of a secretive organization." Perhaps here we find the "underlying impulse," the "deepest fantasies about social life" that Fredric Jameson suggests infuse our interactions with cultural artifacts.[32]

In these hints that readers might like to see and participate in the tribulation, we also see a changing orientation to the modern world. Rather than an immediate escape from the world, the desire that compelled many fundamentalists for generations, contemporary tribulation eschatology suggests a new engagement with the world. Readers hint that the world is a place worth fighting for. Perhaps this is linked to evangelicalism's political and social power emerging in recent decades. A gradual transformation is taking place in eschatology, shaping it into something considerably less "other-worldly" and considerably more impassioned about this world and its battles. Through the centuries-old practice of reading the signs of the times, evangelicals hear a new message, one that compels not their separation from but their engagement with the world.

6

Making Prophecy Live

"Truth" is ideological. It is derived from what Louis Althusser calls one's "lived relation to the real."[1] While people sometimes hold on to truth as if it were unchanging, they live it in everyday life as more flexible, contextual, and relational. Because truth is simultaneously considered immutable and lived in the dynamics of life, it must be protected and reinforced. Just as identity requires what Angela Mc-Robbie calls "acts of identification," truth requires acts of truth making; truth needs to be made and remade in the course of life experience.[2] We might recall Blaise Pascal's famous injunction that if one wants to believe, one must *act* as though one believed. Through mimicking the practices of faith, faith follows. In a similar way, truth must be acted out in order to be made real.

Most readers of *Left Behind* and believers in the rapture would adamantly disagree with this account of truth. For them, the truth is the truth. God said it. It is written in God's word. A human being has the choice to either accept it or reject it, to be saved or to be damned. Each of these two accounts of truth has a story to tell about the other. To readers, my account is hopelessly relativist, and evangelicalism has blamed relativism for everything from teenage pregnancy to violence in the schools to cultural and moral decline.

On the other hand, categories of immutable truth have to be lived just like any other kind of truth. Because they must be lived, they need to be created and protected in the context of everyday life. For readers, acts of creation and protection include religious rituals of prayer and personal devotions, Bible reading, Bible study, conversations with members of their communities, Sunday worship, Sunday potlucks, listening to Christian music and Christian radio, reading materials published by Focus on the Family, and many other activities that are woven into the fabric of everyday life. Readers acknowledge this when they talk about someone who has fallen away from the faith—someone who has lapsed in these practices of identification and confirmation, who has found other ways of truth making.

The specific truth that concerns readers of *Left Behind* is the truth of prophecy. Prophecy is an odd kind of truth because its realization remains always in the future. One must live toward it, rather than in it. But evangelical prophecy—the prophecy of rapture and tribulation—also has much to say about how one should live now, in this moment. As we saw in the last chapter, it can provide a script for social living and a script for the reading of human history. As a script, prophecy guides the reading of other texts, especially the newspaper and the television newscast. It puts seemingly random events and chaotic world events into a coherent scheme. If Israel is at war or at peace, if Russia is friend or foe, if China is stable or unstable: all of these world conditions can be "read" in biblical prophecy. With prophecy as a tool for what Wahneema Lubiano calls "world-making," believers receive a script not only through which they can interpret world events, but also through which they can interpret their own lives.[3] Prophecy speaks not only to the course of human history, but also to how this moment should be lived. If the rapture could come at any moment, how does one want to be found living?

Readers find in *Left Behind* a powerful tool for making the doctrine of dispensational premillennialism real to them. The story—its characters, plot, and visual images—comes vividly to life and confirms its truth for many readers. Yet, while prophecy offers certainty, it also conjures doubt, particularly self-doubt. Readers of *Left Behind* constantly question their own salvation and that of loved ones. They seek out in the act of reading confirmation and affirmation. They seek to reassure themselves against the fear of being left behind. Readers engage this narrative in their lives as a way of conceiving and confirming vital truth that shapes their worlds into coherence, but the truths derived from this narrative become as individual as readers themselves and take shape within the unique circumstances of each life they touch.

The Truth of Fiction

A manifestation of biblical truth, *Left Behind* is simultaneously fiction. It functions as a means to truth and as truth's confirmation. It conveys "facts" of biblical prophecy while providing a narrative frame and striking visual images that, through fiction, make the facts come alive. *Left Behind*'s status as a fictional conveyor of truth gives it an unusual cultural authority for readers—one that is both undermined and reinforced by the books' status as fiction.

Over and over again in interviews, I ask the question, "Are these books accurate? Is this the way the world is going to end?" Over and over again, I receive the same answer, "Yes, but they are just somebody's interpretation. They are only fiction."

This "yes, but" lends the books cultural authority, authority to speak the truth, but then takes that authority away, undermining it so that the books remain within the realm of entertainment and play. Yes, the books are accurate according to what they know of the Bible, but, as many readers remind me, this is "only" fiction, "just one person's interpretation." By raising this crucial "but" in their answers, readers offer a subtle question about the books' authority. For most readers, the Bible is the ultimate authority on biblical prophecy, and they have to judge the books through a received understanding of the Bible. Readers express uncertainty about how much such a fiction can really tell them about "truth."

At the same time, the lightness with which readers accept the books, the lack of authority the novels have because of their status as fiction, paradoxically opens the door wider for the books' ideological work. Readers do not need to study the books with the precision required of the Bible. They do not need to discern the meanings of individual words and images—a process that can lead to uncertainty and multiplicity by its very nature. Instead, they can read for fun, for pleasure, getting caught up in characters' lives and the presentation of images. When they return to the biblical text, these images, received through the innocuous means of entertainment, give shape and meaning to the previously obscure text, making it come alive in a way it previously had not. This lends an authority to *Left Behind* that often goes unacknowledged by readers.

Jason is somewhat suspicious of fiction. He is a thoughtful and articulate person who defends his religious beliefs with quiet reasoning, constantly seeking a middle ground in religious questions. While Jason defies nearly all stereotypes of a fanatical fundamentalist, he is a conservative evangelical. He describes himself as "born again" and his church as teaching the literal truth of the Bible within a "conservative theology." By his own admission, he doesn't read much fiction. He likes his reading to be productive, he says, to be a part of other goals, so he is more attracted to nonfiction, to news, history, and politics. When he was first handed *Left Behind*, he was particularly skeptical. "Kate had been raving about the books and telling me how this was all the rage back in the town where she is from. I didn't know if it was just a local phenomenon. I hadn't heard about them anywhere else yet." Jason was uncertain of the books' quality, their authority, and their ability to convey biblical truth. Yet, when he finally sat down to read the first one, he found himself completely absorbed, reading for hours at a time to the neglect of everything else.

When I ask Jason about the relationship between truth and fiction in *Left Behind* he makes a distinction between what the books say and what any reality of eschatology might be. "It is fiction, but at the same time it does help to bring home a message from the Bible that we believe is imminent, something that is going to happen, we don't know exactly when or how." For Jason, as for many readers, *Left Behind* is a kind of fictional truth or truthful fiction. The fiction effectively delivers the "message" of the end times and serves as a conduit for the truth of biblical prophecy. For the most part, readers remain fully aware that what they are reading is fiction, "just somebody's interpretation," but through the act of reading, they become absorbed in the books' narrative, devoting hours and hours to fictional reading.

Many readers credit *Left Behind* for bringing the Book of Revelation to life for them in a way that has never happened before. Readers admit that Revelation is a struggle for them in their Bible reading because it is full of strange visions and bizarre images. They cannot read it literally but cannot make sense of it symbolically. They attribute to *Left Behind* the bringing of these obscure images "to life," which often means bringing them into a scheme of logic, assimilating them into a cosmic story they can understand. Darren expresses this with particular precision when he says that the books bring the end times into his "visual consciousness." He suddenly sees in his mind's eye the "reality" of the rapture and tribulation, and they seem compellingly real to him. The ability to envision the mysterious prophecies of Revelation is one of the most powerful effects that reading the books has. Readers often describe a kind of fictional hangover when they move from the books back into everyday life with a slightly altered vision. One reader describes turning on the television after a long session of reading and expecting to see news about the Antichrist. Another describes having to "pinch herself" to remember that half of the United States has not been destroyed by an earthquake. These comments and others like them are made casually, usually with laughter, but they emphasize that reading leaves a residue—a series of mental images, the outline of a narrative—that remains even when the immediate force of reading the story fades. One reader takes this relationship to the texts even further, claiming that God has spoken to her through the text.

Ann Marie came to the interview with some hostility toward me as an academic interested in *Left Behind*. She was not at all sure I would be able to understand her powerful appreciation of the books and hesitated to share the spiritual, almost mystical, response she had to them. She had prayed for me before I arrived for the interview, asking God to help her with whatever challenges I might present to her faith. While she had, after much nagging on my part, consented to the interview, she remained hesitant to share with me some of the more powerful spiritual experiences of her life, afraid that I might use them to mock or belittle her.

As she tells me about her experience of reading *Left Behind*, she tentatively raises the connection between spiritual authority and the authority of the fiction. "There have been a couple of times where I . . . and I don't know how you feel about this . . . where I really felt the Holy Spirit speaking to my heart. And I would feel what I think God wanted me to feel from reading the book." I ask her to clarify. Are there specific moments that conjure up this reaction? Ann Marie's answer invokes and dismisses the writers of the series, so that she can focus specifically on God's message, "Just one-on-one with understanding what God was saying, inspiring through this writer. Again, he wanted to speak to my heart." The writer was inspired, but Ann Marie's experience of reading is a "one on one" with God. Ann Marie points to the difficulty of Revelation, "I have always struggled with Revelation because it is so symbolic and all these visions. I mean, I could read it twenty-five times and there are some verses I can get a whole bunch out of and others that I am just kind of like OK, God, I read that. . . ." She gestures toward her confusion. "I had done a couple of studies on it and had learned some but I still struggled because it was so deep."

This difficulty with Revelation, the struggle to understand, has been frustrating for Ann Marie. She is able to piece together many other parts of her spiritual life. She is well read and well studied in biblical texts. But the intensely symbolic nature of Revelation has refused to let her in and seems to repel her attempts at understanding. In the midst of confusion, *Left Behind* intervenes and offers understanding. "But for me, I do know that they are totally fiction books. I do know that I went along with the Scripture at the same time. I made sure the Scripture was what it was supposed to be." Ann Marie reads with *Left Behind* in one hand and the Bible in the other, moving back and forth between the biblical text and the story, sometimes drawing on more than one translation of the Bible. Despite her insistence that "they are totally fiction books," she uses them as a study guide and road map to the biblical texts.[4] She both claims this authority for the books and denies it. "I knew that what he was proposing in this book might not be the way that it is, but it helped me to see it. Before I had tried to picture it, it just wouldn't come clear to me." This struggle to "see" the biblical images and the relief that *Left Behind* offers have become a spiritual experience for Ann Marie; she feels mystically touched by the Spirit through the act of reading. "It just took me into . . . a cross-spiritual realm where I was like, 'God, maybe this is the way it is and here I am seeing it for the first time. I am just glad I am understanding a little bit better, because You have spoken to my heart.' "

She adamantly claims this authority for God, not for the authors of *Left Behind*. She insists that God speaks to her through the books. "Not because Tim LaHaye did, but because God opened it up a little bit and made me say, 'Yeah, maybe that verse could mean that.' " She feels the need to separate God's authority from the authors' authority in order to give the books a more forceful articulation as "truth." If the books are fiction alone, they remain outside the realm of the communication of biblical truth. But if God speaks to her through these books, if God's authority interrupts the fiction and uses it to give her access to the truth, then they transcend their position as "totally fiction" and give her the ability to interpret the biblical texts.

For Ann Marie, this happens in a mystical context. God transforms the books from fiction into truth. For other readers, the books function as truth without direct divine intervention. Because they make the biblical texts vivid and provide images and language through which the biblical texts can be understood, they open the door for readers to accept them as "truth" on several levels. They are a true representation of biblical prophecy, offering a road map of God's cosmic plan. But they are also a true representation of human relationships, telling the truth about Christian leadership and Christian community. Because readers can return to the Bible to examine the details of what the authors propose to be biblical truth, they can accept the authors' authority on other matters.

Matt, a relatively new convert, sheepishly admits that he has never read the Book of Revelation and that he relies on his wife's assurance of the novels' validity. He describes the role his wife played in his interpretation: "I don't know much about the Bible. But every time Sarah reads [*Left Behind*], she says it is amazing how it is following exactly the Book of Revelation. The men at the Wailing Wall, the attacker from the north, the seven signs. I don't think Sarah would ever lie to me about church, Jesus, God, any of that. So whatever she says to me, I believe. I'm not saying she's . . . I'm not saying I'm a computer and she is programming me."

Matt ascribes to Sarah a powerful role in conveying to him the truth of what he reads. But he also expresses some concern that her authority is too great and that he sounds too passive. His concern that I might understand him as a "computer" that Sarah programs gives voice to some uncertainty about his own relationship to faith and the Bible. In evangelicalism, where each believer is encouraged to seek biblical knowledge through personal study, Matt feels uncomfortable acknowledging that he relies heavily on his wife's knowledge. Unlike Ann Marie, who had engaged with rapture eschatology for many years, Matt is an open slate for biblical interpretation. Whatever the books say must be true because he has no alternatives for comparison. Confirmed by Sarah, the books have a powerful role in forming his biblical interpretation.

Some readers have significant experience in rapture eschatology, raised on it since they were children, encountering it in many forms, both fiction and nonfiction, so that they are able to distance themselves to some degree from the narrative. They have other representations they can use to compare and contrast this particular version. For Matt, this simply is not so. When he became a believer, he accepted as truth his wife's faith. When I ask him if he could imagine someone being a believer but not accepting the rapture, he looks at me puzzled.

"You have to believe that Jesus is your savior, that he will rapture the church, that you will have to stand before him, stand before God, and answer to him. Yeah, yeah. That is it."

"That's key."

"That's not the key. It's the key, it's the house, the car, the mansion. That's everything."

"So, if someone said to you, 'I'm a Christian, but I don't believe in the rapture. The rapture is not an important part of the Christian faith to me. Jesus matters, but the rapture is not important.'"

"Jesus is the rapture. I mean . . . it wouldn't make sense. That's like saying the Dallas Cowboys are going to win the World Series. You have to accept Jesus 100 percent. Everything."

For Matt, the logic of the rapture is indelibly tied to his faith. He cannot separate the two, and the books' presentation of this eschatology is woven into his understanding of that undeniable truth. By combining the books' images with his wife's reassurances of their biblical reliability, Matt builds a framework for faith with the rapture narrative as an inseparable element.

Betty expresses concern that the books have become too powerful for her, that the line between fiction and truth has become indelibly blurred. Like Ann Marie, she moves back and forth between the Bible and the fictional text and finds herself amazed at the correspondence.

"I borrowed Ken's and then I bought it. I read it and I mean I couldn't put it down. I would go back to Scripture and I thought, 'I wonder if it really could mean this.' Because Revelation is a hard book to understand, and I had never . . . I had tried to read, but I could never . . . make sense of it. It became so real to me. I mean, I could see this happening. . . . I had to remember this is fiction. . . . It was hard for me to keep it separate, to know that this is a fiction book. I mean it brought Revelations to life for me. This is what it did, it brought Revelations completely to life. And I couldn't read them quick enough."

A friend cautioned Betty that she was making too much out of a fictional work. "I was walking with the girls, it was about six or seven of us, and we would share different things. One of the girls, Jody, she went to our church; in fact, she grew up in our church. And she said she wouldn't read them. I don't think it was anything against the books or anything, but she said, 'Betty, these are not the Bible.' I didn't feel that way, because everything that they've quoted in there, I've looked up. It's pretty much the Bible."

Even at the time of our interview as she recalls her conversation with Jody, Betty is still torn between whether the books are "just fiction" or as authoritative as the Bible. "I said to her, 'I realize that these are fiction.' But what Jody was saying was true. I was so drawn in; I couldn't wait to tell them what was happening the next morning when we went walking. . . . She was worried that I might take that as the truth instead of the Bible. And I would say, 'Jody, I am looking this up, I'm looking it up in the Bible.' I said, 'Jody, I realize these are fiction.' But at that time, I don't think I realized how much they had drawn me in. I said, 'I realize these are just fiction.' And she said, 'I just want to make sure you realize these are just fiction.' "

Betty's repeated insistence that "these are just fiction" expresses her more deeply rooted uncertainty about the line between the books and the Bible. On the one hand, as she puts it, "it's pretty much the Bible," and on other hand it is just fiction. While she is trying to allow both to be equally true, her friend, who refused to read the books, thought that she had confused them and pushed Betty to a place of discomfort about her reading. Even Betty has come to feel that she had been drawn in too deeply and confused truth with fiction.

Readers like Jason, Matt, Ann Marie, and Betty ascribe to *Left Behind* significant authority. Even while undermining that authority in speech by claiming that the books are "only" fiction, they then affirm it by giving the books both divine and cultural authority to convey the message of God's coming judgment. The books make the Book of Revelation come alive. They map the dispensationalist narrative onto the biblical text and give themselves the power to "see" its truth and experience it in a way that is almost visceral. Many readers express a profound imaginative experience reading *Left Behind*, but not all. For those readers who do not find their imaginations engaged, the problem is often one of belief. They do not share the authors' account of truth and therefore are uncompelled by the authors' fiction.

Too Much Fiction

I get off on the wrong foot with Jackson right away. I arrive during the second half of a football game in which his team is losing by three touchdowns and a field goal. "I waited around for you all morning," he grumbles as he keeps one eye on the television.

I inquire about the game, trying to engage with him, and he responds gruffly. Finally, although he is turned toward the television and not looking at me, I decide to attempt an interview. Rather than beginning with my usual formalities, I decide to start a casual conversation. "So you read the *Left Behind* novels?"

"I read them all."

"Did you like them?"

"Too much fiction in them," Jackson says.

"What do you mean?"

"What do I mean? It's fiction. Too much fiction in them."

"You don't like fiction?"

"Oh, I love fiction, but you expect them to stick more to the truth of the Bible, and I don't think they did. . . . There's nothing in the Bible that tells me that salvation is going to be rampant after the rapture. Salvation after the rapture, I believe, is going to be very uncommon. . . . As much as I'd like to see their version, it's not biblical."

Jackson's objection to the failure of the fiction to capture the "truth" of the Bible to some extent harms his pleasure in reading. He wants his books to be either "fiction" or "truth," not a hybrid. He has continued to read the *Left Behind* series, but with an overall air of disapproval and disappointment for the liberties they take with the biblical account as he understands it. Like many who disagree with the books in some fundamental way, Jackson finds it difficult to remember characters or plot. He has no vivid images of the rapture and tribulation lent to him by the books. At the same time, Jackson seems pleased that he can read and disagree. It gives him a sense of superiority over the books and confirms the rightness of his own beliefs, and he continues to read them despite his disagreement.

Michael disagrees for a different reason. Michael appears to have read the *Left Behind* series in a distracted way. Like Jackson, he barely remembers characters or events, and the books have meant little to him. Like many other readers, he reads *Left Behind* to keep abreast with what others in his church are interested in, although the books fail fundamentally to hold his attention. He disagrees on one major point—he rejects the idea of the secret rapture entirely: "I'm thinking that when Jesus comes back there will be no doubt that Jesus is back. I feel like the book is entertaining and maybe it opens up some possibilities, but I don't think that's the way it will be. . . . I think that some people just have very vivid imaginations, and I don't know as I'm going to worry about what might be. As I say, I feel like when Jesus comes, he'll be here and there will be no doubt."

Michael goes further to ascribe Revelation itself to the realm of fantasy and John as one of those with "vivid imaginations." "A lot of it is a dream by John, right? Or a vision, if you will. On Patmos Island, I think it was. He was an exile there. I'm not sure what to make of all that, but from what I read in the Gospels when Jesus is talking, Jesus says he'll return and when he returns, there will be no doubt."

Michael is a conservative Christian and goes to a church dominated by the dispensationalist narrative, but he firmly holds to his own reading of the Bible and rejects the *Left Behind* series. Perhaps even more than Jackson, his inability to embrace the series as truth interferes with his experience of it as pleasure. Even when he suggests that the books are "entertaining," I sense that he, himself, does not find them so, only that he has seen that response in others. When he talks about other things that he has read—poetry that he keeps in his wallet and other pieces that he recites to me from memory, a book called *Walk across America* in which a young man sets out to restore his faith in America, the Bible story of Daniel in the den of lions—Michael's eyes light up and he speaks with enthusiasm, even moving both of us to tears with his descriptions. With *Left Behind*, he expresses primarily boredom. "Some of it was all right. Some of it got kind of long and I was thinking, why are you going into this?"

Michael and Jackson suggest that the process of making prophecy live for a reader involves consent. A reader arrives ready to embrace the truth of the fiction and finds himself or herself suddenly able to see what was before obscure. Without this consent, without a prior investment in the books' account of truth, this act of imagination does not seem to take place. The truth of dispensational premillennialism does not come alive. Reading is a form of interaction, a transaction between text, author, and reader. While a fictional text offers plot, characterization, and description, the reader's imagination brings these devices to life and does the work of transforming the narrative into a vivid form of truth. When this transaction fails, when the reader's imagination is not profoundly connected, the books seem to have little impact on truth making.

Find whatever they're into

Food
Serve recipes that hit the spot from top brands you trust.

Health & Wellness
Care for them with easy prescriptions, vet diets & supplements.

Treats
Bring the snacks you know they crave & try new surprises.

Toys & Supplies
Set them up with bowls, leashes & all their must-haves.

Start saving now at Chewy.com

$20 off

Your first pet food, supplies or pharmacy order of $49 or more. Use code at checkout:

Plus **fast, free delivery.**

ZXNG5C94F

chewy
where pet lovers shop

Making and Protecting Prophecy

Religious belief takes shape in a diverse and often conflicting landscape. Religious beliefs, even when rigorously guarded, are still subject to change, to subtle influences, and to transformation over time. Readers use *Left Behind* to insulate their worldviews, to protect the "truth" that gives meaning to their lives and to human history. By reading *Left Behind* readers can be assured that they remain within the boundaries of the evangelical worldview, within the truth. If the narrative makes them "see" biblical prophecy for the first time, it also restricts their vision within secure limits. In fact, vision is made possible by putting these limits into place, by offering a very particular narrative and framework into which biblical images can then be incorporated. Dispensational premillennialism lives because other interpretations are excluded. In earlier rapture fiction, authors occasionally included footnotes or prefaces that they used to express the significant diversity of opinion among believers about the rapture narrative.[5] *Left Behind* includes no such alternatives. It distills these controversies into one cosmic plan for the end of history. Readers vary widely in their commitment to this one account of truth. Some feel the need to invest unquestioningly in the authors' account of biblical truth in order to maintain a relationship with the books. Others interpret *Left Behind* within a much broader stream of culture where the books have the power to comment on contemporary life, but not dominate it.

Fran is a fifty-five-year-old retired government worker. As she tells me her story, it is clear how vigorously Fran feels she needs to guard the boundaries of her religious belief. She rigorously avoids ideas that contradict those on which she has already settled. She became a Christian at age eighteen, shortly before her marriage, and has belonged to the same church in rural Virginia ever since. Fran believes that reading can be dangerous. She describes an incident from the early days of her conversion that solidified her view of reading.

"I was sitting there reading one of those true-romance magazines once. I was a teenager not having nothing to do, trying to mark time. The minister walked in there and asked me what I was doing. I said, 'Oh, I'm just reading a magazine. Just stories about romance.' He said, 'Is that doing you any good? What are you reading it for?' I says, 'Well, just to mark time.' 'Why don't you read something that will do you some good?' I just shrugged it off, you know."

Fran's husband was in the military, and he was transferred to Germany. "Guess what was there in stacks and stacks in the apartment we had? True-romance magazines. I read and read until I got downright depressed. I took those things and threw them in the trash can and went to the library on the base. First book I got was Norman Vincent Peale, *The Power of Positive Thinking*." She laughs with some self-deprecation at her first choice. "The second book was *In His Steps*. That got me started more in the right direction."

From that experience, Fran decided that reading could be a powerful force in her life, and she decided to be more cautious about what she read. Even so, Fran reads constantly. She reads *Guideposts Magazine*, *Reader's Digest*, books she buys from Christian bookstores, and books she orders through the mail. Since she has retired, she reads "every chance I get," and seems to organize her life around her reading. As a volunteer, she spends hours with elderly people in a nursing home reading with and to them.

Fran discovered *Left Behind* through a friend in her church. She has become an enthusiastic fan, buying each new book in hardcover as soon as it comes out. This is a luxury she rarely allows herself. More often, she chooses only less expensive paperbacks and used books. Even though she reads often, one cannot say that she reads widely. She rigidly restricts her reading to things she feels sure she will already agree with. As she describes her reading habits, she says, "If I see something in a book that I feel could—that is against what I believe, I stop reading it, set it aside, give it away, throw it away." Books represent both intense pleasure and a deep anxiety. As a window to other worlds, they are also windows to other ways of thinking and other modes of belief. She breaks off the phrase, "If I see something in a book that I feel could. . . ." In that blank, Fran expresses fear that she might be changed. That fear is produced by a strong sense of division between her church and the world. If she were insidiously influenced by a book that comes from the world "out there," beyond the secure boundaries of the church, she is at risk of losing her place within it, of losing her salvation and her identity. Fran fills in the blank she left with a significantly more stable phrase, "that is against what I believe." The first, broken thread reflects uncertainty. The second, completed thread offers security. It asserts belief against the influences of the hostile world, against the devil who might whisper through the pages of a book. If she can discern what remains within the realm of belief and what remains outside, then she is safe.

Not only does Fran restrict her reading, but she also strives to buttress her faith by surrounding herself with believers and then convincing herself that they believe exactly what she does. She adamantly asserts that a pre-tribulation rapture is the only possibility, but I am surprised to see her acknowledge disagreement.

"I've asked everyone when they think the rapture is going to come. Because there are a lot of different ideas among the different denominations—if it is going to come before the tribulation, during the tribulation, or at the end of the tribulation. Everyone I've talked to so far believes and hopes that it is going to come before the tribulation."

Fran faces considerable anxiety around the question of diversity of belief. Her informal poll was work she did to confirm and secure her own belief in the face of potential difference. It is not so much confrontation with difference as a way to defend herself against the intrusion of uncertainty.

For clarification, I repeat what she has just told me. "So you believe the rapture is going to come before the tribulation?"

"Yes, I have, even before I read these books."

"Do you think if the books had been advocating another position, if they had been post-tribulation or—"

Fran interrupts. "I wouldn't have read them."

"You wouldn't have read them."

"No."

"Why is that?"

To answer my inquiry, Fran returns to the minister who had first warned her about the potential dangers of reading. "The minister that I worked for for years told me to be careful of what I read because it could confuse me in what I believe. So if I see something that is against what I believe, I don't dip into it. It's just like, are you going to open a door to an intruder, someone that you know is going to harm you? Or are you going to say, 'I'm sorry, I'm not going to open this door to you?'"

Fran makes the connection between reading and danger explicit. Different ideas, opinions, and orientations are dangerous "intruders." They have the potential to cause harm and bring about chaos. Fran sums up the danger they present by saying, "They might confuse me in what I believe." To prevent this confusion, to stave it off and protect her worldview from invasion, Fran has to avoid the slightest difference in opinion, even the difference between pre-tribulation rapture and post-tribulation rapture. All difference, anything that might challenge the fragile structure of belief Fran has created, needs to be avoided. Since Fran surrounds herself with like-minded people and fills her life with activities that will confirm her beliefs, reading is one of the few places where alternatives might creep in. She is sure to keep this window—as, it appears, all windows of her faith house—tightly shut and locked.

Fran finds *Left Behind* effective in securing her realm of belief. It confirms her worldview, strengthens and solidifies her apocalyptic orientation, and gives her a secure sense of being among the few who know the truth and will go up in the rapture. While Fran seems absolutely certain that this is the case, her certainty masks a deeper anxiety about the nature of belief and its potential for change. She cannot give voice as Susan did to the fear "What if I'm . . . I am

... I don't want to be left behind," but that same sense of fear and the potential that salvation might be under threat pervade Fran's anxiety about reading and about her community. The uncertainty that Susan expressed in a previous chapter is unsurprising, given her marginal position within evangelicalism and her decision to spurn the social institution of the church. Fran, on the other hand, has been in her church for more than thirty years. It is as securely her "home" as her own house. She has the support and confirmation of the entire congregation. Her confidence in her faith should be secured by all of these things and yet she remains uncertain, anxious about intruders, and always alert to prevent difference from entering in.

Ken, on the other hand, reads *Left Behind* within a much broader world-view. He keeps up with the series, buying each new installment as it comes out. He is instrumental in sharing the series with members of his church, where he is an active participant in the congregation. Yet, outside of the *Left Behind* series, Ken consumes a wide range of cultural objects. In his house, the television is often on. He watches movies on his new DVD player and also goes out to movie theaters frequently. He listens to music, especially country and contemporary Christian music, and listens to hours of Christian radio. Not only does he consume movies, television, and music, but he also reads widely. He reads popular fiction and religious devotional books. More recently, he has started to read some Christian classics—the works of Tolstoy appeal to him in particular. Also within the last few years, he has started to read a considerable amount of evangelical fiction including westerns, historical novels, and the *Left Behind* series. Through all of this cultural consumption, Ken has a fairly critical theory of the influence of popular culture. He says that he reads quickly and mostly just for entertainment. He often forgets what he has been reading the moment after he sets the book down.

At the same time, Ken asserts that books, movies, and television have a powerful effect on their audiences: "Good stories serve their entertainment purposes. I'm sure they do affect us in more subtle ways, too. That's why it became important for me to switch to more Christian fiction because in subtle ways they do affect how we think." By suggesting this important cultural influence, Ken acknowledges that books go beyond mere entertainment. They shape and alter how he understands the world. By "switching" to Christian fiction, which Ken has done only partially, he can be sure that what he is reading will not subtly change the worldview to which he is committed. Reading Christian fiction is a way of insulating and protecting his worldview. He gives an example of how popular culture's sinister influence could take place, "Like if you see a movie that has a lot of racing in it, then it is hard to get in your car and drive the speed limit. You get home and you're not in the movie anymore. Sometimes attitudes you can pick up in a movie, I think you can pick up the same things in a book."

Ken is self-aware of how reading might be detrimental to his moral life—how it might subtly convey "attitudes or goals or ideals" that might undermine his worldview. Even though Ken is an active, committed evangelical Christian, he is aware of being vulnerable to the larger culture, which he perceives as potentially hostile. Ken relies on the cultural authority of books like *Left Behind*. He seems to hint at the fragile nature of belief and strives to protect himself through a turn to Christian products and Christian culture. Ken senses that individual agency is weak, that we are not finally autonomous individuals, but, at least in part, products of our culture. He does not trust his own ability to remain unaffected by products of secular culture.

On the other hand, Ken also consumes large amounts of secular culture. If he is concerned about the impact these cultural objects might have on him, he does not allow it to shape his behavior dramatically. Ken displays a certain confidence about his ability to discern truth from falsehood. He is an astute and critical reader. He has several complaints about the *Left Behind* series, both its form and its content. He criticizes the way the writers seem to be dragging out the plot and laughs that they are clearly motivated by a desire to make money. Like Sarah's minister and Jackson, he does not think people will get a second chance after the rapture. Those souls left behind will merely suffer the tribulation without recourse to salvation. All of these disagreements with and hesitations about *Left Behind* do not undermine his pleasure in reading the books. In fact, they engage him more deeply in religious questions.

At times in our interview, Ken seems to repeat verbatim ideas that he has heard on Christian radio or has picked up from reading Christian materials. He speaks confidently of the "right" ideas that true Christians should hold—about evolution, divorce, and American politics. Still, at other times, I am struck by the depth of his analysis, his willingness to continue to mull over questions without shutting down avenues of discourse. He is remarkably open and interested in conversation without needing to always be certain of his opinion. Reading as much as he does is a way of educating himself, and talking about what he has read is a way of engaging other people in order to enrich the questions he has found himself asking. Ken has strong ideas and strong opinions, but he enjoys subjecting these to the analysis of others. For this reason, he is a skilled and admired Bible study and Sunday school leader in his church.

Many readers use *Left Behind* as a means to buffer their worldview. Reading is an act of confirmation in which dispensational premillennialism receives the narrative investment it needs to survive in the imagination. Whether they read *Left Behind* to the exclusion of other things or draw *Left Behind* into a broad stream of cultural consumption, reading helps to protect and secure belief. At the same time, the salvation that reading helps to secure remains in question. Many readers express a fundamental anxiety about their own salvation that helps to cultivate their fascination with the rapture and their interest in *Left Behind*.

A Certain Uncertain Salvation

The state of "being saved" is crucial to evangelicalism. "Being saved" is the very thing that separates believers from unbelievers, and the rapture is the very moment when the saved are known and the unsaved are left behind. For many readers, this is the primary distinction through which they interpret their own place in the world, and in a complex and fluid culture, it is a way of sorting through conflicting meanings. When readers question me about my own beliefs, they try to determine my state of salvation. Am I saved, they want and need to know. My own inability to make this distinction and to answer this question clearly marks me, for them, as someone in need of salvation.

The problem with salvation as a marker, however, is that it has no necessarily tangible form. Salvation, in the evangelical imagination, often "happens" at a particular moment in time. It involves an act of going forward at a church service to "accept Christ" or the recitation of a formulaic prayer, often called the "sinner's prayer," in which the sinner confesses sin and asks Jesus to enter into his or her heart. At this moment, many evangelicals believe, an invisible transformation takes place. The "sinner" is "born again" to new life in Christ and her salvation is assured. On the one hand, this moment is so crucial in evangelical belief that nothing can ever transform it. If the sinner asks with a sincere heart, then Christ will enter into that person's heart and life and never leave. On the other hand, this moment must be maintained through prayer, Bible study, and interaction with other believers.

On the other side of this transformation, however, salvation has few outward signs. In the most dramatic accounts of salvation, a believer testifies to absolute depravity before the moment of salvation and a completely transformed life thereafter. Evangelicals thrive on these kinds of testimonies, welcoming the stories of depravity and salvation as proof of the transformation that Christ brings. But for most believers, there is little they can point to in their own lives as conclusive proof of salvation. While the state of "being saved" should lead a person to live a moral life, to witness to others, and to "bear spiritual fruit," none of these things is decisive evidence of salvation. "Being

saved" is a state of grace that cannot be confirmed by action; the most inauthentic person can pretend to be a Christian, and one might never know. Likewise, one's own authenticity can be in doubt. Once the initial glow of salvation
fades, how can one be sure that it was real?

Angela McRobbie points out that a subject never achieves complete and
final identity; identity is not a location in which a subject can finally rest.
Instead, identity is a dynamic process that is always in the midst of being
forged: "Identity requires acts of identification, and this, in turn, implies agency
and process."[6] Inside evangelicalism, there are few acts that confirm one's
identity as "being saved." Rapture eschatology and the rapture narrative play a
crucial role here. In rapture eschatology, the moment of the rapture is the final
proof. Those who are taken up will be shown to be the true Christians. Those
left behind, no matter what acts of goodness, no matter what pretenses of
righteousness, will be revealed as hypocrites and failures.

In *Left Behind*, the role of the inauthentic Christian is given to Pastor
Barnes. Pastor Barnes, a minister at Irene Steele's church, is left behind. When
the rapture occurs, he realizes immediately what has happened and is not at
all surprised to find himself among the hypocrites: "In church and at school,
I said the right things and prayed in public and even encouraged people in
their Christian lives. But I was still a sinner. I even said that. I told people I
wasn't perfect; I was forgiven. . . . I had a real racket going . . . and I bought
into it. Down deep, way down deep, I knew better."[7] The inauthenticity of Pastor
Barnes's salvation is intriguing. Presumably, his public display of faith was
flawless, his actions impeccable. Even his own wife did not suspect. He said
and did "the right things." He, himself, on a certain level, believed in his own
salvation, "buying into" his own display. Only "down deep, way down deep"
did he know better. In other words, Pastor Barnes was not an evil deceiver. He
did not play with people's faith out of some desire to hurt or confuse them.
He was entirely sincere and yet completely inauthentic at the same time. The
alchemy of salvation, whatever that entails, had not successfully transformed
him.

Stories like Pastor Barnes's work to confirm the insecurities that readers
already face about their own salvation. Are they a "Pastor Barnes" for whom
faith is merely a show? As the moment of "being saved" fades, doubts about
salvation creep in. Some evangelicals find themselves "rededicating" their lives
over and over to keep that spiritual fervor alive. Because the certainty of salvation can only be known "down deep, way down deep" and because it has no
necessary form in material life, believers find they can be assailed by doubts.
The rapture, as an event that can happen at any moment and will be the final
determination of the saved and the unsaved, feeds these doubts and leads

believers into a constant assessment and policing of their own position in the religious body.

In contrast to this uncertainty, *Left Behind* portrays "tribulation saints"— those who become Christians after the rapture—as receiving a mark on their foreheads. Through this mark, believers receive assurance of their own salvation, and they can immediately recognize one another. *Left Behind*'s authors offer a fantasy of assurance through this mark that readers cannot have in their daily lives. The mark both answers the anxiety of the uncertainty of salvation, of having no tangible proof that one really belongs, and, at the same time, gives readers a longing for such assurance that has no answer in life on this side of the rapture.

Sarah describes a time in her life when such doubts overwhelmed her. Interestingly, this period of extreme doubt coincided with her marriage. Just as she was securing herself within the evangelical community by marrying a Christian, she became plagued by panic attacks and nervousness. "I've always believed that the devil knows what to say to you and how to get to you. At that point in my life, he was saying to me things like, 'Don't you think if you were really a Christian, you wouldn't be so worried about things? Don't you think, if you were really saved, you wouldn't have all these doubts and fears?' I was really a mess." Sarah's doubts focused on doubt itself. Why, if she were "really saved," would she have doubts about her salvation? In the circling of worry, doubt produced still more doubt. Sarah's mother helped to rescue her from this troubling situation by drawing her back to the moment of her salvation. "My mom was like, 'Sarah, either you lied or God lied. When you said, "Jesus, I want you to be my Lord and Savior," did you lie?' No. 'Well, when God said, "If you ask, I will do it," did He lie?' No. I was like, you have a good point. That helped comfort me a lot."

During this time of confusion, Sarah did not have recourse to anything in her daily life that would help confirm her salvation. She could not point to contemporary practices or to material evidence. Instead, her mother drew her back to a moment when she was a very small child—Sarah sets the date of her "acceptance of Christ" at around the first grade—and used that moment as confirmation that Sarah had indeed "been saved." Sarah may be somewhat anomalous as a believer by attempting to reach back so far into her past for assurance of salvation. In fact, there is something almost sacramental in Sarah's reclamation of the moment at which she accepted Christ as her Savior that is similar to the way that Catholics might hold on to their baptisms as the moment at which they were formally accepted into the family of God. This sacramentalism is something that most evangelicals would reject. More often, evangelicals assess the state of salvation by asking, "Am I trusting in Jesus

Christ as Lord and Savior now?" instead of reaching into the past. Or perhaps more precisely, as Brenda Brasher describes it, salvation may be encompassed in a single moment, but conversion is an ever-ongoing process.[8] On the other hand, Sarah expresses a more general problem that afflicts evangelicals broadly. In order to hold on to confidence in faith—in that which sets them apart, assures their transcendence in the rapture, and provides the basis for current identity—many evangelicals must rely on an intangible spiritual state to answer the question, "How do I know I am saved?"

Sarah poses and then tries to answer this question, "I know I am because I am, because it is real. It's not a . . . I don't want to say it is a feeling because. . . ." She pauses, and I try to fill in the blank. "It doesn't change like a feeling?" "Right, two years ago I was feeling very torn and very upset, but it is a knowledge. No matter what happens or what goes on, there is always some piece, even if my faith is not big enough to let it overwhelm my life, there is this little piece of peace and understanding. You know you will get back to where you were. It may take you a while, but you will be able to get back there."

Sarah describes the movement of faith as "back" toward certainty, back to a confidence that might be lacking in the fluctuations of everyday life. Certainty of salvation is a "knowledge" that Sarah holds onto through the complexity and change inherent in life. In some ways, Sarah struggles to be that little girl again who was overwhelmed by a certainty in her family, in her church, and in God that compelled her forward one Sunday in church. She reaches always backward to that moment of faith that ensures her present path.

Left Behind becomes, for many evangelicals faced with this problem of personal salvation, a way of reading toward confirmation. Even as the story of Pastor Barnes raises doubts about salvation, the story also contains the potential to find those doubts answered. Jay describes a reading practice he uses to engage in this constant process of confirmation.

"When they were walking through the steps of salvation, I find myself double-checking. 'Did I do this? Did I do this?' And I did do it, so I felt like I was pretty secure with. . . ."

"So you found yourself confirming what you believe?"

"Yeah, you know, even when you pick up a gospel tract, you're like, 'Well, have you asked God to come into your heart?' Yeah, I've done all this, so then you know you are a Christian. You know that little cloud of doubt will creep in."

Jay searches in the texts of *Left Behind* for tangible proof that he has indeed done what is required to be saved. As the authors of the books take him through the steps of salvation, he uses these passages as a means to confirmation. As he reads, Jay can remember and reassert his salvation. The fact that this identity requires such a constant and sometimes almost feverish confirmation demonstrates how intangible salvation is, how difficult it is for even a committed believer to be certain where he stands. While salvation may happen in a moment, confirmation of that salvation must be repeated over and over again in ongoing activity and process. Reading *Left Behind* both raises in readers doubts about their salvation and confirms that they are indeed saved, they do in fact have the special "knowledge" that ensures that they will not be left behind.

This constant reproduction of doubt and reassurance is a means by which believers assess the state of their own salvation. It is one act of identification and confirmation in a religious universe that contains too few opportunities for genuine assurance. Even readers deeply grounded in faith, living by all accounts a faithful life, experience moments of tremendous doubt to which the rapture gives profound expression. One woman describes a moment of terror in which she suddenly believed that her daughter and husband had been raptured and she had been left behind. "After I had just read the book, I came home from somewhere in the evening. And I came in and the door to the house was open and Douglas and Christy were gone. I got so upset. I thought, 'I've been left behind. They took the child and they left me.'" Leah tells this story through peals of laughter, both from her and her other listeners. The story did not come up during her interview. It is not until, in a more informal situation, when someone else reminds her, that she tells it. She laughs so hard through the story, she can hardly get the words out. The laughter is a way of answering the anxiety that the event caused. Leah had come home in the evening to find her husband and child gone. Her first thought, her initial reaction to their unexplained absence, was that she had been "left behind," that whatever she had done to be saved was not enough.

Leah's vision was a domestic one. She returned home to find the house empty. She had been out fairly late in the evening, called by other responsibilities. Her response to finding the house empty may have been in part a response of guilt. She had not been at home when the rapture came, not performing family duties. Perhaps this was why she had been left behind? With the rapture as both threat and promise, Leah's self-doubt gave her a momentary question about her place in the community. The fear that she might be "left behind" keeps her answerable at every moment for actions that might impinge on her salvation. Every moment is one in which the rapture might occur. This leaves believers subject to the possibility that they could be left behind, deserted and robbed of the security of family and home.

We should not discount Leah and her listeners' laughter. We are laughing at the absurdity of Leah's self-doubt. Everyone in the room is aware of what an upright person Leah is, how well she fulfills the role of "devoted wife and mother" so important to rapture eschatology. We all feel that if anyone will be left behind, it certainly will not be Leah. At the same time, we laugh out of recognition at the self-doubt Leah expresses. We all understand that kind of self-doubt, that moment of wondering, when everything you think you have built is eclipsed by deeply rooted insecurity. We laugh too, at the way that Leah has been influenced by her reading of *Left Behind*, that it was just after reading the first book that she had this vision. Through the act of reading, Leah has entered thoroughly into the universe of the books. They spark this fear and self-doubt that was waiting for a moment in her life to materialize. Through laughter, Leah is able to acknowledge how seriously she has taken the books, and the lightness of the moment produces the possibility of articulating her fears.

Leah's story effectively illustrates how the story of the rapture disciplines religious subjects. It brings into focus deeply rooted fears about isolation and personal failure; it plays on these fears in order to produce in even very devout people a nagging uncertainty about their own worthiness. If, as I have suggested, evangelicalism draws and holds people through a vision and experience of communal life, it also uses a particular kind of eschatology to conjure up doubts that then secure believers ever more strongly. The ideological power of the rapture's "truth" becomes vivid in Leah's story in the power of the narrative to frighten and discipline her.

The rapture narrative answers anxieties and raises them, simultaneously giving readers an identity within the narrative and giving them reason to question that identity. In this dialectical pull on readers, the rapture narrative establishes its cultural and ideological work. By "bringing Revelation to life," giving readers visual images and a coherent narrative for biblical prophecy, *Left Behind* provides tools readers use to make sense of the world they live in. This reading produces tangible effects. We might think about Betty's changing relationship to technology, Jason's desire to "stick around," and Cindy's television watching as ways that reading *Left Behind* does its work, seeping into readers' lives and taking tangible form among practices. The narrative feeds off of even the instability of religious salvation to draw readers ever more powerfully into its structuring narrative and truth-making consequences.

7

Witness to the Apocalypse

I arrive at Ann Marie's workplace knowing only that I am interviewing a woman who has little interest in sharing her story. She avoided an interview for months and only through regular persistence on my part has the interview been arranged. I am surprised, then, to meet her. She is tall and striking and quickly takes control of the interview. When we are seated at a small table in the break room, she asks, as though she is the interviewer, "Why don't you tell me a little about yourself?" Later, I learn that this assertiveness is in part the result of anxiety about who I am and what my purposes might be in interviewing her. At the end of the interview, she admits that she was concerned when she heard I came from Duke University. In preparation, she prayed for me and for our interview.

"I had prayed about it and I had prayed for you specifically and I thought, 'You know, God, I don't know what she is going to come up with, but I pray you'll help me handle it.'"

Ann Marie listens more carefully than other interviewees to the story that I tell her about myself. She is quiet but attentive, asking a question of clarification here and there. Two hours later, when we have completed the interview about *Left Behind*, she returns to the subject of my spirituality.

"What are your beliefs?" she asks me, and as I fumble for an answer, she continues. "Are you afraid to die? Has anyone close to you ever died? Where do you think that person went?"

My answers are brief, inarticulate, and embarrassing. I feel suddenly trapped and suffocated even as I try to retain the calm and unruffled demeanor of a researcher. I find I have no language to articulate my own eclectic religious beliefs and practices, and I have a keen awareness of how lost I must sound to her. I know as we continue to talk that her fear of me has turned to pity. I also know that she will be praying for my immortal soul, and the thought makes me inwardly cringe.

Susan Harding points out that ethnographic work, by its very nature, opens the researcher to acts of witnessing like Ann Marie's because ethnographic work is about the fine art of listening, while witnessing is about the fine art of telling.[1] As distinctly uncomfortable as Ann Marie's attempts to witness to me make me, they are crucial to the work that I am doing. If I foreclose her line of questioning, I do so only to reestablish the dynamics of power between us in my favor and cease to be a good listener. Though I long to return to the role of expert and scholar, that is a role, given my religious incoherence, that Ann Marie cannot allow me. Instead, she is the expert with important knowledge about the state of my soul. Ann Marie has begun to witness to me and this process continues over several weeks while I attend her church and interview her friends.

As Ann Marie works at realigning my reality and reconstituting my truth, she is also providing herself a confirmation of her own fundamental spiritual knowledge. For dispensationalists, the truth of rapture and tribulation, of an apocalyptic future, has always been, in part, about evangelization. If the rapture is coming soon, then the unsaved need to know about it. They need the opportunity to accept Christ or reject him before the end. I did not anticipate that, in the process of interviewing, I was going to become a part of the most important work that *Left Behind* attempts, the work of witnessing. But it was essential that I did so because *Left Behind*, like rapture texts before it, is partly fueled by this evangelizing urge. It seeks both to convert the unbelieving and to create a sense of urgency among the saved.

Both the producers of *Left Behind* and many of its consumers see witnessing as an important part of the work *Left Behind* can do. Whether or not they engage in such practices, most evangelicals agree that witnessing is a fundamental part of faith. Christian Smith examines what he calls evangelicalism's "personal influence strategy," which intends to bring about social change one person at a time through individual salvation.[2] Through promotional materials and institutional practices, Tyndale House urges readers of *Left Behind* to use the series to bring about the conversion of others. For example, they have started a program called the Underground. Directed at young people, this program motivates youth "to go and save the lost world one friend at a time."[3] In September 2000, Tyndale House issued a mass-market paperback version of *Left Behind*. The primary purpose of this smaller, cheaper version of the novel was to sell the books in large quantities to churches for use in witnessing.[4] Some churches have even developed witnessing programs based on the novels and are training people to "spread the gospel" while sharing the novels.

Readers share this view with the producers of the series. They often see the books as an important tool for witnessing. Because the books are so successful at giving readers a strong sense of community identity, they hope the books might also convince others to join. The expectation of the rapture provides a particular kind of urgency and justification for sharing faith, a reason to press faith on others. Readers in my study describe giving the books away to the "unsaved" people in their lives, to both positive and negative responses. After they became captivated by the series, Katie and her mother bought multiple copies of *Left Behind*. "My mom went out and bought like twenty copies at the bookstore and sent them out to everyone." She laughs. "Then we went to Sign of the Fish . . . and bought a bunch of copies and sent them to people."

"Who did you send them to?"

"Relatives mostly and people who we knew weren't saved, but we just thought it might be a way to get their interest."

A more extreme example comes from Tyndale House itself. In an advertisement to Christian bookstore owners, the publisher tells of receiving a letter from a reader who writes that she gave the first book to her stepmother, who then "was so touched she went out and ordered 500 of them and passed them out to everyone. Even strangers."[5] This particular advertisement was part of a campaign telling Christian bookstore owners that *Left Behind* was helping Tyndale House fulfill its mission to "minister to the spiritual needs of people, primarily through literature consistent with biblical principles." Ministering to people's spiritual needs includes both being a company that "witnesses" to Christ's salvation and encouraging Christian consumers to do the same.

Witnessing, at least in the case of *Left Behind*, is synonymous with the attempt to expand Tyndale House's market base. Conversion means more consumers for their products—more books, tapes, comic books, and so on. While we might view this as a cynical, money-driven motivation on the part of Tyndale House (as several readers did), Tyndale House sees it differently. Expanding markets mean expanding faith; Christians are fulfilling their call to spread the Gospel through the production, consumption, and sharing of Christian books. As Colleen McDannell puts it, "advertising and witnessing become interchangeable."[6] Advertising is profoundly important as a religious act. Tyndale House makes no distinction between the secular marketplace and their religious intentions; rather they skillfully use the marketplace for religious purposes. Similarly, consumption is not materialistic, self-serving, or greedy. In-stead, it too is a religious act, done not only for one's own good, but also for the good of others.

Readers often feel that *Left Behind* calls them to action; they insist that *Left Behind* makes them urgently feel the need to witness to their neighbors, un-saved family members, and friends. Witnessing—sharing their faith with oth-ers—is the most potent form of action that they can imagine. While embedded in consumer culture, they never describe this action as a political, social, or economic one; rather it rises from a profound concern for the salvation of others' souls. Bobbi insists that *Left Behind* has convicted her. The point of *Left Behind*—its most significant message to her—is that she needs to tell other people about salvation through Christ and the coming of the rapture. Oddly, however, she finds herself unable to act on this message. "It should make me want to go out and tell everybody about salvation, the salvation planned. But I'm still too timid. . . . It's very encouraging to read the books and I think, this is something I should be doing. It convicts you, whether you actually do it or not." She laughs, "It does convict you."

Bobbi describes an urge to witness as the primary effect of *Left Behind* on her life. This is in part because once a person has become a Christian, the most important thing they can do, the act that will attest to their faith more than any other, is the act of witnessing. Bobbi laughs with self-deprecation and guilt when she says that while *Left Behind* should make her more open to witnessing, she is "still too timid." What Bobbi does instead is make purchas-ing and reading the books an act of public display. She buys her books at Sam's Club and starts conversations with people there. "It's funny," she says, "but as soon as someone sees you pick up the book, they'll ask you about it." And she recommends the books to everyone she knows, insisting that they will make a difference in people's lives.

For readers still "too timid" to share their faith using direct methods like Ann Marie's, *Left Behind* can play a role. Matt explains why he shared the book with his closest childhood friend, someone he feels certain isn't saved.

> Josh is my best friend in the world. I want to be in heaven with him. I do. At least I can say, "Hey, Josh, man, let me tell you about what is happening in my book!" I tell him, you know, and that maybe starts a dialogue. He might ask me a question. Or we'll start talking. Whereas if I said, "Hey, Josh, let me tell you about the Bible!" that might come off as a little more forward. This way, I ease into it with, "This is so cool, this one thing." That has actually prompted he and I to talk for about an hour about God and Jesus and stuff that

doesn't pertain in the books, what's going on in the books, but we talk about the Bible. I love Josh. He is like a brother to me, and these books help me talk to him.

Many readers feel that the books provide an opening, a casual and non-threatening way to present their faith to others. The Bible is too intimidating a place to begin, so readers turn to fiction to offer their faith to their friends. And not only friends, but strangers too. Readers purposely read the books in public places so that they can be questioned about their contents. Laura describes reading *Left Behind* on a plane and finding an opportunity to speak with others about her faith. First she spoke with the flight attendant and then with the person sitting next to her. "When I was talking with the stewardess, the person next to me was interested in what we were talking about, so that I was able to explain to her about the novels. Not so much that she will ever read the book, but we were discussing about what might happen after the rapture. So it provided a spark to be able to talk to somebody about Christ."

Like Matt, Laura reasons that the *Left Behind* series is easier to talk about than the Bible, and she uses the books to talk with strangers if the opportunity arises. "Maybe its less-officialness makes it easier to discuss, and it sparks the conversation a little more than if I am sitting there reading the Bible. It's got those cool fiery balls on the front and somebody could say, 'Oh, *Apollyon*, I never heard of that. What's that?' Then you can say something, and I love opportunities like that!"

For many evangelicals, the stranger is always someone in need of Christ, someone to whom the Christian should witness. Readers of *Left Behind* who use their reading as a form of witnessing almost always assume that the general public is lost. By casting the stranger in the role of other, of non-Christian, would-be evangelizers create a sense of distinction for themselves and a sense that they have an urgent, special message for the world. Ironically, much of this form of witnessing is silent. They merely read in public. Sarah carries her book to work and keeps it on the top of her desk. Betty reads the book while standing in line at the bank. Laura takes the book on trips to visit her mother. Only if they are approached will they speak, but they feel they are fulfilling their duty to witness to their faith nonetheless.

While most readers are enthusiastic about the witnessing potential of *Left Behind*, they report much less successful results. The most positive response comes from Katie. Her husband, David, gave the book to all of his groomsmen before their wedding and two of them responded positively.

[David bought the books for his groomsmen] because he really had very much of a spiritual revival, more so than he'd ever had in his life before. Mostly all of his groomsmen weren't saved, and he wanted to take the opportunity to tell them about his faith. They had been friends forever, but he had never really been open about his faith. They knew what he believed and he would argue with them on an intellectual level . . . but never really from his heart. One guy— he's an atheist, and they argue all the time about it. So he bought them all a *Left Behind* book with a letter, just kind of sharing his heart, how much he's changed and all that. David didn't hear back from them, so he was really worried. He didn't know if they were offended, and so over Christmas he ran into the one guy, Jim. He said, "Oh, I'm really sorry I didn't get back to you. All I've been do- ing is reading the books. I'm on the third book." So it was neat to see that it really caught his attention. And then the atheist, he lives in Hong Kong and it just happened over the next couple of months that David had a lot of trips to Hong Kong. They would talk for hours about the books and the guy said that it really makes him think about the Bible in different ways, you know, read the Book of Revelation and try to figure out. . . . He said, "I'm not going to go out and buy these books, but if you keep sending them to me, I'll read them."

Most readers, however, face far more frustrating outcomes. Sarah gave the book to a family member and was deeply disappointed.

I thought, maybe coming out of somebody else's mouth, it would sound different and she would be able to hear it. And I was so dis- appointed because when she was finished reading the book, I thought, "Good. This is going to give us the perfect platform to talk about these things." She said, "Oh, that was some nice stories." To her, it was totally and completely fiction. There were no realities. When I tried to talk about the reality of it, in her mind it was still fiction.

Sarah is frustrated that the message of truth she was trying to convey through fiction comes across in her relative's mind as only fiction. While fiction is a relatively nonthreatening way to communicate faith, the witnesser runs the risk that the attempt to share the urgency of faith will be lost in a purely fictional message. This is indeed what happened for Sarah. Likely, the object of Sarah's intentions knew perfectly well that she was being witnessed to—as Margaret did when her daughter Rachel gave her the books—and the fiction of the books was a place where she could retreat. Just as Sarah tried to obscure her intention by cloaking her message in fiction, the reader could also obscure her response by commenting on the "nice stories." The real exchange—an offering and a rejection—was shaded by the fiction. Sarah is frustrated by her relative's refuge in the book's fictional premise, but this is an escape she herself has provided.

Sarah is fortunate, however, that the target of her attempts actually read the book. Many others find that their gifts go unread. Lila gave the book to her mother, whom she describes as a "closet Christian," hoping that her mother would read the book, share the urgency, and become more visible in her faith, especially with Lila's father. Again, the mission failed.

> So I figured, *Left Behind*, it's fiction so it's not like I'm shoving any-
> thing down her throat. I thought that it might be something that
> made her think, "If this happens in any way like this, then we need
> to be really concerned about my dad and where he is going to spend
> eternity." I don't think she worries enough about that. . . . So I gave
> it to her for Christmas, also thinking that if she liked it—this was
> very manipulative of me—my dad might read it too. I knew I
> couldn't give it directly to him. . . . My mom opens it and she says,
> "Ooo, *Left Behind*—that doesn't sound like a very fun book." I've
> asked her since then and I've said to her, "It's a fictional book. It's
> fun. An easy read." I asked her if she read it. She said, "No, I don't
> really read that much while I'm working. Maybe I'll read it this
> summer." I would be willing to bet she will never read it. I think it
> is threatening to her. Because my dad is not a Christian it would
> make her have to face that head on, and she just likes to bury her
> head in the sand.

Sarah, Lila, and many others find that while *Left Behind* seems to provide an opening for them to share their faith with unsaved loved ones, the books rarely have the desired effect. The books do not seem capable of persuading the unpersuaded into a position more amenable to faith. The more powerful effect seems to be on the believer who finds his or her own life profoundly touched and feels deeply and passionately the need to share the message.

This is true in the many settings where evangelicals are urged to share their faith. While directed at others, the effect of the message is often on the believer, not the unbeliever. In nearly all of the churches of readers, an invitation is issued at the end of each service to bring unbelievers into the fold. In my visits very rarely does anyone go forward during these services and never do I see a spontaneous conversion, but I witness over and over again the ritual of self-confirmation that the moment of invitation provides. In her study of fundamentalism, Nancy Ammerman points out that the ritual of invitation at the close of every fundamentalist service fills two roles. On the one hand, it provides a model for listeners to follow, confirming them in their role as tellers as well as hearers of the word. On the other hand, it confirms a sense of distinction; it provides a feeling, in the midst of an otherwise confusing cultural terrain, of identification.[7] During my fieldwork, this distinction was invoked many times for the clarity it brings to the sometimes murky matters of faith in a diverse and market-driven culture. The invitation ostensibly offered to nonbelievers articulates for speakers and listeners a confirmation of identity. At one church, after a fiery sermon, the minister concludes by asking the congregation to close their eyes. He says, "Everyone here who has accepted Jesus Christ as personal Lord and Savior, who knows that transformation and that healing that I am talking about, and if you haven't experienced that transformation, you won't know, raise your hands." There is a swift rustling all around me. I keep my hand down.

"Now if you haven't experienced that, but you would like me to pray for you; if you want to say, 'Pastor, pray that I might know Jesus'; if you need help carrying your burdens, raise your hand, just raise your hand." He pauses and then acknowledges into the microphone the hands he sees. "Thank you, sir. I see you. Thank you." I feel conspicuous. Although all eyes are supposedly closed, I feel distinctly watched. There is only one category left over for me—those choosing to be damned—but he does not ask us to raise our hands.

The minister has created a universe in which there are only two answers—either you have accepted Jesus Christ and are saved, "and if you haven't experienced that transformation" then you cannot know what it feels like. Or you are damned and in need of salvation. For most of his listeners, the invitation to raise their hands provides a moment of confirmation. I am surprised by the effect this either/or rhetoric has on me, an unaffiliated listener. I find myself struggling within the minister's logic, not immediately recognizing it as a logic, but instead trying to place myself within the given categories. Several minutes pass as the minister asks us to stand and sing the invitation hymn and encourages the unsaved to come forward before I am able to think outside this particular logic, before I am able to reject the logic itself. This yes or no, damned or saved rhetoric of salvation is a powerful one within evangelicalism because it creates a universe inside which one must articulate an answer. Either you are saved or you are damned. Since "damned" is an unacceptable alternative, one must answer yes. Even with a long history both inside and outside evangelicalism, I find myself temporarily drawn in to this logical universe, trying to make sense of my position within its terms.

During his sermon, the minister of this particular church invokes both the rapture and death as potential creators of the eschatological moment when the saved will be separated from the damned. Both of these events force a moment of final confirmation and are effective rhetorical means to the sense of urgency that a decision for salvation requires. When he asks for a physical demarcation of the damned and the saved through the raising of hands, he is creating the moment of the rapture in speech. He is asking his listeners to decide if they will go or if they will stay, and then encouraging a visible symbol of that separation. The effect this logic has on me is the powerful effect of inclusion and exclusion. He forces me into a moment of choice as well—I have to choose to be excluded.

At the same time, this pastor's message is delivered in a church in which the unsaved visitor is a rare event. Visitors certainly come with long-time church members, but this particular church has a stable membership of nearly four hundred people, a church school where the children of the congregation attend, and it seems to be largely a self-contained universe. While the minister's rhetoric appears on the surface to be directed at me—the unsaved—its more general purpose is probably self-confirmation for the congregation. He provides them the opportunity to acknowledge themselves as believers and to enact that identity in the ritual raising of their hands.

Left Behind serves a purpose very similar to this preacher's sermon and to the practices of invitation and witnessing in general. If, as I argue in the first chapter, evangelicalism exists in a very complex field of faith and evangelicals make their way through the broader culture without experiencing much alienation, invitations and witnessing provided opportunities to experience the distinction and identity of faith. They are acts that give truth an opportunity to be expressed and confirmed and therefore shape the believer's world perhaps even more importantly than the unbeliever's to whom the message is often directed.

While giving *Left Behind* to unbelievers is a method of witnessing to others about faith, a more common method in evangelicalism is the telling of one's own story. This method is frequently called a "testimony." When believers offer their stories as a testimony, they hope that it will provide a model for others to follow and bring about others' conversion.[8] Within the context of conducting interviews for this study, I hear many conversion stories, some told with the explicit purpose of witnessing to me. The books themselves—theoretically the center of the interview—move to the periphery as readers take the opportunity of my presence to present their conversion narratives. Darren's story, told to me within the context of an interview yet also polished and refined as a tool for witnessing, illustrates one of the story's common forms.

I was raised in a Presbyterian church. . . . We went to church every Sunday. I was raised in a Christian family, but it never really made any sense to me. I kind of went through the motions of Presbyterianism. . . . Although I heard about Jesus, I really didn't understand any significance to him. . . . For a long time I would have told you that I was scared of dying. I mean as a kid, I would go to bed thinking, I am going to die tonight and I always imagined that as me sitting in a coffin conscious with nothing to do. That scared me. I was terrified. . . . But later, I began to suppress that fear. I was much more a follower throughout high school. I started drinking, using drugs in high school and college. I would never say it was abusive, but it was one of those things I was using to fill up. It was something that was a suppressor; it made me feel good, at least a temporary high at the time. And it was enough just to keep that . . . scary question [away], and I just didn't want to deal with it.

So I went through college really filling myself with relationships with women, with drugs, with friends. It was pacifying. . . . I started working with my father and then success became one of the things I started to fill myself with and money. I was totally unconscious of all this. . . . [Then] a real good friend of mine—I used to go see him play on Saturday nights—was in a really good band. One time he invited me to go see him play on Sunday morning. I was like, "Where in the world is he going to play on a Sunday morning?" He said, "Well, I'm on a music team at this church. Why don't you come see me?" And I said, "OK." I wasn't afraid of church. I hadn't had bad experiences in church; it was more like milquetoast to me. So I went and I remember this distinctly; it was in March. It was as if the space inside of me had really been cleaned out and I could feel a real emptiness inside me. The pastor was doing a message on the lust of the eyes, the lust of the flesh, or you know, the things of this world. I really felt like, "Gosh, if there were nobody else in here, he's talking to me." I remember getting this really big lump in my throat like oh no, there's something really wrong in my life. I felt something was wrong. I was very aware of it. I came back the next week, of course. I remember coming back and thinking, "This is that question that had been suppressed for me for a very long time." I wasn't aware of it. I wasn't conscious. I just knew this was going to the first-order questions for me. There's life, there's a purpose to it and you are coasting through life without any acknowledgement of what is happening. And then my friend invited me to a small group. He said, "Why don't you come? A bunch of us meet on Wednesday night and talk about the things that matter in life."

So I remember going to his small group. . . . It had a little worship time, and stuff. And the worship time seemed to me like campfire songs, you know, it just seemed kind of silly. But the people there were all people I could trust and that I could relate to. It wasn't like I was sitting in on some sappy Christian thing. I don't remember what we were studying, but I remember that the leader was real aware of where I was. I was almost belligerent. . . . Sometimes I would go to small group and be distracting and sarcastic. One night, I remember saying, "You all are talking about Jesus like he is so important. What's the big deal?" I remember thinking about that as kind of a silly question, but I didn't realize that that was the question. I mean that *was* the question. I became a Christian over the next month. It wasn't one moment in time. I began to realize there was a huge gap. I said, "OK, God, this may be true." All this stuff they are talking about . . . I'll give it a shot. I'll just say it is going to be true. If it is not true, what have I lost? I'll just go back to the way I was. I didn't realize that that itself was the first step of faith—just saying, "OK, I'm going to let you into my life and clear out that space so that you can begin to come in."

Darren's story tells of his life before conversion—drugs, sex, alcohol, and a spiritual emptiness. Then he presents the invitation to faith and his initial attraction and rejection. Finally, prompted by a crisis—this one internal—he finds faith and embraces it. His story is first of all personal—it is the story of a personal struggle and confrontation with ultimate truth. At the same time, the story follows a familiar conversion formula, and it is carefully crafted. It is organized around the themes of emptiness and fulfillment directed to convey Darren's primary message to me: don't be satisfied with earthly things. In his interview, he begins with this message, telling me, "God created a God-shaped vacuum inside us and until that is filled we attempt to fill it. . . . He wants you to find Him, but, being human, we try to fill that with almost anything else, but it always comes up a little bit short." His testimony then becomes an illustration of this point, crafted, he hopes, to speak to my fears and desires.

In *Left Behind* characters repeatedly tell the stories of their conversions to other characters in the same way that readers repeatedly tell me the stories of their conversions. Rayford's testimony to Mac McCutcheon in *Soul Harvest* is a typical example. Mac, another pilot, invites Rayford to speak and encourages his story with frequent questions. Like Darren, Rayford details his life of sin-fulness, hearing the truth and rejecting it, followed by a crisis event (in this case, the rapture) that causes him to reconsider the truth and leads to his transformation. Finally, he extends the truth to his listener, laying out the plan of salvation and biblical support for the need of personal transformation.[9]

Scenes like this allow the series to perform a role that is simultaneously modeling for believers and witnessing to nonbelievers. Believers see how they might tell their own stories and Rayford's words arm them with appropriate Bible passages and pithy phrases. The passages also carefully lay out the "plan of salvation"—our separation from God, God's gift of Jesus as atonement for our sin, the need for sinners to accept that gift, and finally, a version of the "sinner's prayer" in which the converted asks God's forgiveness and asks Christ into his or her heart. Someone who has not converted to evangelical Christianity would find the process of conversion clearly articulated and easy to follow. At the same time, the passages give readers both a language and a structure to follow when telling their own stories to unbelievers. In the books, these stories are always, eventually, effective means of "bringing others to Christ." In real life, however, witnessing can be a frustrating and ineffectual task.

Specters of Conversion

In the November 2001 issue of Tyndale House's *Left Behind* e-newsletter, the publisher reports that two weeks after its release, the ninth book in the series, *Desecration*, is the number-one selling book on the *New York Times*, *USA Today*, *Wall Street Journal*, and *Publisher's Weekly* best-seller lists. "While the sales numbers are spectacular," the newsletter says, "the most important thing is that millions of people's eternities have been altered because of fans like yourself sharing *Left Behind* with your friends."[10] Tyndale House routinely claims that *Left Behind* has brought thousands, perhaps millions, of people into the Christian faith. Their evidence is the letters, e-mail, and postings to the *Left Behind* message board from readers who have "accepted Jesus Christ as their savior" through the reading of the novels and written to testify about it. In the Christian booksellers' trade publication, Jerry Jenkins expresses feeling "overwhelmed" by the success of the series. "What's gratifying are the letters we've received. Christians have said the message in the books has helped them be more aggressive in their faith. And about 2,000 people have written to say they've accepted Christ because of the books."[11]

As I conducted my research, I searched in vain for a person who could testify to a life changed through the reading of *Left Behind*. Surely, if Christian conversion is an important outcome of reading the books, as producers claim, I would be able to find someone who could physically embody this process for me and teach me about the relationship between reading fiction and seeking religious truth in the form of conversion. While many readers are strongly influenced by the series, none rest their religious faith or the transformation of being "born again" on the reading of the novels. Furthermore, no one knew of anyone personally who had become a Christian because of reading. Some had heard of these conversions, but none had been personally connected to one. Frustrated at being unable to find an embodied reader, I turned to other sources. I asked Tyndale House if they would be willing to share some of their letters on salvation and I received a packet of seven such letters. Of these, four are letters reporting the conversion of others: "Praise God! Because of your wonderful novels, my daughter-in-law has become a Christian." Three actually tell their own stories.

With such a weak body of evidence from which to draw conclusions, I wonder why the connection between reading *Left Behind* and conversion to evangelical Christianity is so elusive. What is conversion? How do we know it when we see it? How does it take place? The vocabulary of Christian conversion involves several words and phrases that may seem particularly opaque to the noninitiated reader. Jerry Jenkins, for example, talks about "accepting Christ." Readers talk about "asking Jesus into your heart" and "finding God." They talk about being "saved," "drawn," and "born again." Yet the precise transformations that these words indicate can be difficult to grasp. This is partly because the inner transformation's most important effect is unseen—the converted now go to heaven and not to hell when they die. But changes also take place in outer behavior as well; they begin to attend church and Bible study, and spend time in daily prayer and Bible reading. Gradually friendships may change. The converted also report changes in more subtle behavior—maybe they are kinder, more peaceful; maybe they stop drinking or smoking. Many come to these times of transformation through personal crises—struggles in their marriages, the sickness of a child, the death of parents or loved ones. Many report "accepting Christ" as children or teenagers, but not really being faithful until much later, perhaps provoked by a life crisis or drawn by a new friendship.

As a researcher, I take the stories people tell me of their conversions as accounts of real transformations in their lives. At the same time, I find I cannot share their language for what has taken place. Susan Harding describes conversion as a shift in language. The listener begins to internalize the language of the one who has witnessed to her and begins to use that language to tell stories about her own life.

The process starts when an unsaved listener begins to appropriate in his or her inner speech the saved speaker's language and its attendant view of the world. The speaker's language, now in the listener's voice, converts the listener's mind into a contested terrain. At the moment of salvation, which may come quickly and easily, or much later after great inward turmoil, the listener becomes a speaker. The Christian tongue locks into some kind of central, controlling, dominant place; it has gone beyond the point of inhabiting the listener's mind to occupy the listener's identity.[12]

Identity is changed through a transformation in language. The speaker's words produce a dissonance in the listener's mind, a "divided self," and the dissonance is resolved only when the listener perhaps gradually, perhaps instantaneously, tells her own story in a new way. Were I able to share readers' language for what took place, I would myself be converted. Conversion involves precisely that acceptance of the language used to tell the story. Readers and I are, then, often at an impasse. I can only be a listener to their stories, and I very often struggle to find a language we can share to tell my own.

This inability to share the language used to tell stories of conversion contributes to the difficulty of recognizing conversion when it happens and sharing readers' stories here. What interpretation can the unconverted offer that does not undermine the integrity of the converted stories, that does not change their language into something they would find unacceptable and unrecognizable? While this question remains at the center, perhaps, of the specters of conversion that I offer here, I find a considerable dissonance between the stories that producers of the *Left Behind* series tell about conversion and accounts that readers give of their own lives. For most readers, this dissonance goes unrecognized. Readers accept the novels' accounts of salvation and the reports of many converted by the books as true and reasonable. Yet when they tell their own stories, the patterns are very different than the books describe and the publishing house claims. To understand these differences, I offer four versions of conversion—the novels' account through the stories of characters, the producers' account through marketing materials, the readers' accounts in interviews and, finally, my own. Each account, except my own, shares a certain premise—that Jesus Christ enters the hearts of believers, dwells there, and causes a transformation that leads to eternal salvation. In every account, conversion takes place because someone has shared their faith with someone else—the act of testimony or witness. And in all accounts, conversion involves some kind of changed life—before conversion, life was different than it was after. Yet the layers of life experience offered by readers stand in contrast to the more facile stories that the producers tell.

In the novels of *Left Behind*, conversion takes place through the testimony of others. Rayford is converted because of the videotaped testimony of raptured believers. Alone in his living room, after watching the videotape, he gets down on his knees in front of the television and asks Jesus into his heart. His testimony then brings about the conversions of many others: Chloe, Buck, Hattie, Ken, Mac, and so on. Like him, they hear his story and then go off to be alone. Alone, they pray, receive Jesus into their hearts, and become Christians. Salvation is a mixture of the social interaction of hearing the Good News from someone else and then retreating to pray in private. Salvation takes place in solitude and then is reported to other believers. The moment of conversion involves something that evangelicals call the "sinner's prayer," in which the new believer asks forgiveness for her sins and then asks Jesus to come into her heart. In the series, these prayers are offered spontaneously by the new believer, as if discovered anew with each converted soul. As the tribulation progresses, believers receive a mark on their foreheads documenting the transformation in their souls.

Early in the series, Jenkins repeatedly refers to these conversions as "transactions." As Rayford looks down from a helicopter at the destruction caused by an earthquake, he thinks about Hattie and hopes for her conversion. "Was it possible she might have received Christ before this? Could there have been somebody in Boston or on the plane who would have helped her make the transaction?"[13] The language of transaction seems to alter the traditional, organic metaphors of conversion—"washed in the blood," "born again"—and set salvation into a language of commodity exchange. The primary metaphors become those of consumer culture.

Rather than "born again," believers are "brand new." They conduct a "transaction" of faith that leads them to a secure place in the market of heaven. The mark on their foreheads becomes a receipt, proof that the transaction is complete.

In an interview with Jerry Jenkins, I ask about the use of the language of transaction for religious conversion. His answer does not stray far from traditional explanations of Christian salvation. It emphasizes human sin and Christ's gift of salvation, but he extends the metaphor. "Transaction" is an easy transition from the language of "paying" the penalty and the receipt of eternal life.

We believe that God offers salvation to people who will receive it. They acknowledge to God that they are sinners in need of forgiveness and salvation, and when they accept the gift of His Son having already paid the penalty, the Bible says that "to as many received Him to them gave he the power to become sons of God, even to them that believe on His name" (John 1:12). Sons of God are joint-heirs with Christ, so they get what He gets, primarily eternal life.[14]

In Jenkins's mind, the logic of salvation has not changed; the metaphors used to describe it have been slightly altered. For him, these metaphors in and of themselves are insignificant. At the same time, even here the language shifts. Jenkins speaks of "getting" what Christ gets, eternal life. Becoming a "son" of God involves something modeled on consumer culture—a commodity exchange with salvation as that commodity.

For Tyndale House, commodities are also very important in conversion, but in this case, the commodity is not metaphoric. The commodity is the book itself. Tyndale House believes that the *Left Behind* series is an important tool for "spreading the Gospel" and bringing about Christian conversion. They believe that reading the series can lead someone to the "sinner's prayer" and thus to a life transformation. As in *Left Behind*, producers see conversion as the result of testimony, and they believe *Left Behind* can aid in testimony. The letters that Tyndale House sent me are a selection from their "salvation" file, where they place every account they receive of conversion through the novels. A large portion of these accounts, it appears, are stories of a third person telling about the conversion of someone else. Some of these letters use a language of difference, rather than conversion. A pastor writes about his son, "He started reading *Left Behind*, and stayed up late into the night for several nights—and by the time he had finished it, something was different." A woman writes, "My children are good kids, but I noticed a difference in them both and in myself after reading these blessed books." Further third-person testimony comes from an advertisement in *CBA Marketplace* where Tyndale House offers excerpts from the letters they have received via the Internet. "I wanted to share with others who have lost loved ones who are not saved how the Left Behind Series has brought my husband into the family of God. . . . He revealed to me just yesterday that reading those books helped the Bible make sense to him. Thank you Jerry and Tim."[15] It is very difficult to know precisely what these third-person accounts mean. How would the person being talked about describe what happened? Would the son agree that he was "different"? Would the husband agree that he was now "in the family of God"? Beyond perhaps the certainty that the *Left Behind* books have exerted some kind of influence, these accounts tell us very little. We do not gain insight into the relationship between conversion and "difference" or into the precise meaning of these transformations.

Tyndale House also shared first-person accounts with me. In one letter, a reader nicknamed Rookie offers his story: "I grew up in the deep South and off and on visited the local Baptist Church, but never made the final step in excepting [sic] Jesus into my life. I was just in the local bookstore here when I got the overwhelming feeling I needed to buy the first book. I did, took it home, and read it. From there I have now been saved by the Blood of the Lamb and have a new outlook on life."

For Rookie and in the producers' account of conversion, there is a direct connection between the reading of the novels and the transformation that leads to salvation. God has so inspired these novels that someone can get an "overwhelming feeling," a divine inspiration, to purchase a book and then become a Christian. The correspondence between reading and believing is transparent and "witnessing" through a novel is sufficient for conversion to take place. But for the outside observer, the questions multiply. What was Rookie's life history before this conversion? Had he ever heard of the series or did he spontaneously discover it one day? What other influences were at work in his life? What does his "new outlook" involve? To what does the vague phrase "from there" indicate in his account? What exactly transpired between the reading of the book and his salvation? In the accounts offered by Tyndale House, conversion is ephemeral. Acts of conversion are asserted and then retreat between the lines of the letters. Obviously, Tyndale House has no reason or means to inquire into the validity or meaning of the thousands of letters they receive. They have created only one category—salvation—in which to put all of these accounts.[16]

The stories that readers tell about their own lives, however, involve processes of conversion so intricate and extending over so many months and even years that it calls into question the direct relationship that producers assert. While they maintain a "before and after" structure to tell their stories, readers talk about a series of events that lead to a life transformed. Michael, for example, never speaks about becoming a believer; in fact, he never speaks about belief at all. Rather, he describes a series of activities that led him deeper and deeper into a Christian life.

I had been aware of God my whole life and also Jesus, but that is not to say that I depended on them much. I was doing other things. Not that I felt like I was actually a bad person. Didn't feel like I was an ax-murderer or a rapist or anything like that. I certainly had a good time. I certainly knew how to have a good time, at least according to the world's standards. Been through various marriages. Never bothered to ask God about any of them. The last one, February, if I make it to February, middle of February, that'll be six years I been single. The last six years I've tried hard to live a life that has been pleasing to God, or live a Christian life so to speak.

Anyway, my wife left and I'm in debt. Mom and Dad invited me to church. So I started driving them to church. They'd been going to Grace for years and years. Over the years, I had been invited to go— my wife went to church some—but I just . . . I liked rum and Coke. I didn't feel like having my rum and Cokes and going to church too. Anyway, she left and I am all brokenhearted. Wondering what I am going to do next. In debt and just built a new house, didn't know what she was planning to do. When she left, I said, "Lord, I am just so tired of fighting this, I am just so tired. You need to help me if you will." The day she left was the day I quit drinking. I'm not kidding you. February, the middle of February, it'll be six years and not one rum and Coke. Not one. Since then, been going to church regular, mainly just as an observer. Then after I went a while, the preacher and myself became good friends and some of the men invited me to go to Sunday school with them. Started going to Sunday school. Somewhere in the first year or two I was invited to sing in the choir, so then I've been singing in the choir. A little while later, they asked me if I would consider being a deacon, so I was a deacon for three years. At the end of my time there, I went back to singing in the choir. I've been involved in the Promise Keepers. There's another church that I play guitar with some of their youth.

Michael's story is about an ongoing process of change. He began what I am calling his conversion—he never uses the term—in the midst of a crisis, but he describes the coming to faith as a series of actions that follow one after the other. He began hesitantly and yet embraced greater commitments at each step along the way. His conversion is the story of trying, after heartbreaks and loss, to find a better way. It is also a process, as Brenda Brasher describes, that "offers a Buddhist-like release from suffering that is a byproduct of a new relationship with God."[17] Again, however, I am left to infer this because he never mentions this or puts his story into these terms.

Michael became involved in the life and activity of the church, building new friendships and accepting new responsibilities, but he does not articulate the specific beliefs he accepted along the way. While he never mentions conversion, his story shares elements with other conversion stories—he follows a before-and-after narrative. Before, he drank rum and Cokes; after, he did not and he pursued a life in the church. Also, he includes something that resembles a sinner's prayer—"Lord, I am just so tired of fighting this, I am just so tired. You need to help me if you will." Yet Michael's story is not based on belief. His only reference to belief is in the opening statement, "I had been aware of God my whole life and also Jesus, but that is not to say that I depended on them much. I was doing other things." Beyond that, the new structure of his life is more significant than new beliefs, and for him, activity is far more important than the vocabulary of conversion.

If asked, I am not certain that Michael would consider this the story of his conversion, but he would certainly consider it his testimony. Through the interview flows a current I cannot quite articulate until I ask him this question, "Do you ever witness?"

"Well," he answers with a gentle smile under his thick mustache, "I think I am witnessing to you right now." Suddenly, I see the interview in a different light. To some extent, I took his frankness, the emotion with which he tells his stories, and the light in his eyes as a kind of flirtation. In his comment, I realize that what I took as flirtation, he sees as witnessing. In witnessing, he gives me an account of how he has come into a better life. This is not to say that the story is one or the other. Indeed, very likely it is a combination of desires that leads his story to be powerfully told and leads me to experience it in such a profound way.

As in Michael's story, social connections play a significant role in Jill's religious transformation. For her, an important friendship led directly to her conversion.

"I was brought up Catholic. . . . I received First Communion and was confirmed in the church. . . . I always felt that I knew God, I knew who he was, but I never felt like I had any relationship with him because of all the ritual in the Catholic Church. I was really kind of disillusioned with that. . . . When I was twenty I was involved in a very serious car accident. I remember seeing the car just before it hit me. I was driving and I remember thinking, 'God, I don't know you. I haven't done anything for you. I don't want this to be the end.' I remember taking my hands off the steering wheel and seeing everything in slow motion. I obviously survived the accident. From that point on, there was a series of events in my life over sixteen years where God was drawing me. I didn't attend a church, I didn't understand that you could converse with God. . . . I was clueless. . . . When I was thirty-six, I joined a Bible study, just around a kitchen table like this."

"What caused you to do that?"

"Ann Marie. We had known each other for a long time by then and had many spiritual conversations. Her son had gone through some really hard times, and we traveled together in business and had many conversations. She was incredibly patient and loving. God really spoke through her. . . . I was very unhappy professionally; I didn't know what I wanted to do. It was a really a time of turmoil in my life. So I joined this Bible study, it was a Beth Moore Bible Study, and I had never needed friends. I had always been autonomous, had always been driven and ambitious. Anyway, from on about July until December, I was involved in this Bible study and started attending church. I started attending a Southern Baptist church, and you know, a Catholic walking into a Southern Baptist church was . . . unusual. On December 8, they had their Christmas cantata. I was married, and we knew [medically] that we couldn't have children before we were married. What hit me most in that presentation and of course it was a very classical presentation of the birth of Jesus. I had never seen it done with live people. It had never been real to me. It had always been this story and of course I had never read it in the Bible. I saw Joseph lean down and kiss this baby and even now, my heart just leaps. Jesus was a human being. And Joseph was an adopted father. That was so overwhelming. I couldn't sit still. I went forward in church and that was I think the culmination of many months of God drawing me. People say, 'Well, when was your salvation experience?' I'd have to say that was it; however, over a period of six months, there was an awakening and the Holy Spirit was drawing me."

Perhaps most important to Jill's story of her conversion is her deepening connection with other people. Her friendship with Ann Marie broke a cycle of "autonomy" and "ambition" that allowed her to join a Bible study and led to her conversion. Also her desire for children that she is unable to bear found an emotional release in the story of Jesus' humanity. For Jill, faith was a process of God "drawing" her, a process that ranged from six months to sixteen years, depending on when she starts counting. Faith reconciled sadness and dissatisfaction that she had encountered and gave her a new way of telling her life's story.

Both the act of witnessing and the possibility of conversion emerge out of a set of social circumstances. Despite the universal "empty place" that Darren urged me to see and the sudden transformations that Tyndale House claims take place through reading *Left Behind*, both the desire to convert and the language that makes conversion possible exist in a confined social space, constrained by particular sets of social relations. As a language-dependent, strategic, activity-oriented process, conversion is inherently social. The stories of readers' conversions teach us that while *Left Behind* can serve as a means to conversion, it can only be part of a much larger process of conversion that involves a richer social context than being handed a book on a street corner might suggest.

Doom and Destruction or a Message of Hope?

Central to this story has been how readers understand the book that falls into their hands, how they connect their own stories to the story offered by the novels. Readers are active and able interpreters of texts. Even passionate fans of the series often discriminate between their own views and the views offered by the books. The books provide a forum for disagreement, debate, and difference. At the same time, the books bring to life in vivid pictures a story of the end times that, for all the theological disagreements and the protest of biblical scholars, has vast popular support extending far beyond evangelicalism.[18]

While most of those who protest against the *Left Behind* series take the very idea of the rapture to be self-righteous and escapist, readers do not always see it that way. Some readers transform the gloom and doom scenario that *Left Behind* appears to offer into a message of profound hope. Because one can be converted even after the rapture, some readers find reason not to preach doom, but to offer comfort.

Betty tells me, "I think the rapture is going to happen. But for the ones that are left behind, that don't believe that come to believe, there's a hope. They are not going to be deceived. . . . I think I was more worried about things before I read this book."

"More about what? The end of the world?"

"Yes, and the signs. Because you know I'd been hearing this for years. Even growing up, we heard my father say, 'The world's getting to be a bad place.' You know they've been predicting the end of the world as long as I can remember. And I think it was a big whoopdeedoo, this year, 2000, it's going to be the end of the world. But I don't know. I think it give[s] me a lot of hope. I think it opened up some for me Revelations and I think it give[s] me a lot of peace and hope. It is going to be terrible. But it is not going to be like being separated from God. For me, I think that would be horrible.

"There is such a message of hope in these books. There's such a message of hope. Even the ones that don't know Christ, some will come to know Christ. And even though they might have a hard time, they might be martyred, there's still going to be an eternity for them."

I am surprised to see Betty turn the books' apocalyptic message into one of hope. Rather than urgency, doom, and destruction, Betty reads into them a profound sense that God offers her unsaved loved ones hope. Rather than stirring up fear and worry, the books calm Betty. She uses the books to teach herself something she already wants to learn—that God is loving and will give everyone a second chance.

For nearly all readers of *Left Behind*, the books leave them with an urge to action—to witness to the strange truth of the rapture, to share their faith with the lost. They share this truth in their social networks with those who agree and with those who resist the message. They weave the story of Rayford, Chloe, Buck, and the Tribulation Force into their own stories to tell of destruction or hope, the wrath or the love of God. For them, *Left Behind* is a living text, a testimony to the truth and a witness to the future.

8

Fear, Desire, and the Dynamics of *Left Behind*

On Jerry Falwell's talk show *Listen America*, Timothy LaHaye used stark language to describe the state of the nation: "We're in a religious war and we need to aggressively oppose secular humanism; these people are as religiously motivated as we are and they are filled with the devil."[1] His religious war includes antigay, antiabortion, and antipornography campaigns, as well as campaigns for prayer and creationism in the schools. He believes that secularists are in a quest for "world domination" and that Christians have no choice but to fight back. This kind of aggressive political speech has fueled the public image of *Left Behind* as reactionary and even dangerous. Outside evangelical circles, *Left Behind* is frequently viewed as evidence of a perilous shift toward apocalyptic, fanatical, fear-based thinking on the part of the American public. Many believe that *Left Behind* participates in hate-mongering and coddles people's worst fears so that they will embrace a conservative political agenda. Rhetoric like LaHaye's divides the nation into two groups—the good and the evil. Such division eliminates all shades of gray, all room for various understandings, and the viability of diversity of opinion. From there, many conclude that LaHaye's fictional series also promotes hostility and a politics of fear.

Although LaHaye is listed as an author of the series, he himself has not written a word of the text. Officially, the idea of *Left Behind* and the prophetic outline belong to LaHaye while the stories belong to writer Jerry Jenkins, who from all appearances is less politically driven and certainly less visible.[2] Still, with LaHaye's name on the cover, the series places itself firmly in the camp of one of the most conservative wings of the religious right. Criticism of the books' political agenda has emerged from many corners, and yet critics all speak with a similar concern—that *Left Behind* is a pernicious presence in the cultural scene.

Indeed several anti–*Left Behind* books take issue with the theology of the series, its biblical interpretation, and dispensational premillennialism in general. One of the first to speak was Gary DeMar, the president of an organization called American Vision. American Vision very much shares LaHaye's politics and believes in "returning America to its Biblical foundations."[3] DeMar critiques *Left Behind* because it does not take the Bible literally enough. If the series were actually to take the Bible literally as it claims to, DeMar argues, there would be no rapture, no Antichrist, and no tribulation. These are not biblically rooted ideas, but figments of active popular imagination. DeMar has little difficulty with the politics of the book, but he worries that people will imagine the fiction of the series to be literally true. "*Left Behind* is a work of fiction. As long as it's read with this point in mind, there is no harm. But if the interpretive methodology set forth in the series is embraced as the Bible's method, then I believe many people will be disappointed and disillusioned when the scenario outlined by LaHaye does not come to pass."[4] DeMar is concerned less about social messages than about religious ones, and he imagines readers to be drawn in by falsehoods. This is a traditionally fundamentalist position reiterating an early divide in fundamentalism over the prophetic belief in the rapture and tribulation.

DeMar, however, is joined in rejecting the religious foundations of *Left Behind* by such nonfundamentalist religious organizations as the Presbyterian Church U.S.A. and the Lutheran Church–Missouri Synod, which have both passed resolutions telling their congregations that they do not agree with the apocalyptic scenario that the series promotes. The Presbyterians are concerned that *Left Behind* is causing "confusion and dissension" in congregations and ask ministers to address these issues in their churches. Similarly, the Lutherans advise their congregants that *Left Behind* contains "very serious errors about what the Bible really teaches."[5] Anti–*Left Behind* statements can be found from Wesleyans to Catholics. Even those who claim the label "evangelical" have taken issue with the series. Tom Sine, an evangelical writer, argues that *Left Behind* is "fear-mongering" in the form of fiction. Because it is presented as fiction, he argues, the *Left Behind* series causes people "to unwittingly buy into some of those assumptions, not just in eschatology but in politics."[6] Theologian Marva Dawn argues that *Left Behind* encourages "sadism, indifference to suffering, and 'our lust for power.' "[7] Biblical scholar Craig Hill takes issue with the way that rapture belief suppresses social action, particularly on issues of social justice, because of the passivity such belief cultivates in its believers. The writings of LaHaye and others teach us that "nuclear war is inevitable, that the pursuit of peace is pointless, that the planet's environmental woes are unstoppable, and so on."[8] Such beliefs are, in Hill's mind, untenable with the Christian faith, which requires active response to suffering. All of these examples demonstrate that opposition to *Left Behind*—particularly by clergy, biblical scholars, theologians, and denominational structures—has been strong.

In secular cultural criticism, the apocalyptic beliefs on which *Left Behind* is based and the evangelical tradition from which it comes are simplistically understood, rarely engaged, and readily dismissed. The "official story" about evangelicalism is that it fosters oppression and fear-based politics and works to consolidate the status quo at all costs.[9] Marie Griffith points, in particular, to the way that traditional religion is perceived to interact with gender: "Religion, particularly in its more traditional forms, is viewed as a tool of preserving patriarchy, suppressing women's energies and talents, and imbuing them with 'false consciousness' in which hope for a better life is deferred toward expectations of heaven."[10] Evangelicalism as a form of false consciousness, whether in relationship to gender specifically or politics more broadly, dominates secular understanding of the world out of which *Left Behind* emerges. This image of evangelicalism fuels both fear of and distaste for *Left Behind* itself.

In popular culture, *Left Behind*'s image is also controversial. An often-cited article in *Time* magazine, for example, notes that sales of *Left Behind* increased 60 percent after the September 11 attacks.[11] *Time* pairs the article on the *Left Behind* series with articles about al-Qaeda, Osama bin Laden, and suicide bombers, giving the entire issue an apocalyptic and menacing tone. While in part reporting on *Left Behind*, *Time* also contributes to the atmosphere of fear that it claims has fed *Left Behind*'s popularity. Other media references to *Left Behind* are frequent and often negative. An editorial in the *New York Times* casually mentions *Left Behind* among the factors helping the Bush Administration create a "theocracy."[12] Conservative columnist Cal Thomas calls *Left Behind* "intellectual comfort food" that offers people solace in a time of cultural breakdown but is ultimately ineffective.[13] Writer Anne Lamott writes that *Left Behind* is "hard-core right-wing paranoid anti-Semitic homophobic misogynistic propaganda—not to put too fine a point on it."[14]

In another *New York Times* editorial, Nicolas Kristof points out that one of the deepest divides in our society is the divide that separates evangelicals from secular society.[15] And indeed the fear and dislike on both sides runs deep. While followers of LaHaye may believe that "secularists" are "filled with the devil," on the other side of the divide runs a suspicion that *Left Behind* is part of a

conservative movement that plays on people's fear, excites their doomsday beliefs, and entrenches them more deeply in cultural and political bunkers. *Left
Behind*, many believe, places readers in a position of fear where they can be
more easily manipulated by both religious leaders with a thirst for power and
market forces that encourage them to take out their pocketbooks and spend as
a means to allay fear. During my research, I often heard refrains of these
concerns from many who encountered the *Left Behind* series. Little of this is
new to the controversial history of dispensational premillennialism, which, as
we have noted, never cast its lot with those in positions of institutional power
but always sought acceptance among laypeople and in lay belief. Objections by
institutions, academics, and the media, however significant such objections
might be, have rarely stemmed the tide of rapture belief.

To some extent, such fears of *Left Behind* are justified. Timothy LaHaye is
unquestionably a political figure. The Institute for the Study of American Evangelicals named him the most influential evangelical leader of the past twenty-
five years, more influential than Billy Graham, because of his ability to mobilize
the political energies of evangelicalism.[16] The politics of the books are also
right-leaning. Long passages are devoted to pro-life messages, portraying abortion clinic workers, for example, as preying on women's desperation in a desire
to make money. Feminism is a target of the books, as is homosexuality. The
books are anti-Semitic in that conflicted way that evangelical texts often are,
portraying an Israel too stubborn to see that Jesus is the Messiah and making
heroes of Jewish converts to Christianity. In addition, the books can clearly be
understood to be portraying a racially charged American chauvinism. White
American men are the "natural" leaders of the Tribulation Force and all "others"—African Americans, Arabs, Asians, people from many nations and converts to Christianity from many faiths—submit to their leadership, sometimes
in scenes of disturbing capitulation.[17] There is little question that if we train
our eye solely on the political messages of the series, we see a conservative,
patriarchal, even racist agenda that mirrors the agenda of the Christian Right.
And critics are correct that the enormous popularity of the novels should cause
us to reflect on the communicability of those messages and their resonance in
popular culture.

At the same time, one thing that nearly all of these objections to the *Left
Behind* series have in common is a perceived passivity on the part of the audience. Nearly all accounts of *Left Behind* from these various cultural locations
suggest that the audience for *Left Behind* is passively manipulated by the books
and that the very apocalyptic and religious content of the books paves the way
for such capitulation. The audience is subject to such ideological force that it
can do nothing but bend in the face of it. Tom Sine's language above hints at

the easy compliance of the audience that "unwittingly" accepts both the political and religious assumptions of the books' message.

Theories of *Left Behind's* danger are often based on a model for transaction between text and audience that emphasizes audience passivity. They echo theories of mass culture that are suspicious of its effect on audiences. In the 1940s, the Frankfurt School established an understanding of mass culture that many now take for granted. Max Horkheimer and Theodor Adorno argued that mass culture destroys the people's own art-making capabilities. It turns them into mere consumers of art created for them by people with almost complete power over them. Consumers are passively manipulated by an industry that seeks to render them helpless: "Pleasure always means not to think about anything, to forget suffering even where it is shown. Basically it is helplessness. It is flight; not, as is asserted, flight from a wretched reality, but from the last remaining thought of resistance."[18] If mass culture, in general, has the power to manipulate its audiences, religious mass culture increases this risk. There, in addition to the market forces and political forces shaping people's response to cultural forms, we add the power of religious ideology. In this case, structures of religious power pair with capitalism in order to generate mass culture that readers then passively consume. As consumers, they are likewise dupes of this oppressive system.[19]

In the multitude of criticism cited above, it is often unclear whether critics see *Left Behind* as dangerous because of the unconscious but deleterious effect that it has on its audience or because it confirms worldviews in which readers have already invested. Yet both possibilities stem from understanding mass culture as the realm of domination and manipulation by those with cultural, financial, and religious power over those who are inactive and passive consumers. These theories of *Left Behind's* success are based on a largely unidirectional model of reception that is concerned about the audience—particularly about the damaging effects of reading the series—but dismissive of it at the same time. The audience of *Left Behind* is assumed rather than investigated.

In this book I have tried to refocus our attention from the text to the readers. I have suggested that when we place the reading of *Left Behind* in social situations and assume that the interactions between text and reader take place in social contexts, such unidirectional theories are untenable. Instead, the flow of meaning is multidirectional. While it does flow from the text to the reader, it moves into an already dynamic social setting where the reader must do the work of making sense of the text in light of the social circumstances into which the book is received. This process reflects back on the text and creates from it other avenues of meaning. The interpretive communities of readers, in Stanley Fish's terms, are frequently plural and not always in agreement about the meaning of the text.[20] In other words, texts are deciphered not in one interpretive community, but often in several at once. The work of interpretation, in which readers must actively engage, involves social settings that are almost always divided and dynamic.

Many of the stories readers in this study tell indicate that *Left Behind* cultivates fear. Susan speaks of how *Left Behind* causes her to articulate self-doubt, Leah tells of entering her empty house and fearing that she has been left behind, Carissa says she needs to "get right." Each of these readers articulates personal fear, and an anxiety about self, nation, and world permeates the interaction that many have with *Left Behind*. While these fears most certainly have multiple sources, they also have commonalities. In various ways, from Susan's "what if?" to Jay's practice of reassuring himself of salvation while reading, readers express a fear of being themselves left behind. Fear of being left behind is fear of separation and isolation; it is fear of failure and loss. In a culture of that emphasizes individualism above community ties, the threat of social isolation may be felt more broadly than by evangelicals alone. Readers of the series use the books to reach out to friends, relatives, and strangers in part because they sense the power of the rhetorical claim that one does not want to be "left behind." The books themselves both evoke this anxiety and mitigate it by depicting a post-rapture community of believers that binds together to share their suffering. Indeed this vision of communal Christianity is deeply appealing for many readers, and they use the books to help develop these communities of shared identity.

While the community created through this apocalyptic narrative provides security, it also makes demands on its adherents. It makes demands on thought, speech, and action, disciplining people within the community's stories. Perhaps it would be tempting then, in light of this apparently rigid social structure, to claim individual autonomy as superior to this kind of community. But this is a false choice. Philosopher Iris Marion Young notes that the dichotomy of individual and community is simply an untenable one: "Each entails a denial of difference and a desire to bring multiplicity and heterogeneity into unity, though in opposing ways. Liberal individualism denies difference by positing the self as a solid, self-sufficient unity, not defined by anything or anyone other than itself. . . . Proponents of community, on the other hand, deny difference by positing fusion rather than separation as the social ideal."[21] If we were to deny the appeal of these communities and insert instead the value of individual autonomy and freedom, we would be drawn into the very false dichotomy to which Young points. Both ideals of autonomy and community fall short in their ability to recognize the social fluidity of the self, its shifting place within the complexity of social relations. As interpreters of *Left*

Behind's place in the culture we need to understand the way that readers situate themselves in rhetorics of both freedom and connection, and we need to be mindful of the longing for community relationships to which the reading of *Left Behind* speaks.

Related to a fear of social isolation among readers of *Left Behind* is a fear of social change. Schooled in dispensational premillennialism, rapture believers tend to think that the world is descending into evil. Social change, especially that which affects the structure and function of the family, is frightening. Readers in my study find "signs" of the end of the world in areas of social transformation—the changing role of women, the globalization of the economy, the increasing openness of homosexuality. What is it about social change that readers fear? This study was not large enough to track whether certain kinds of concerns belonged to certain social and economic demographics, although it hints at this possibility. For example, Betty's fear of computers and Jason's wholehearted embrace of them stem in part from very different social positions. Yet an investment banker and a mechanic alike express fear of globalization, and readers from a broad spectrum express concern about homosexuality. Certainly the relationship between social position and fear of social change is a highly complex one that deserves further careful study.

If reading *Left Behind* is in part about fear, then it is both fear's expression and antidote. While the series feeds apprehension of social change, it also feeds a desire for release from the oppressive conditions of the contemporary moment. While it is invested in consolidating power for some, it also negotiates power for others. The authority of the books oversteps the authority of pastors, parents, teachers, and mentors. Readers repeatedly comment on the way that reading *Left Behind* helps to strengthen their faith. If there is anything they admire about the Tribulation Force and the characters in the novels, it is the "strength" of faith that they display. Readers express a desire to learn and model such strength. They desire the ability to endure through difficult times "like Buck" or "like Rayford." *Left Behind* helps readers to articulate their fears and models a community of shared belief and of people engaged in a courageous response.

Readers of *Left Behind* connect to one another and use the books to provide ground for those connections. The popularity of *Left Behind* lies in its passage from hand to hand.[22] Readers read *Left Behind* in networks that extend beyond particular churches, particular denominations, and religious organizations. In order to participate in these networks, the readers in my study are willing to endure boredom, frustration, and disbelief. They are willing to set aside personal objections that range from dislike of the books' theology to frustration with poor writing in order to read what others are reading. By no means does

Left Behind foster undivided communities; it often provides the very ground for disagreement. Yet at the same time, the series allows readers to imagine and desire such communities and facilitates connections with other readers. The interpretive communities of readers are not communities of monolithically shared belief. Their foundations are far more complex and involve a considerable amount of room for disagreement and disbelief. Even in the most monolithic of social situations—Katie's family, for example—we see how the family has to make sense of others who do not believe and incorporate disbelief into its narrative of the books' meaning. Far more common, however, are disagreements—between family members, between clergy and laypeople, between friends and congregation members—that enrich rather than destroy the texture of these communities and yet still interrupt relations of power (as in Sarah's case) or provide a space of imaginative connection (as in Betty's case).

When I chose to conduct a small, qualitative study of readers of *Left Behind*, I wanted to disrupt the totalization of *Left Behind's* audience. By focusing on the nuances of individual circumstances and individual interpretations, I could allow for a multiplicity of responses, intentions, and stories that I hoped might make it impossible to see only one thing when looking at the phenomenon of *Left Behind*—whether that one thing be theological mistake, political disaster, or conspiratorial takeover by conservatives. Stories leave room for interpretation. Perhaps this is even a reason for the popularity of *Left Behind* itself, why it is far more successful than Timothy LaHaye's nonfiction prophetic texts have ever been. As fiction, *Left Behind* attracts a broad audience because in its very nature as a story it invites multiplicity. A story is multisided and reflexive. It mirrors back onto its reader and creates a prism of stories inside of only one. Even a story as black and white as the rapture that appears on the surface to be only about the saved and the damned turns out to have a multitude of stories within its story—stories about family life, about finding meaning, about negotiating power, creating truth, and sharing truth.

Often what readers express through the story of rapture and tribulation is not about "the end" at all, but about the creation of meaning in the present moment. They forage in the present and sort through what is available to construct meaning and identity. They create a space in modern life for traditional religion and negotiate with diversity in order to make a place for absolute truth. The stories of readers also make clear that identification and identity are processes, not end points, and that reading plays a role as an "act of identification."[23] Readers engage with *Left Behind* as a part of processes that form their subjectivity and create complex identities. Belief in the rapture requires acts of identification; it requires a process by which believers secure themselves in the belief of that which cannot yet be experienced. Reading provides vivid imaginative ground for this creation of meaning to take place, and this imaginative engagement draws readers into a world that renders rapture belief plausible and even urgent.

If we think of *Left Behind* as a monolithic force and its readers as merely deceived, then we ourselves can have no response to the series but fear. We fall easily into the very apocalyptic rhetoric that we condemn in the books by creating a black and white division between the "we" who have escaped the domination of this form of popular culture and the "they" who remain helpless in the face of it. If, on the other hand, we see the series as the multiple, dynamic, contradictory system that I have argued it is, then there are cracks and fissures, places to enter and cultivate the imaginative desires that some readers express as a part of their reading. As imaginative engagement, reading *Left Behind* has the potential to open doors as well as to close them.

Given this picture of *Left Behind* and its readers, we need to reconsider the models we use to think about the role of evangelicalism in popular culture. The model that has been most frequently employed is a subcultural model that implies that evangelicals and evangelicalism can be rather neatly sifted out from the rest of the population. Their "sacred umbrellas," as Christian Smith calls them, are of a distinctive color that separates them out from the broader culture.[24] To some extent, of course, this is undeniably true. American evangelicalism has a particular history, a particular language, and a particular interpretation of its role in American society that together contribute to the theory of subculture. At the same time, however, because this model emphasizes the distinctiveness of evangelicalism, it leads to theories of eruption. Phenomena like *Left Behind* "erupt" from this subcultural position into the mainstream, drawing attention for a short time to evangelicalism and then returning underground again to wait for the next eruption. This is perhaps why *Left Behind* could surprise scholars, the media, and even its own publisher with its popularity.

But this model for understanding the place of evangelicalism in American culture has its limits. It prevents us from seeing just how broad and diffuse evangelicalism is in American culture. It prevents us from seeing the multidirectional flow of meaning that transforms both the subculture and the broader culture. The evangelical readers who participated in my study are frequent consumers of popular culture, and only a very small percentage of what they consume is explicitly "Christian." While some, like Ken, are wary of the impact that this so-called secular culture has on them, they nonetheless watch movies and television and read popular novels and popular magazines without inhibition. In so doing, they likewise create the meanings of these phenomena by incorporating them into their worldviews.

Gauri Viswanathan notes that when scholars force religious believers to the margins of the culture, they allow religion to be modernity's "estranged self" and thereby contribute to the very construction of fundamentalism.[25] The apocalyptic rhetoric of *Left Behind* thrives on the creation of a rhetoric of separation and distance from the larger culture. The perpetuation of this image of rapture believers in both scholarship and the media feeds the very apocalypticism that it claims to abhor. As the number of professed evangelicals grows in the United States, scholars must consider studying evangelicalism differently. We need studies that consider the relationship between evangelicalism and American popular culture, that contemplate the role of evangelicalism in shaping the broader culture that we all share. We need to stop expressing surprise at phenomena like *Left Behind* and to start investigating the complex links and the fluidity of cultural influence that facilitate such popularity. We need to understand evangelicalism as sharing the field of popular culture, shaping it, and being shaped by it. It does not materialize and then disappear but exists in constant relationship with American popular culture. When *Left Behind* leaves the *New York Times* best-seller list, we may mistakenly presume that its role in American culture is complete. But readers of *Left Behind* will remain persistent and eager participants in popular culture and will continue to exert influence on that arena.[26]

Reconfiguring our understanding of both the interpretation of *Left Behind* by readers and reconsidering the place of *Left Behind* in the cultural arena also have broader implications for the study of religious identity. Because it is highly malleable and transient, religion plays a frustrating role when we try to understand how identity is formed. Not only can conversion transform one's religious position and often, therefore, one's politics and one's place in the social arena, but also less dramatic transformations can take place within religious identity that are far more difficult to map. At the same time, we need to recognize religion as part of complex processes of identity construction that are currently defined by race, class, gender, and sexuality. Religion is inextricably intertwined with these aspects of identity formation, but it is not reducible to them. Whether a child is christened, circumcised, dedicated, or welcomed at the temple, these early acts of identification, done without the child's consent, inscribe on the child a certain cultural and religious identity that will shape him or her from before her earliest memories in ways that an analysis of gender, race, and class alone will simply miss. At the same time, people do not merely inherit religious identity; they also actively create it in the everyday moments of their lives. As Robert Orsi puts it, "All religious ideas and impulses are of the moment, invented, taken, borrowed, and improvised at the intersections of life."[27]

We need to understand religious belief as dynamic, fluid, and flexible as it functions in people's everyday lives. We need a theory of belief that allows us to see its multiple functions, its work to confirm, disrupt, and transform identities. Perhaps, we need to consider why the category of "belief" is a helpful one at all. Daniel Lopez points out that discussions of belief often mask material concerns, hiding material investment behind esoteric claims of belief.[28] Other scholars have pointed out that belief as a category of religious study became important only after the Enlightenment as individual subjectivity arose as the main location of meaning and truth. In his anthropological study of belief, Rodney Needham concludes, "Yet the deeper and more minutely we go into the meaning of 'belief,' the harder it is to concede it any discrete character or any empirical value as an index to the inner life of men."[29] In her study of theories of religious ritual, anthropologist Catherine Bell agrees and suggests that its erratic nature makes religious belief a very troublesome object of study.[30] People may have eclectic and incompatible beliefs within very coherent forms of religious practice. Beliefs are unstable, constantly under revision and rarely subject to systemization. If belief is so erratic, so difficult to grasp, and so volatile, why not discard it in favor of more concrete religious forms like ritual, practice, or performance?

Indeed, recently many religious studies scholars have shied away from belief as the site of investigation in part because the study of "belief" has been a mechanism used to separate out the religious from the realm of everyday life. Belief systems and theological ideas have been used to abstract religion from the quotidian in order to maintain the distinction between sacred and profane so crucial to the classical study of religion. Scholars of American religious history have turned to the study of practice, understanding that religious belief makes no sense outside the contexts in which it is lived. Anthropologist Michael Turner points out that beliefs have "no stable or intrinsic truth values that can be defined outside contexts of use."[31]

Yet belief is the primary category through which readers of *Left Behind* explain to me their religious lives. Belief, however unstable, is important for their self-understanding of commitments and choices and often the ground for speaking to me. Readers often challenge me, not on my religious practice, not on churchgoing, Bible study, or prayer, but on my beliefs. "What are your beliefs?" they want to know. Whether or not beliefs are an "index to the inner life of man," they certainly, as Daniel Lopez points out, have historical effects. Beliefs are an indelible part of the formation of subjectivity—not just for religious believers, but for everyone; they become interwoven with practices, not always as the cause of practices, nor always as the result, but, as philosopher Elizabeth Anscombe describes the role of testimony in creating belief, like "the

flecks and streaks of fat that are often distributed through good meat."[32] Belief
and practice, for the readers I interviewed, cannot be cut away from each other,
divided with the fine point of a knife. They help to shape the inner and outer
lives of readers. As a researcher, I cannot shy away from the category to which
readers would give the most emphasis. What you *believe* will get you into
heaven. What you practice is merely the fruit of your belief. I may not agree
with this cause-and-effect version that is common sense for many readers, but
I must still come to an understanding that will allow me to engage a category
of fundamental importance to readers themselves.

In order to remove religious belief from its reification both in the rhetoric
of believers and in the rhetoric of scholars, we need to see religious traditions,
religious belief, and religious persons as interacting with and within a diverse
and complex culture. The complexity of belief stems in part from the fact that
the articulation of religious belief and the practices of religion are forms of
interaction and are always formed in community relations. Beliefs are ways in
which believers situated in societies that contain both religious and secular
elements work out the complexities of the cultural landscape, make distinctions
between contradictory teachings and impulses, and answer conflicting desires.

For the most part, religious people are extremely active in the construction
of their religious lives. They reason, study, explain, absorb, teach, interpret,
compare, reject, and so on. In interviews with readers, I found that this was
as true for people whose political positions I found disturbing and distasteful
as it was for people whose opinions I admired. All are actively working out
what it means to be religious, to be human, and to live in a human society,
and they are using the material around them, including texts, to do this. This
work is constrained by ideology and worked out in somewhat inflexible environments where the consequences for choosing alternative understandings are
alienation and loss of intimacy. All the same, we need to recognize the agency
present in such formations. We are often anxious to locate agency in groups
whose positions we have reason to support politically. If they are working
against the establishment, practicing forms of resistance, or finding freedom
within restrictive cultural mediums, we are happy to point out their agency.
But when people actively work out their subjectivity in ways we find problematic or distasteful, we are less quick to champion these people as "agents." By
affirming the agency of even conservative evangelicals in working out their
religious beliefs, I do not mean to dismiss the powerful elements of ideology
nor the limits that our environments place on our worldviews. I merely want
to suggest that people are actively engaged in the formation of their subjectivity
and that the result of such activity is not necessarily consistency and complete-
ness, nor is it always to our liking. By seeing religious conservatives as "dupes"

or as "fearful and ignorant," we fail to see the ways they are engaging with the culture and transforming it.[33] If we affirm the agency of evangelical believers, we gain the advantage of creating a space for increased understanding and dialogue. We can see the potential for change as well as the potential for shared concerns, even if the answers we reach are radically different. Fundamentalists and people of conservative religion in the United States have remained what Susan Harding calls "modernity's repugnant Other."[34] Yet, I would argue, there is value in pursuing even this "repugnant" connection; by doing so, we gain a more complicated view of the culture in which we live, we come to better understand ourselves, and we have hope that, as in every encounter, each one who encounters is changed.

Furthermore, we need to understand religious subjectivity as formed within a context at once highly structured and frequently playful. On the one hand, there is no question that strictures of power and authority often bind religious people to certain institutions. The religious discipline to which readers in this study are subjected is both conscious and unconscious. The story of rapture and tribulation has a policing function, and readers conform to expectations placed on them from outside through fear, insecurity, and religious fervor. At the same time, readers' interaction with the narrative of rapture and tribulation is creative and responsive to the demands of everyday life. Readers use the narrative to remind themselves of their inner strength, to build relationships with others, to interact playfully with human history and current events, to imagine spaces of greater freedom, to question their beliefs, to critique consumer culture, and for many other purposes nearly as individual as readers themselves.

Each religious expression is a mixed site of resistance and discipline; each religious subject is formed in a complex relation to religious structures and contemporary culture.[35] *Left Behind* as a powerful expression of the religious force of popular culture in the United States is no different. For some readers, the narrative of the rapture is primarily about exclusion. It helps to create a faith house made of secure walls and few doors, where only those with the right answers will be allowed inside. Yet for many, the narrative also promises hope—hope that what is now divided will then be reconciled, hope that what is now lost will be saved, hope that tears will turn to laughter, mourning to dancing. While this is a utopian vision, it is also a distinct vision for social life, fraught as all forms of social life are with questions of power and problems of freedom. It is also a vision that articulates a desire for human connection. We need to acknowledge this desire and the complexity of religious identities; we need to foster the development of a vocabulary that can speak to the dynamic nature of religious phenomena.

Notes

INTRODUCTION

1. Charles Strozier, *Apocalypse: On the Psychology of Fundamentalism in America* (Boston: Beacon, 1994), 11.

2. Virginia Ramey Mollenkott, *Women, Men, and the Bible*, rev. ed. (New York: Crossroad, 1988).

3. Ien Ang, *Desperately Seeking the Audience* (London: Routledge, 1991), x.

4. For a discussion of this problem, see Susan Friend Harding, "Representing Fundamentalism: The Problem of the Repugnant Cultural Other," *Social Research* 58 (1991): 373–393.

5. In this way, this project joins the work of other scholars like R. Marie Griffith, *God's Daughters: Evangelical Women and the Power of Submission* (Berkeley: University of California Press, 1997); Judith Stacey, *Brave New Families: Stories of Domestic Upheaval in Late-Twentieth-Century America* (New York: Basic Books, 1991); and Brenda Brasher, *Godly Women: Fundamentalism and Female Power* (New Brunswick, N.J.: Rutgers University Press, 1998). And, to a lesser extent, Linda Kintz, *Between Jesus and the Market: The Emotions That Matter in Right-Wing America* (Durham, N.C.: Duke University Press, 1997).

6. Readers' names and certain details have been changed to protect participants' privacy.

7. Janice Radway explores metaphors of consumption for the description of pleasure reading in "Reading Is Not Eating: Mass-Produced Literature and the Theoretical, Methodological, and Political Consequences of Metaphor," *Book-Research-Quarterly* 2.3 (1986): 7–29.

8. See Janice Radway, *Reading the Romance: Women, Patriarchy, and Popular Literature* (Chapel Hill: University of North Carolina Press, 1991); Ien Ang, *Watching Dallas: Soap Opera and the Melodramatic Imagination*, trans. Della Couling (London: Methuen, 1985); and Wahneema Lubiano, "Black Nationalism and Black Common Sense," in *The House That Race Built*, ed. Wahneema Lubiano (New York: Random House, 1997). Each of the above discusses a different medium—romance novels, television, and popular music. Yet each is concerned with the problem of how popular culture becomes a means to the production of meaning, what Lubiano calls "world making."

9. Martin Buber, *I and Thou*, trans. Ronald Gregor Smith (New York: Collier, 1987).

10. Stephen O'Leary, *Arguing the Apocalypse: A Theory of Millennial Rhetoric* (New York: Oxford University Press, 1994), 11.

CHAPTER 1

1. Lee Quinby, *Anti-apocalypse: Exercises in Genealogical Criticism* (Minneapolis: University of Minnesota Press, 1994), xv.

2. Catherine Keller, *Apocalypse Now and Then: A Feminist Guide to the End of the World* (Boston: Beacon, 1996), xi, 9.

3. For discussions of American apocalyptic culture, see Keller, *Apocalypse Now and Then*, and Quinby, *Anti-apocalypse*, as well as Sacvan Bercovitch, *The American Jeremiad* (Madison: University of Wisconsin Press, 1978); Michael Barkun, "Divided Apocalypse: Thinking about the End in Contemporary America," *Soundings* 66 (1983): 257–280, and *Disaster and the Millennium* (New Haven, Conn.: Yale University Press, 1974); Malcolm Bull, ed., *Apocalypse Theory and the Ends of the World* (Oxford: Blackwell, 1995); Adela Yarboro Collins, "Reading the Book of Revelation in the Twentieth Century," *Interpretation* 40 (1986): 229–242; O'Leary, *Arguing the Apocalypse*; Douglas Robinson, *American Apocalypses: The Image of the End of the World in American Literature* (Baltimore: Johns Hopkins University Press, 1985); Charles B. Strozier, *Apocalypse: On the Psychology of Fundamentalism in America* (Boston: Beacon, 1994); Daniel Wojcik, *The End of the World as We Know It: Faith, Fatalism, and Apocalypse* (New York: New York University Press, 1997); and Lois Parkinson Zamora, ed., *The Apocalyptic Vision in America: Interdisciplinary Essays on Myth and Culture* (Bowling Green, Ohio: Bowling Green University Popular Press, 1982).

4. Barkun, *Disaster and the Millennium*, 91.

5. See Thomas Robbins and Susan J. Palmer, eds., *Millennium, Messiahs, and Mayhem: Contemporary Apocalyptic Movements* (London: Routledge, 1997).

6. R. Laurence Moore, *Religious Outsiders and the Making of Americans* (New York: Oxford University Press, 1986), xi.

7. See Ernest Sandeen, *The Roots of Fundamentalism: British and American Millenarianism 1800–1930* (Chicago: University of Chicago Press, 1970), for a thorough discussion of Darby's life and work.

8. See George Marsden, *Fundamentalism and American Culture: The Shaping of Twentieth-Century Evangelicalism: 1870–1925* (Oxford: Oxford University Press, 1982), for a description and discussion of dispensationalism. See also Sandeen, *Roots of Fundamentalism;* Timothy Weber, *Living in the Shadow of the Second Coming: American Premillennialism* (New York: Oxford University Press, 1979); and Paul Boyer, *When Time Shall Be No More: Prophecy and Belief in Modern American Culture* (Cambridge: Belknap Press of Harvard University Press, 1992).

9. Sandeen, *Roots of Fundamentalism,* 62–70.

10. Approximately fifty novels based on the rapture and tribulation were published in the United States between 1909 and the present. See the bibliography for a complete listing of the novels involved in this study.

11. Joel Carpenter asserts these roles for dispensationalism in *Revive Us Again: The Reawakening of American Fundamentalism* (New York: Oxford University Press, 1997), 71.

12. Alisdair MacIntyre, "The Virtues, the Unity of a Human Life, and the Concept of a Tradition," in *Why Narrative? Readings in Narrative Theology,* ed. Stanley Hauerwas and L. Gregory Jones (Grand Rapids, Mich.: Eerdmans, 1989), 101.

13. 1 Thess. 4:16–17 NASV.

14. Anthony A. Hoekma, *The Bible and the Future* (Grand Rapids, Mich.: Eerdmans, 1979), 164 n. 3

15. Sandeen, *Roots of Fundamentalism,* 73.

16. Stewart arranged for the publication of *Jesus Is Coming* and it became the most popular of its kind. Eventually, at least 691,000 copies were printed and the tract was translated into thirty-one languages. Sandeen, *Roots of Fundamentalism,* 191.

17. Joel Carpenter details this movement in *Revive Us Again.* See also Virginia Lieson Brereton, *Training God's Army: The American Bible School, 1880–1940* (Bloomington: Indiana University Press, 1990).

18. See Marsden, *Fundamentalism and American Culture,* 55–62.

19. Sandeen, *Roots of Fundamentalism,* 222. Oxford University Press has sold well over two million copies since 1967, 85 percent of them leather bound. Randall Balmer suggests that this is "an indication that the overwhelming majority of copies are sold for personal, devotional use rather than for use in libraries." Randall Balmer, *Blessed Assurance: A History of Evangelicalism in America* (Boston: Beacon, 1999), 125, n. 27.

20. Brereton, *Training God's Army,* 20.

21. Carpenter, *Revive Us Again,* 206.

22. *Modernity* is a broad and complicated term. In order to make any arguments about the conditions of "modernity" one must separate out one modernity from other, follow certain strains of the modern and ignore others. In this section, I will be discussing modernity as a certain projection by American conservative Protestants. I will be using the term to describe the conditions of modern life as they perceived them—particularly economic and social changes that transformed religious life.

23. Weber, *Living in the Shadow of the Second Coming,* 84.

24. Historian R. Laurence Moore describes this transition in *Selling God: American Religion in the Marketplace of Culture* (New York: Oxford University Press, 1994). See also Douglas W. Frank, *Less Than Conquerors: How Evangelicals Entered the Twentieth Century* (Grand Rapids, Mich.: Eerdmans, 1986), 167–231, and James Davison Hunter, *American Evangelicalism: Conservative Religion and the Quandary of Modernity* (New Brunswick, N.J.: Rutgers University Press, 1983), 37.

25. Betty A. DeBerg, *Ungodly Women: Gender and the First Wave of American Fundamentalism* (Minneapolis, Minn.: Fortress, 1990), 7.

26. Susan Harding, *The Book of Jerry Falwell: Fundamentalist Language and Politics* (Princeton, N.J.: Princeton University Press, 2000), 63.

27. Carpenter, *Revive Us Again*, 201.

28. Randall Balmer examines the role of these films and of Thompson himself in chapter 3 of *Mine Eyes Have Seen the Glory: A Journey into the Evangelical Subculture in America* (New York: Oxford University Press, 1989), 48–70.

29. Many readers of *Left Behind* mention these films in interviews and remember having seen them as young people; one woman reports showing them to the youth group of which she is now a leader.

30. Brasher, *Godly Women*, 23.

31. Statistic quoted in Steve Rabey, "No Longer Left Behind," *Christianity Today*, April 22, 2002, 28.

32. Robert Wuthnow, *The Restructuring of American Religion: Society and Faith since World War II* (Princeton, N.J.: Princeton University Press, 1988).

33. Carpenter writes, "It had become very important, for the identity and coherence of fundamentalism, to be able to tell who was an insider and who was an outsider. The behavioral code was becoming an indispensable tool for boundary-setting" (*Revive Us Again*, 61). Betty DeBerg attributes this turn to rules as primarily directed at controlling the behavior of women (*Ungodly Women*, 102–105). DeBerg writes, "In [popular fundamentalist] materials, 'morality' is often just a code word for sexual and gender impropriety" (122).

34. A Barna Research Group survey suggests that 57 percent of *Left Behind's* readers are female and 43 percent are male; 85 percent are white, 9 percent are Hispanic, 7 percent are black; 65 percent attend a non-mainline church, 26 percent are Baptist, 14 percent are mainline churchgoers; 8 percent are Catholic (accessed October 31, 2002). Available at www.leftbehind.com. My own research group was 67 percent female and 33 percent male; 3 percent Latino, 3 percent African American, and 94 percent white; 50 percent had a college education and an additional 23 percent had earned a degree beyond college; of the remaining 27 percent, all had completed high school. The affiliations were 19 percent Baptist, 34 percent nondenominational, 23 percent Presbyterian, 7 percent Catholic, 7 percent Mormon, and 10 percent with no church affiliation.

35. Robert Wuthnow notes that this move to complexity has been a recent and important development in the study of American religion. Many are turning to ethnographic methods and qualitative research to attempt to give the macrohistories of a previous generation of scholars more nuances. See "The Cultural Turn: Stories, Log-

ics, and the Quest for Identity in American Religion," in *Contemporary American Religion: An Ethnographic Reader*, ed. Penny Edgell Becker and Nancy L. Eisland (Walnut Creek, Calif.: Alta Mira, 1997).

36. One study cited in the *Christian Century* suggests that up to half of the readers of *Left Behind* are nonevangelicals. See John Dart, "'Beam Me Up' Theology," *Christian Century*, September 25–October 8, 2002, 8–9. This is misleading, however. Dart refers to the Barna survey cited above. The details of this survey say that 41 percent of readers are "evangelicals," but 81 percent are "born again." This suggests a problem with labeling, but it does not suggest that *Left Behind* is read by a large percentage of unaffiliated readers. Barna writes, "The survey suggests that nearly one-tenth of the audience for the series are atheists and people associated with non-Christian faiths while more than two million of the readers are individuals who consider themselves to be Christian but have never accepted Jesus Christ as their savior." See www.barna.org (accessed October 31, 2002).

37. Harding, *The Book of Jerry Falwell*, 232.

38. Boyer, *When Time Shall Be No More*, 2–3.

39. See Hunter, *American Evangelicalism*, Carpenter, *Revive Us Again*, and Christian Smith, *American Evangelicalism: Embattled and Thriving* (Chicago: University of Chicago Press, 1998).

40. Smith, *American Evangelicalism*, 89.

41. In order to define evangelicalism but also to solve problems of doctrinal hairsplitting, Smith asked respondents in his extensive sociological survey to label themselves. His group of researchers gave survey respondents a choice between the following labels: evangelical, fundamentalist, mainline Protestant, liberal Protestant, Catholic, nonreligious, or other. Through in-depth interviews with 130 self-proclaimed Protestants, the researchers produced what they called "identity maps" that helped respondents locate themselves within a variety of statements about religious beliefs. He writes, "We concluded that—while they are ill-equipped to explicate religious history and complex theological controversies—most ordinary Protestants are capable of relying on their own mental and emotional associations and sentiments about various religious traditions to locate themselves accurately on a Protestant identity map" (*American Evangelicalism*, 234). Smith and his researchers took careful steps to determine that these labels were not "forced or arbitrary" (236). Yet at the same time, he does little within the study to acknowledge fluidity among categories, even among those with the most "focused" identities (236).

42. Smith, *American Evangelicalism*, 27.

43. Ang, *Desperately Seeking the Audience*, 156.

44. Wade Clark Roof, *Spiritual Marketplace: Baby Boomers and the Remaking of American Religion* (Princeton, N.J.: Princeton University Press, 1999), 4.

45. Roof, *Spiritual Marketplace*, 17–19.

46. Harding, *The Book of Jerry Falwell*, 152.

47. See Harding, *The Book of Jerry Falwell*, for a more extensive discussion of this development, especially chaps. 2 and 5.

48. The first such novel was published in 1905: Joseph Birkbeck Burroughs, *Ti-*

tan, Son of Saturn: The Coming World Emperor, a Story of the Other Christ (Oberlin, Ohio: Emeth, 1905).

49. See DeBerg, *Ungodly Women*, Margaret Bendroth, *Fundamentalism and Gender, 1875 to the Present* (New Haven, Conn.: Yale University Press, 1993), and Brasher, *Godly Women*. See also chap. 4 in this book.

50. Paul Apostolidis discusses the role of the forgiving victim in Christian right ideology in *Stations of the Cross: Adorno and Christian Right Radio* (Durham, N.C.: Duke University Press, 2000), 205–207.

51. An interesting exception to this rule is in Don Thompson's film *Thief in the Night*. In the film, a woman is left behind while her husband is raptured. She goes on to play a role common to women in rapture fiction, that of victim and martyr of the Antichrist's regime.

52. Examples of this include Mother Collins in Ernest Angley's *Raptured: A Novel of the Second Coming of the Lord* (Akron, Ohio: Winston, 1950) and Miriam Kolzon in Forrest Loman Oilar's *Be Thou Prepared, for Jesus Is Coming* (Boston: Meador, 1937).

53. Randall Balmer, *Blessed Assurance*, 72. Among scholars there is some disagreement on this point. In *Fundamentalism and Gender*, for example, Bendroth argues that fundamentalists actually reversed the Victorian formula, giving the most prominent religious role to men. Fairly consistently in rapture fiction, however, women are pious and churchly while men are worldly and corrupt.

54. Timothy LaHaye and Jerry Jenkins, *Left Behind: A Novel of Earth's Last Days* (Wheaton, Ill.: Tyndale House, 1995), 1.

55. Examples from the history of rapture fiction include Hester Bell Wilson compared to Jim Collins in Angley's *Raptured;* Jane Kolzon compared to her brother Frank in Oilar's *Be Thou Prepared;* the abused women compared to their husbands in Joshua Foster's *The Judgement Day: A Story of the Seven Years of Great Tribulation* (Louisville, Ky.: Baptist World, 1910).

56. Timothy LaHaye and Jerry Jenkins, *Tribulation Force: The Continuing Drama of Those Left Behind* (Wheaton, Ill.: Tyndale House, 1996), 226.

57. See Kintz, *Between Jesus and the Market*. Kintz uses the language of tenderness in a very specific way to describe a kind of emotional expression that does not conflict with masculinity. See chap. 4, "Tender Warriors." Also see Dane Claussen, ed., *The Promise Keepers: Essays on Masculinity and Christianity* (Jefferson, N.C.: McFarland, 2000).

58. Timothy LaHaye and Jerry Jenkins, *Soul Harvest: The World Takes Sides* (Wheaton, Ill.: Tyndale House, 1998), 307–312.

59. See James Davidson Hunter, *Evangelicalism: The Coming Generation* (Chicago: University of Chicago Press, 1987). Hunter claims that "feminist sensibilities are, nevertheless, ingrained within substantial sectors of Evangelicalism" (106).

60. Kintz, *Between Jesus and the Market*, 55.

61. Colleen McDannell has noted similar signs of negotiations in the publications of Focus on the Family. She notes that publications directed at women and girls emphasize connection and relationship over conflict and controversy. She writes, "Although Dobson may be increasingly involved in right-wing politics and

more rigid in his opinion, what attracts women and girls to Focus on the Family is more than Christian certitude. . . . Focus on the Family supports conservative Christians because it shows them how to be faithful and still enjoy the benefits of modern life." "Beyond Dr. Dobson: Women, Girls, and Focus on the Family," in *Women and Twentieth-Century Protestantism*, ed. Margaret Lamberth Bendroth and Virginia Lieson Brereton (Urbana: University of Illinois Press, 2002), 128.

62. See Moore, *Selling God*, and Carpenter, *Revive Us Again*.

63. Harding writes, "We know now that strict Bible belief in America did not diminish but rather flourished during the middle half of the twentieth century; also that it was always more heterogeneous, more urban, more middle class, more educated and more nationally engaged than it was represented to be in popular and academic discourses; and that it became more heterogeneous, urban, upwardly mobile, educated and nationally engaged—right along with the rest of the country—after World War II" (*The Book of Jerry Falwell*, 75).

64. LaHaye and Jenkins, *Soul Harvest*, 159.

65. LaHaye and Jenkins, *Left Behind*, 382.

66. Timothy LaHaye and Jerry Jenkins, *Nicolae: The Rise of Antichrist* (Wheaton, Ill.: Tyndale House, 1997), 45–46.

67. Harding writes, "Although we cannot foresee how Bible prophecy will mutate anew as the third millennium begins, we know that shifts in prevailing apocalyptic scenarios matter. If we listen carefully to them, to their details and nuances, we may learn how born-again Christians are resituating themselves as agents in and of history. We may read their politics, and perhaps also perceive the present and future from their point of view" (*The Book of Jerry Falwell*, 245).

CHAPTER 2

1. Nancy Gibbs, "Apocalypse Now," *Time*, July 1, 2002, 43–44.

2. Daniel Boyarin, "Placing Reading: Ancient Israel and Medieval Europe," in *The Ethnography of Reading*, ed. Jonathan Boyarin (Berkeley: University of California Press, 1993), 11.

3. The radio drama is broadcast on "more than 700 radio stations," reports its producer GAP Digital. Available at www.gapdigital.com (accessed October 31, 2002).

4. Emile Durkheim, *The Elementary Forms of Religious Life*, trans. Carol Cosman (New York: Oxford University Press, 2001).

5. "Congregational women not only had power but could exercise it to change a major pattern of congregational life. Yet they did so in a way that left the form of traditional male authority norms intact. The women effectively maneuvered within the bifurcated realms of meaning their community supports, and drew upon the symbolic resources available there to influence the structures and practices of congregational life. Thus a crisis affecting the morale of the congregation lifted the curtain on what might best be described as a delicate dance between male authority and female power in church life." Brasher, *Godly Women*, 76.

6. Brasher, *Godly Women*, 165.

7. Carpenter, *Revive Us Again*, 61.

8. Sarah's logic implies that the saints cannot be Jews. The relationship between dispensational premillennialism and Judaism is a complex subject beyond my scope here. For historical background, see Yaakov Ariel, *On Behalf of Israel: American Fundamentalist Attitudes toward Jews, Judaism, and Zionism, 1865–1945* (New York: Carlson, 1991). See also David A. Rausch, *Fundamentalist-Evangelicals and Anti-Semitism* (Valley Forge, Pa.: Trinity Press International, 1993).

9. Jane Tompkins, *Sensational Designs: The Cultural Work of American Fiction, 1790–1860* (New York: Oxford University Press, 1985). See the introduction.

10. Rachel's use of this metaphor has a semantic relationship to the more common Christian evangelical expression that when a person becomes a Christian she is "born again."

11. Angley, *Raptured*, 105.

12. See Daniel P. Resnick and Lauren B. Resnick, "Varieties of Literacy," *Social History and Issues in Human Consciousness: Some Interdisciplinary Connections*, ed. Andrew Barnes and Peter Stearns (New York: New York University Press, 1989), 171–196.

13. Alberto Manguel, "Private Reading," *A History of Reading* (Toronto: Knopf, 1996), 153. See also Steven Gilbar's preface to *Reading in Bed* (Boston: David R. Godine, 1995).

14. Victor Nell, *Lost in a Book: The Psychology of Reading for Pleasure* (New Haven, Conn.: Yale University Press, 1988), and Janice Radway, *A Feeling for Books: The Book-of-the-Month Club, Literary Taste, and Middle-Class Desire* (Chapel Hill: University of North Carolina Press, 1997).

CHAPTER 3

1. Mark Taylor, "News," www.leftbehind.com (accessed July 12, 1999).

2. These questions arise from arguments in reception theory about the process of engaging with texts. In his classic essay "Encoding/Decoding," Stuart Hall suggests three codes that audiences use to "decode" producers' messages—a "dominant" code, a "negotiated" code, and an "oppositional" code (*Culture, Media, Language*, ed. Stuart Hall, Dorothy Hobson, Andrew Lowe, and Paul Willis [London: Hutchinson, 1980]). Recently, Virginia Nightengale has taken issue with Hall's system arguing that the encoding/decoding model itself severely undertheorizes the moment of decoding. It assumes that the message is stable and must merely be decoded in order to be understood. She suggests that, instead, audiences participate in the very construction of the message, interactively relating to the text and developing its meaning (*Studying Audiences: The Shock of the Real* [London: Routledge, 1996]). My understanding of audiences' relationship to texts is closer to Nightengale's, but at the same time, especially in a case like *Left Behind*, I think we need to take the ideological context in which reading is formed very seriously.

3. Westboro Baptist Church is the organization that became infamous for picketing at the funeral of Matthew Shepard and conducting a national antihomosexuality campaign.

4. I interviewed Samantha quite early in my research and, as I describe in the introduction, before I learned to make clear my own position on the novels. This left Samantha at a disadvantage until around the middle of the interview, when I declared myself sympathetic with her views. This offered her a considerable amount of relief. Until that point, she had censored herself and sidestepped difficult issues. Samantha's interview was very influential in the restructuring of my approach in later interviews.

5. See chap. 7 in this volume.

6. LaHaye and Jenkins, *Nicolae*, 281.

7. LaHaye and Jenkins, *Nicolae*, 88.

8. Guy Blod's scenes are scattered throughout the eighth book in the series, *The Indwelling: The Beast Takes Possession* (2000). The final mention occurs on p. 349: "People, including Guy Blod and his assistants, shrieked and fell prostrate, peeking at the image."

9. See Maxine Montgomery, "The Fire This Time: Apocalypse and the African American Novel Tradition," in *African Americans and the Bible: Sacred Texts and Social Textures*, ed. Vincent L. Wimbush (New York: Continuum, 2000), 489–500.

10. See Albert G. Miller, "The Construction of a Black Fundamentalist Worldview: The Role of Bible Schools," in Wimbush, *African Americans and the Bible*, 712–727.

11. See Michel de Certeau, "Reading as Poaching," in *The Practice of Everyday Life*, trans. Steven Randall (Berkeley: University of California Press, 1984), 165–176.

CHAPTER 4

1. Eve Sedgwick, "Introduction," *Novel Gazing: Queer Readings in Fiction* (Durham, N.C.: Duke University Press, 1997), 4.

2. The main sources for this chapter are DeBerg, *Ungodly Women;* Bendroth, *Fundamentalism and Gender;* Brasher, *Godly Women;* Gail Bederman, "The Women Have Had the Charge of the Church Work Long Enough: The Men and Religion Forward Movement of 1911–1912 and the Masculinization of Middle-Class Protestantism," *American Quarterly* 41 (September 1989): 432–465; Randall Balmer, "American Fundamentalism: The Ideal of Femininity," in *Fundamentalism and Gender*, ed. J. S. Hawley (London: Oxford University Press, 1994); Griffith, *God's Daughters;* Hunter, *Evangelicalism;* Kintz, *Between Jesus and the Market;* Stacey, *Brave New Families.*

3. Brasher, *Godly Women*, 129.

4. Linda Kintz offers an analysis of the contemporary rhetoric in *Between Jesus and the Market*. Betty DeBerg offers an historical analysis of the rhetoric of fundamentalist leaders and their interest in questions of gender in *Ungodly Women*.

5. Susan Harding writes, "Both fundamentalism and the modern evangelical movement had been Christian men's movements from their beginnings, that is, movements led by conservative Protestant male leaders who self-consciously articulated a male point of view intent on protecting and cultivating male headship at home and in the church" (*The Book of Jerry Falwell*, 155).

6. Bendroth, *Fundamentalism and Gender*, 3.

7. See chap. 1 above.

8. "Rapture," *Oxford English Dictionary*, 2d edition. Prepared by J. A. Simpson and ESC Weiner, vol. 13 (Oxford: Clarendon, 1989), 193.

9. Rev. 19:7 NASV.

10. Bendroth, *Fundamentalism and Gender*, 52.

11. Bendroth, *Fundamentalism and Gender*, 7. "The movement, as always, depended on the willing participation of its predominantly female constituency. But the resulting numerical imbalance created some potentially awkward contradictions between strict standards of female subordination and relatively permissive customs. Although fundamentalist doctrine prohibited women from teaching doctrine, the practical needs of evangelism demanded their skills in religious education, Bible teaching and foreign missions" (9).

12. Many examples could be offered here. Some classics are Timothy and Beverly LaHaye, *The Act of Marriage: The Beauty of Sexual Love* (Grand Rapids, Mich.: Zondervan, 1995); Beverly LaHaye, *The Desires of a Woman's Heart* (Wheaton, Ill.: Tyndale House, 1993); James Dobson, *Love for a Lifetime: Building a Marriage that Will Go the Distance* (Portland, Oreg.: Multnomah, 1987).

13. I draw the word *tender* from Linda Kintz, who believes that this new Christian man is a mask for even greater male domination. I would argue, however, that experientially, women have found good reason to embrace this emotional turn in their husbands and partners. The "tender" Christian man is supposed to be more sensitive to women's needs, more able to listen and respond emotionally and more open to intimacy. If that is the case, we should not find it mysterious that women have promoted and embraced movements like the Promise Keepers.

14. Brasher, *Godly Women*, 30–31.

15. Stacey, *Brave New Families*, 56–57.

16. This is Harding's phrase; see *The Book of Jerry Falwell*, 155.

17. Robert Cole, "Promising to Be a Man: Promise Keepers and the Organizational Constitution of Masculinity," in *The Promise Keepers: Essays on Masculinity and Christianity*, ed. Dane Claussen (Jefferson, N.C.: McFarland, 2000), 128.

18. Stacey, "Epilogue: Taking Women at Their Word," *Brave New Families*, 272–278.

19. In her study of women's reading groups, Elizabeth Long writes something very similar to what can be said about evangelical readers: "Literature affects [readers] differently because they appropriate it, or engage with it, motivated by a different set of needs and with a conception of the text almost diametrically opposed to that held by modern literary scholars." "Women, Reading, and Cultural Authority: Some Implication of the Audience Perspective on Cultural Studies," *American Quarterly* 38.4 (1986): 609.

20. James Kavanaugh, "Ideology," in *Critical Terms for Literary Study*, ed. Frank Lentricchia and Thomas McLaughlin (Chicago: University of Chicago Press, 1990), 310.

21. See chap. 6 in this book.

22. De Certeau, "Reading as Poaching," 165–176.

23. De Certeau, "Reading as Poaching," 174.

CHAPTER 5

1. Ruth Alden Doan, *The Miller Heresy, Millennialism, and American Culture* (Philadelphia: Temple University Press, 1987), 21. See also O'Leary, *Arguing the Apocalypse*, 93–110.

2. Sandeen, *The Roots of Fundamentalism*, 54.

3. O'Leary, *Arguing the Apocalypse*, 139.

4. Boyer, *When Time Shall Be No More*, 83.

5. See Boyer, *When Time Shall Be No More*, for the origins of this prophetic practice, esp. chap. 1, "Origins of the Apocalyptic," and chap. 2, "Rhythms of Prophecy Belief."

6. LaHaye and Jenkins, *Tribulation Force*, 67.

7. See O'Leary, *Arguing the Apocalypse*, 139; Sandeen, *Roots of Fundamentalism*, 211; Weber, *Living in the Shadow of the Second Coming*, 229.

8. LaHaye and Jenkins, *Left Behind: A Novel of Earth's Last Days*, 210–216.

9. This practice of invitation is one that comes into contemporary evangelicalism from fundamentalism. Joel Carpenter describes the "altar call" as the "high and holy moment" of fundamentalism. "Fundamentalist preachers regularly gave the invitation for people to step forward and publicly profess Christ as their savior, and many pastors insisted on giving this 'altar call' at every service. Their reason for doing this was that it was their evangelistic duty, but this ritual, performed with the musicians softly playing, the congregation singing or praying, and the leader speaking in an almost liturgical cadence, had become the high and holy moment of the fundamentalist church service, the time when miracles happened" (*Revive Us Again*, 77).

10. Jean Leclerq, O.S.B., *The Love of Learning and the Desire for God: A Study of Monastic Culture*, trans. Catharine Misrahi (New York: Fordham University Press, 1961), 90, quoted in Wesley Kort, *"Take, Read": Scripture, Textuality, and Cultural Practice* (University Park: Pennsylvania State University Press, 1996), 23.

11. Anselm of Canterbury, *Anselm: Opera Omnia*, vol. 3, trans. and ed. F. S. Schmitt (Edinburgh: Thomas Nelson and Sons, Ltd., 1946), 84, quoted in Paul J. Griffiths, *Religious Reading* (New York: Oxford University Press, 1999), 43.

12. Kort, *"Take, Read,"* 23.

13. Kort, *"Take, Read,"* 36.

14. "Frequently Asked Questions," www.leftbehind.com (accessed July 12, 1999).

15. Marsden, *Fundamentalism and American Culture*, 56.

16. Angley, *Raptured*, 91.

17. LaHaye and Jenkins, *Left Behind*, 214.

18. Harding, *The Book of Jerry Falwell*, 28.

19. Rev. 9:7–10 NASV.

20. Hal Lindsey, *Apocalypse Code* (Palos Verdes, Calif.: Western Front, 1997), 166–167. Thanks to Hal Lindsey Web Site Ministries for this reference.

21. Boyer, *When Time Shall Be No More*, 178, 275–276.

22. John Cawelti, *Adventure, Mystery, and Romance: Formula Stories as Art and Popular Culture* (Chicago: University of Chicago Press, 1976), 3.

23. Cawelti, *Adventure, Mystery, and Romance*, 35–36.

24. Harding, *The Book of Jerry Falwell*, 232.

25. Colleen McDannell, *Material Christianity* (New Haven, Conn.: Yale University Press, 1995), 223.

26. This practice has been widespread enough to cause controversy in the Christian bookselling community. Christian retailers have been provoked by the fact that Tyndale House has allowed discount retailers to sell the books so cheaply. Also, discount retailers have sold the books before the declared "street date," also giving them an advantage. See the trade journal *CBA Marketplace*, beginning in September 1999.

27. Rev. 13: 16–18: "And he causes all, the small and the great, and the rich and the poor, and the free men and the slaves, to be given a mark on their right hand, or on their forehead, and he provides that no one should be able to buy or sell, except the one who has the mark, either the name of the beast or the number of his name. Here is wisdom. Let him who has understanding calculate the number of the beast, for the number is that of a man; and his number is six hundred and sixty six" (NASV).

28. Oilar, *Be Thou Prepared*; Salem Kirban, *666* (Wheaton, Ill.: Tyndale House, 1970).

29. Carpenter, *Revive Us Again*, 180.

30. Only one novel explores this view in fiction: John Myers, *The Trumpet Sounds* (New York: Pageant, 1965).

31. Timothy LaHaye and Jerry Jenkins, *Are We Living in the End Times?* (Wheaton, Ill.: Tyndale House, 1999).

32. Fredric Jameson, "Reification and Utopia in Mass Culture," *Social Text*, no. 1 (1979): 130–149.

CHAPTER 6

1. Louis Althusser, "Ideology and Ideological State Apparatuses (Notes toward an Investigation)," in *"Lenin and Philosophy" and Other Essays*, trans. Ben Brewster (London: New Left, 1971), 164–165.

2. Angela McRobbie, "Post-Marxism and Cultural Studies," in *Cultural Studies*, ed. Lawrence Grossberg, Cary Nelson, and Paula Treichler (New York: Routledge, 1991), 723.

3. Wahneema Lubiano, "Black Nationalism and Black Common Sense," in *The House that Race Built*, ed. Wahneema Lubiano (New York: Random House, 1998), 246.

4. Tyndale House has encouraged this kind of reading through the advertisement of charts and a timeline that lay out the biblical foundation of dispensational premillennialism. One advertisement for *A Visual Guide to the* Left Behind *Series* in the *Left Behind* e-mail newsletter reads, "These colorful charts show how each Left Behind Series book fits into the end-times biblical timeline. It makes understanding the Bible and the Book of Revelation fun and easy, while giving you a deeper understanding of the Left Behind series" (fall 2001).

5. Examples are Sydney Watson, *In the Twinkling of an Eye* (Los Angeles: Biola

Book Room, Bible Institute of Los Angeles, 1918); Oilar, *Be Thou Prepared;* Myers, *The Trumpet Sounds.*

6. McRobbie, "Post-Marxism and Cultural Studies," 723.

7. LaHaye and Jenkins, *Left Behind: A Novel of Earth's Last Days,* 196.

8. Brasher, *Godly Women,* 37.

CHAPTER 7

1. Harding, *The Book of Jerry Falwell,* 57.

2. Smith, *American Evangelicalism,* 38, 187.

3. "New Join the Underground," www.leftbehind.com (accessed March 12, 2001).

4. In March 2001, Tyndale House issued an announcement about the mass-market paperback to readers of their eNews e-mail list. "This Easter, we want to give you the opportunity to use the Left Behind Series to spread the Good News to your community. This vision is for you to use the Left Behind Mass Paperback book as a tool to invite members of your local community to your church's Easter service. An invitation card will be provided with each copy of Left Behind so that you can include a personal message and details about the special church service" (March 14, 2001).

5. Tyndale ran an advertising campaign in *CBA Marketplace* in which they excerpted actual fan mail they had received. This particular letter was quoted in an ad in the *CBA Marketplace* (November 1999).

6. McDannell, *Material Christianity,* 266.

7. Nancy Ammerman, *Bible Believers: Fundamentalists in the Modern World* (New Brunswick, N.J.: Rutgers University Press, 1987), 129–130.

8. Brasher, *Godly Women,* 38.

9. LaHaye and Jenkins, *Soul Harvest.* Rayford's witnessing and Mac's conversion take place over several episodes in chaps. 6, 7, and 9.

10. Left Behind Series eNews 11.2 (November 2001).

11. *Bookstore Journal,* December 1999, 24.

12. Harding, *The Book of Jerry Falwell,* 34.

13. LaHaye and Jenkins, *Nicolae,* 407.

14. Interview with Jerry Jenkins via e-mail, November 29, 1999.

15. *CBA Marketplace,* November 1999.

16. More recently, too late to be included in this study, Tyndale House has released a book, *These Will Not Be Left Behind: Incredible Stories of Lives Transformed after Reading the* Left Behind *Series* (Wheaton, Ill.: Tyndale House, 2003). This collection documents the publisher's evidence of the impact of the *Left Behind* series: excerpts from e-mails, message boards, and letters. Rather than solving the question of *Left Behind*'s ability to spark conversions, the book compounds the problem. The stories told in each chapter are highly glossed versions, told in third person. The e-mail excerpts that are in first person are only one or two lines long. While I do not think that Tyndale House is being intentionally evasive, I do think that the evidence I am looking for and that which they are able to provide do not match.

17. Brasher, *Godly Women*, 55.

18. Some of these controversies are summarized in Dart, "'Beam Me Up' Theology," 8–9. See also the critique of *Left Behind* in Gary DeMar, *End Times Fiction: A Biblical Consideration of the Left Behind Theology* (Nashville, Tenn.: Thomas Nelson, 2001).

CHAPTER 8

1. LaHaye quoted in Jane Lampman, "Apocalyptic—and Atop the Bestseller Lists," *Christian Science Monitor*, August 29, 2002, 14.

2. Many critics of *Left Behind* have failed to note the way that this division of responsibility creates a divided and tension-filled text, full of self-contradiction and political and social maneuvering. I briefly discuss these divisions in chapter 1, but more could be said about the relationship between LaHaye and Jenkins and the effect that produces on the story *Left Behind* tells.

3. See www.americanvision.org (accessed March 10, 2003). DeMar also points out that he has no basic political differences with LaHaye (*End Times Fiction*, xviii).

4. DeMar, *End Times Fiction*, 207.

5. Dart, "'Beam Me Up' Theology," 8.

6. Sine quoted in Lampman, "Apocalyptic," 14.

7. Dawn quoted in Jeffrey Macdonald, "Theologian Rebuts 'Left Behind' Series of Revelation Intent," *Oregonian*, September 28, 2002.

8. Craig Hill, *In God's Time: The Bible and the Future* (Grand Rapids, Mich.: Eerdmans, 2002), 208.

9. Secular criticism infrequently mentions or engages *Left Behind* directly. Some examples of how simplistically religious belief is understood can be found in Mary Kelley, "Taking Stands: American Studies at Century's End, Presidential Address to the American Studies Association, October 29, 1999," *American Quarterly* 52.1 (March 2000): 1–22, and Quinby, *Anti-apocalypse*, esp. the preface.

10. Griffith, *God's Daughters*, 203.

11. Nancy Gibbs, "Apocalypse Now," *Time*, July 1, 2002, 43.

12. Paul Krugman, "Gotta Have Faith," *New York Times*, December 17, 2002.

13. Thomas quoted in Gibbs, 49.

14. Anne Lamott, "Knocking on Heaven's Door," *Traveling Mercies: Some Thoughts on Faith* (New York: Pantheon, 1999), 60.

15. Nicholas Kristof, "God, Satan, and the Media," *New York Times*, March 4, 2003.

16. Lampman, "Apocalyptic," 14.

17. See specifically *Apollyon*, 110–113; *The Mark: The Beast Rules the World* (Wheaton, Ill.: Tyndale House, 2000), 24–28; *The Indwelling*, 70.

18. Max Horkheimer and Theodor Adorno, "The Culture Industry: Enlightenment as Mass Deception," *Dialectic of Enlightenment* (New York: Continuum, 1987), 144.

19. See a discussion of the metaphor of "consumption" as passivity in Janice Radway's "Reading Is Not Eating: Mass-Produced Literature and the Theoretical, Methodological, and Political Consequences of a Metaphor," *Book Research Quarterly* 2.3 (fall 1986): 7–29.

20. Stanley Fish, *Is There a Text in This Class? The Authority of Interpretive Communities* (Cambridge, Mass.: Harvard University Press, 1980).

21. Iris Marion Young, *Justice and the Politics of Difference* (Princeton, N.J.: Princeton University Press, 1990), 229.

22. Tyndale House has astutely recognized this. *Left Behind's* Web site notes, "The Left Behind Series is a word-of-mouth phenomenon. An incredible 64.7 percent of readers first heard about the series from friends or relatives. Research shows that LBS readers want to share their experience with someone they know. 43 percent of buyers have given the books as gifts. Nearly two-thirds of LBS readers (63 percent) have recommended the series to a friend." See www.leftbehind.com (accessed October 31, 2002).

23. McRobbie, "Post-Marxism and Cultural Studies," 723.

24. Smith, *American Evangelicalism*, 106.

25. Gauri Viswanathan, *Outside of the Fold: Conversion, Modernity, and Belief* (Princeton, N.J.: Princeton University Press, 1998), xii.

26. In *Culture, Power, Place,* Akhil Gupta and James Ferguson argue that the very language of "culture" creates the problem I am articulating here. Culture implies a false boundary and fails to note the shared historical processes that simultaneously differentiate and interconnect various groups and peoples. We need to stop thinking of evangelicalism as a subculture and start to think about the multiplicity of personal, national, and global relationships that construct evangelicalism as an entity. See Akhil Gupta and James Ferguson, "Beyond 'Culture': Space, Identity, and the Politics of Difference," *Culture, Power, Place: Explorations in Critical Anthropology,* ed. Gupta and Ferguson (Durham, N.C.: Duke University Press, 1997), 46.

27. Robert Orsi, "Everyday Miracles: The Study of Lived Religion," in *Lived Religion in America: Toward a History of Practice,* ed. David D. Hall (Princeton, N.J.: Princeton University Press, 1997), 8.

28. Daniel Lopez, "Belief," in *Critical Terms for Religious Studies,* ed. Mark C. Taylor (Chicago: University of Chicago Press, 1998), 28.

29. Rodney Needham, *Belief, Language, and Experience* (Chicago: University of Chicago Press, 1972), 234.

30. Catherine Bell, *Ritual Theory, Ritual Practice* (New York: Oxford University Press, 1992), 185.

31. Michael Jackson, *Paths toward a Clearing: Radical Empiricism and Ethnographic Inquiry* (Bloomington: Indiana University Press, 1989), 65. Quoted in Orsi, "Everyday Miracles," 16.

32. G. E. M. Anscombe, "What Is It to Believe Someone?" in *Rationality and Religious Belief,* ed. C. F. Delaney (Notre Dame, Ind.: Notre Dame University Press, 1979), 143.

33. See Angela Dworkin, *Right-Wing Women: The Politics of Domesticated Families*

(New York: Coward, McCann, and Geoghegan, 1982), 34. Quoted in Griffith, *God's Daughters*, 204–206.

34. Susan Harding, "Representing Fundamentalism: The Problem of the Repugnant Cultural Other," *Social Research* 58 (1991–1992): 373–393.

35. This is a point made eloquently by Robert Orsi in "Everyday Miracles," 11–15.

Select Bibliography

PRIMARY SOURCES

Adams, Wayne. *No Mark*. Self-published, 1996.

Angley, Ernest. *Raptured: A Novel of the Second Coming of the Lord*. Akron, Ohio: Winston, 1950.

Balizet, Carol. *The Seven Last Years*. Toronto: Bantam, 1980, c1978.

BeauSeigneur, James. *Birth of an Age*. Rockville, Md.: Selective House, 1997.

———. *In His Image*. Rockville, Md.: Selective House, 1997.

———. *Acts of God*. Rockville, Md.: Selective House, 1998.

Betzer, Dan. *Beast: A Novel of the World's Future Dictator*. Lafayette, La.: Prescott, 1985.

Brenneman, Jean. *Virtual Reality (It's No Dream)*. Lima, Ohio: Allendale, 1997.

Burroughs, Joseph Birkbeck. *Titan, Son of Saturn; The Coming World Emperor, a Story of the Other Christ*. Oberlin, Ohio: Emeth, 1905.

Cerullo, Morris. *The Omega Project*. San Diego: World Evangelism, 1981.

Cohen, Gary. *The Horsemen Are Coming*. Chattanooga, Tenn.: AMG, 1987, 1991.

Collier, John. *Choices: The Story of Three Young Men, Friends and Recent High School Graduates Whose Lives are Changed by the Rapture and the Following Tribulation Period*. Columbus, Ga.: Brentwood Christian Press, 1996.

Dolan, David. *The End of the Days*. Grand Rapids, Mich.: F. H. Revell, 1995.

Everest, Mortimer. *What Will Have Happened*. Johnstown, N.Y.: Mortimer Everest, 1936.

Folkee, Norman. *The Last Trumpet*. Monterey, Calif.: Nachman, 1978.

Foster, Joshua. *The Judgement Day: A Story of the Seven Years of Great Tribulation*. Louisville, Ky.: Baptist World, 1910.

Gale, Judith. *A Promise of Forever*. Pittsburgh: Dorrance, 1997.

Gardner, Jim. *Time, Times and Half a Time: The Beginning of the Great Tribulation*. New York: Vantage, 1997.

Graham, Billy. *Approaching Hoofbeats: The Four Horsemen of the Apocalypse*. Waco, Tex.: Word Publishing, 1983.

Grant, Jean. *The Revelation: A Novel*. Nashville, Tenn.: Thomas Nelson, 1992.

Harriss, Nellie Scott. *Ruth's Rapture: The Book of Revelation in Story*. Los Angeles: privately printed, n.d.

Hill, Grace Livingston. *Dwelling*. Philadelphia: J. B. Lippincott, 1938.

Kirban, Salem. *666*. Wheaton, Ill.: Tyndale House, 1970.

———. *Matthew: The Beginning of Sorrows*. Chicago: Moody, 1972.

———. *1000*. Chattanooga, Tenn.: Future Events, 1973.

LaHaye, Tim, and Jerry Jenkins. *Left Behind: A Novel of Earth's Last Days*. Wheaton, Ill.: Tyndale House, 1995.

———. *Tribulation Force: The Continuing Drama of Those Left Behind*. Wheaton, Ill.: Tyndale House, 1996.

———. *Nicolae: The Rise of Antichrist*. Wheaton, Ill.: Tyndale House, 1997.

———. *Soul Harvest: The World Takes Sides*. Wheaton, Ill.: Tyndale House, 1998.

———. *Are We Living in the End Times?* Wheaton, Ill.: Tyndale House, 1999.

———. *Apollyon: The Destroyer is Unleashed*. Wheaton, Ill.: Tyndale House, 1999.

———. *Assassins: Assignment: Jerusalem, Target: Antichrist*. Wheaton, Ill.: Tyndale House, 1999.

———. *The Indwelling: The Beast Takes Possession*. Wheaton, Ill.: Tyndale House, 2000.

———. *The Mark: The Beast Rules the World*. Wheaton, Ill.: Tyndale House, 2000.

———. *Desecration: The Antichrist Takes the Throne*. Wheaton, Ill.: Tyndale House, 2001.

———. *The Remnant: On the Brink of Armageddon*. Wheaton, Ill.: Tyndale House, 2002.

LaHaye, Timothy, Norman B. Rohrer, and Jerry Jenkins. *These Will Not Be Left Behind: Incredible Stories of Lives Transformed after Reading the Left Behind Series*. Wheaton, Ill.: Tyndale House, 2003.

Lalonde, Peter, and Paul Lalonde. *Apocalypse*. Niagara Falls, N.Y.: This Week in Bible Prophecy, 1998.

———. *Revelation*. Niagara Falls, N.Y.: This Week in Bible Prophecy, 1999.

Lindsey, Hal. *The Late Great Planet Earth*. Grand Rapids, Mich.: Zondervan, 1970.

———. *Apocalypse Code*. Palos Verde, Calif.: Western Front, 1997.

———. *Blood Moon*. Palos Verde, Calif.: Western Front, 1997.

Maddoux, Martin. *Seal of Gaia: A Novel of the Antichrist*. Nashville, Tenn.: Word Publishing, 1998.

Martin, Irene. *Emerald Thorn*. Oklahoma City, Okla.: Hearthstone, 1991.

McCall, Thomas, and Zola Levitt. *Raptured*. Eugene, Oreg.: Harvest House, 1975.

Myers, John. *The Trumpet Sounds*. New York: Pageant, 1965.

Oilar, Forrest Loman. *Be Thou Prepared, for Jesus Is Coming.* Boston: Meador, 1937.

Peretti, Frank. *This Present Darkness.* Wheaton, Ill.: Crossway, 1986.

————. *Piercing the Darkness.* Wheaton, Ill.: Crossway, 1989.

Robertson, Pat. *The End of the Age.* Dallas, Tex.: Word Publishing, 1995.

Stine, Milton H. *The Devil's Bride: A Present Day Arraignment of Formalism and Doubt in the Church and in Society, in the Light of the Holy Scriptures. Given in the Form of a Pleasing Story.* Harrisburg, Penn.: Minter, 1910.

Wade, Ken. *The Orion Conspiracy: A Story of the End.* Boise, Idaho: Pacific, 1994.

Watson, Sydney. *In the Twinkling of an Eye.* Los Angeles: The Biola Book Room, Bible Institute of Los Angeles, 1918.

————. *The Mark of the Beast.* New York: F. H. Revell, 1918.

————. *The Scarlet and the Purple, a Study of Souls and "Signs."* New York: F. H. Revell, 1933.

Young, Kim. *The Last Hour.* Phoenix, Ariz.: ACW, 1997.

SECONDARY SOURCES

Althusser, Louis. *For Marx.* Translated by Ben Brewster. New York: Pantheon, 1969.

————. "Ideology and Ideological State Apparatuses." *"Lenin and Philosophy" and Other Essays.* Translated by Ben Brewster. London: New Left, 1971.

Ammerman, Nancy Tatom. *Bible Believers: Fundamentalists in the Modern World.* New Brunswick, N.J.: Rutgers University Press, 1987.

————. "North American Protestant Fundamentalism." In *Fundamentalisms Observed,* edited by M. E. Marty and R. Scott Appleby. Chicago: University of Chicago Press, 1991.

————. "The Dynamics of Christian Fundamentalism: An Introduction." In *Accounting for Fundamentalisms: The Dynamic Character of Movements,* edited by M. E. Marty and R. Scott Appleby. Chicago: University of Chicago Press, 1994.

Ang, Ien. *Watching Dallas: Soap Opera and the Melodramatic Imagination.* Translated by Della Couling. London: Methuen, 1985.

————. *Desperately Seeking the Audience.* London: Routledge, 1991.

Apostolidis, Paul. *Stations of the Cross: Adorno and Christian Right Radio.* Durham, N.C.: Duke University Press, 2000.

Aune, David E. "The Apocalypse of John and the Problem of Genre." *Semeia* 36 (1986): 65–96.

Bakhtin, M. M. *Problems of Dostoevsky's Poetics.* Translated by Caryl Emerson. Minneapolis: University of Minnesota Press, 1984.

————. *The Dialogic Imagination: Four Essays.* Translated by Caryl Emerson and Michael Holquist. Austin: University of Texas Press, 1981.

Balmer, Randall. *Mine Eyes Have Seen the Glory: A Journey into the Evangelical Subculture in America.* New York: Oxford University Press, 1989.

————. "American Fundamentalism: The Ideal of Femininity." In *Fundamentalism and Gender,* edited by J. S. Hawley. London: Oxford University Press, 1994.

————. *Blessed Assurance: A History of Evangelicalism in America.* Boston: Beacon, 1999.

Banta, Martha. "American Apocalypses: Excrement and Ennui." *Studies in the Literary Imagination* 7 (1974): 1–30.

Barkun, Michael. *Disaster and the Millennium*. New Haven, Conn.: Yale University Press, 1974.

———. "Divided Apocalypse: Thinking about the End in Contemporary America." *Soundings* 66 (1983): 257–280.

Barthes, Roland. *Image, Music, Text*. London: Fontana, Flamingo, 1977.

Becker, Penny Edgell, and Nancy L. Eiesland, eds. *Contemporary American Religion: An Ethnographic Reader*. Walnut Creek, Calif.: Alta Mira, 1997.

Bederman, Gail. "The Women Have Had the Charge of the Church Work Long Enough: The Men and Religion Forward Movement of 1911–1912 and the Masculinization of Middle-Class Protestantism." *American Quarterly* 41 (September 1989): 432–465.

———. "The Men and Religion Forward Movement." In *A Mighty Baptism: Race, Gender, and the Creation of American Protestantism*, edited by S. Juster and Lisa MacFarlane. Ithaca, N.Y.: Cornell University Press, 1996.

Behar, Ruth. *Translated Woman: Crossing the Border with Esperanza's Story*. Boston: Beacon, 1993.

———. *The Vulnerable Observer: Anthropology That Breaks Your Heart*. Boston: Beacon, 1996.

Bell, Catherine. *Ritual Theory, Ritual Practice*. New York: Oxford University Press, 1992.

Bendroth, Margaret. *Fundamentalism and Gender: 1875 to the Present*. New Haven, Conn.: Yale University Press, 1993.

Bendroth, Margaret, and Virginia Lieson Brereton, eds. *Women and Twentieth-Century Protestantism*. Urbana: University of Illinois Press, 2002.

Benjamin, Walter. "Theses on the Philosophy of History." In *Illuminations*, translated by Harry Zohn. New York: Schocken, 1968.

Bercovitch, Sacvan. *The American Jeremiad*. Madison: University of Wisconsin Press, 1978.

Berger, James. *After the End: Representations of Post-apocalypse*. Minneapolis: University of Minnesota Press, 1999.

Berland, Jody. "Cultural Technologies." In *Cultural Studies*, edited by Lawrence Grossberg, Cary Nelson, and Paula Treichler. New York: Routledge, 1992.

Bhabha, Homi. "Interrogating Identity: The Post-colonial Prerogative." In *Anatomy of Racism*, edited by David Theo Goldberg. Minneapolis: University of Minnesota Press, 1992.

Blaising, Craig A., and Darrell L. Bock. *Progressive Dispensationalism*. Wheaton, Ill.: Victor Books, 1993.

Blodgett Jan. *Protestant Evangelical Literary Culture and Contemporary Society*. Westport, Conn.: Greenwood, 1997.

Bloom, Harold. *The American Religion: The Emergence of the Post-Christian Nation*. New York: Simon and Schuster, 1992.

Boone, Kathleen. *The Bible Tells Them So: The Discourse of Protestant Fundamentalism*. Albany: State University of New York Press, 1989.

Bourdieu, Pierre. *Outline of a Theory of Practice*. Translated by Richard Nice. Cambridge: Cambridge University Press, 1977.

———. *Distinction: A Social Critique of the Judgment of Taste*. Translated by Richard Nice. Cambridge, Mass.: Harvard University Press, 1984.

Boyarin, Jonathan, ed. *The Ethnography of Reading*. Berkeley: University of California Press, 1993.

Boyer, Paul S. *When Time Shall Be No More: Prophecy and Belief in Modern American Culture*. Cambridge: Belknap Press of Harvard University Press, 1992.

Brasher, Brenda. *Godly Women: Fundamentalism and Female Power*. New Brunswick, N.J.: Rutgers University Press, 1998.

Brereton, Virginia Lieson. *Training God's Army: The American Bible School, 1880–1940*. Bloomington: Indiana University Press, 1990.

Brod, H., and Kaufman, M., eds. *Theorizing Masculinities*. Thousand Oaks, Calif.: Sage, 1992.

Brown, Karen McCarthy. *Mama Lola: A Vodou Priestess in Brooklyn*. Berkeley: University of California Press, 1991.

Brummett, Barry. *Contemporary Apocalyptic Rhetoric*. New York: Praeger, 1991.

Bull, Malcolm, ed. *Apocalypse Theory and the Ends of the World*. Oxford: Blackwell, 1995.

Butler, John. *Awash in a Sea of Faith: Christianizing the American People*. Cambridge, Mass.: Harvard University Press, 1990.

Carnes, M. C. *Secret Ritual and Manhood in Victorian America*. New Haven, Conn.: Yale University Press, 1989.

Carpenter, Joel. *Revive Us Again: The Reawakening of American Fundamentalism*. Oxford: Oxford University Press, 1997.

Cawelti, John G. *Adventure, Mystery, and Romance: Formula Stories as Art and Popular Culture*. Chicago: University of Chicago Press, 1976.

Chakrabarty, Dipesh. "The Time of History and Times of the Gods." In *The Politics of Culture in the Shadow of Capital*, edited by Lisa Lowe and David Lloyd. Durham, N.C.: Duke University Press, 1997.

Chartier, Roger. *The Order of Books*. Translated by Lydia G. Cochrane. Stanford, Calif.: Stanford University Press, 1994.

———, ed. *The Culture of Print: Power and the Uses of Print in Early Modern Europe*. Translated by Lydia G. Cochrane. Princeton, N.J.: Princeton University Press, 1989.

Chidester, David. *Salvation and Suicide: An Interpretation of Jim Jones, Peoples Temple, and Jonestown*. Bloomington: Indiana University Press, 1988.

Clark, Suzanne. *Sentimental Modernism: Women Writers and the Revolution of the Word*. Bloomington: Indiana University Press, 1991.

Clatterbaugh, K. *Contemporary Perspectives on Masculinity: Men, Women, and Politics in Modern Society*. Boulder, Colo.: Westview, 1996.

Claussen, Dane, ed. *Standing on the Promises: The Promise Keepers and the Revival of Manhood*. Cleveland, Ohio: Pilgrim Press, 1999

———, ed. *The Promise Keepers: Essays on Masculinity and Christianity*. Jefferson, N.C.: McFarland, 2000.

Clifford, James, and George Marcus, eds. *Writing Culture: The Poetics and Politics of Ethnography.* Berkeley: University of California Press, 1986.

Clinton, Catherine. *The Other Civil War: American Women in the Nineteenth Century.* New York: Hill and Wang, 1984.

Cohen, Norman J., ed. *The Fundamentalist Phenomenon: A View from Within, A Response from Without.* Grand Rapids, Mich.: Eerdmans, 1990.

Cohn, Norman Rufus Colin. *The Pursuit of the Millennium: Revolutionary Messianism in Medieval and Reformation Europe and Its Bearing on Modern Totalitarian Movements.* 2d ed. New York: Harpers and Row, 1961.

Collins, Adela Yarbro. *Crisis and Catharsis: The Power of the Apocalypse.* Philadelphia: Westminster, 1984.

———. "Reading the Book of Revelation in the Twentieth Century." *Interpretation* 40 (1986): 229–242.

Collins, John J. "Apocalypse: The Morphology of a Genre." *Semeia* 14 (1979): 1–20.

Darnton, Robert. *Kiss of Lamourette: Reflections in Cultural History.* New York: W. W. Norton, 1990.

Davidson, Cathy, ed. *Reading in America: Literature and Social History.* Baltimore: Johns Hopkins University Press, 1989.

Dawn, Marva. *Joy in Our Weakness: A Gift of Hope from the Book of Revelation.* Grand Rapids, Mich.: Eerdmans, 2002.

DeBerg, Betty A. *Ungodly Women: Gender and the First Wave of American Fundamentalism.* Minneapolis: Fortress, 1990.

De Certeau, Michel. *The Practice of Everyday Life.* Translated by Steven Rendall. Berkeley: University of California Press, 1988.

———. "What We Do When We Believe." In *On Signs,* edited by Marshall Blonsky. Baltimore: Johns Hopkins University Press, 1985.

De Lauretis, Theresa. *Alice Doesn't: Feminism, Semiotics, Cinema.* Bloomington: Indiana University Press, 1984.

DeMar, Gary. *End Times Fiction: A Biblical Consideration of the Left Behind Theology.* Nashville, Tenn.: Thomas Nelson, 2001.

Denning, Michael. *The Cultural Front: The Laboring of American Culture in the Twentieth Century.* London: Verso, 1996.

Derounian-Stodola, Kathryn Zabelle, and James Arthur Levernier. *The Indian Captivity Narrative, 1550–1900.* New York: Twayne, 1993.

Dessauer, John P., Paul D. Doebler, and Hendrik Edelman. *Christian Book Publishing and Distribution in the United States and Canada.* Tempe, Ariz.: CBA/ECPA/PCPA Joint Research Project, 1987.

Detweiler, Robert. "Christ in American Religious Fiction." *Journal of the Bible and Religion* 32 (1964): 8–14.

———. *Uncivil Rites: American Fiction, Religion, and the Public Sphere.* Urbana: University of Illinois Press, 1996.

Doan, Ruth Alden. *The Miller Heresy, Millennialism, and American Culture.* Philadelphia: Temple University Press, 1987.

Donoghue, Denis. *The Practice of Reading.* New Haven, Conn.: Yale University Press, 1998.

Douglas, Ann. *The Feminization of American Culture*. New York: Knopf, 1977.

Duke, Judith. *Religious Publishing and Communications*. White Plains, N.Y.: Knowledge Industry Publications, 1981.

Ebersole, Gary L. *Captured by Texts: Puritan to Post-modern Images of Indian Captivity*. Charlottesville: University of Virginia Press, 1995.

Emerson, Michael O., and Christian Smith. *Divided by Faith: Evangelical Religion and the Problem of Race in America*. New York: Oxford University Press, 2000.

Escarpit, Robert. *The Book Revolution*. London: George Harrap, 1966.

Fish, Stanley. *Is There a Text in this Class? The Authority of Interpretive Communities*. Cambridge, Mass.: Harvard University Press, 1980.

Forbes, Cheryl. "Coffee, Mrs. Cowman, and the Devotional Life of Women Reading in the Desert." In *Lived Religion in America: Toward a History of Practice*, edited by David D. Hall. Princeton, N.J.: Princeton University Press, 1997.

Foucault, Michel. *Religion and Culture*. Edited by Jeremy R. Carrette. New York: Routledge, 1999.

Frank, Douglas. *Less Than Conquerors: How Evangelicals Entered the Twentieth Century*. Grand Rapids, Mich.: Eerdmans, 1986.

Frei, Hans W. *The Eclipse of Biblical Narrative: A Study of Eighteenth and Nineteenth Century Hermeneutics*. New Haven, Conn.: Yale University Press, 1974.

———. "The 'Literal' Reading of Biblical Narrative in the Christian Tradition: Does It Stretch or Will it Break?" In *The Bible and the Narrative Tradition*, edited by F. McConnell. New York: Oxford University Press, 1986.

Freund, Elizabeth. *The Return of the Reader: Reader-Response Criticism*. London: Methuen, 1987.

Friedlander, Saul, Gerald Horton, Leo Marx, and Eugene Skolnikoff, eds. *Visions of Apocalypse: End or Rebirth?* New York: Holmes and Meier, 1985.

Gates, Henry Louis, Jr., ed. *"Race," Writing, and Difference*. Chicago: University of Chicago Press, 1986.

Geertz, Clifford. "Deep Play: Notes on the Balinese Cockfight." In *The Interpretation of Cultures*. New York: Basic, 1973.

———. "Thick Description: Toward an Interpretive Theory of Culture." In *The Interpretation of Cultures*. New York: Basic, 1973.

Gibson, James William. *Warrior Dreams: Paramilitary Culture in Post-Vietnam America*. New York: Hill and Wang, 1994.

Gillis, John. *A World of Their Own Making: Myth, Ritual, and the Quest for Family Values*. New York: Basic, 1996.

Goldberg, David Theo, ed. *Anatomy of Racism*. Minneapolis: University of Minnesota Press, 1992.

Gramsci, Antonio. *Selections from the Prison Notebooks of Antonio Gramsci*. Edited and translated by Quintin Hoare and Geoffrey Nowell Smith. New York: International Publishers, 1971.

Griffith, R. Marie. *God's Daughters: Evangelical Women and the Power of Submission*. Berkeley: University of California Press, 1997.

Griffiths, Paul J. *Religious Reading: The Place of Reading in the Practice of Religion*. New York: Oxford University Press, 1999.

Grossberg, Lawrence. *We Gotta Get Out of This Place: Popular Conservatism and Post-modern Culture.* New York: Routledge, 1992.

Grossberg, Lawrence, Cary Nelson, and Paula Treichler, eds. *Cultural Studies.* New York: Routledge, 1992.

Gupta, Akhil, and James Ferguson. "Beyond 'Culture': Space, Identity, and the Politics of Difference." *Culture, Power, Place: Explorations in Critical Anthropology,* ed. Akhil Gupta and James Ferguson. Durham, N.C.: Duke University Press, 1997.

Gutjahr, Paul. "No Longer *Left Behind:* Amazon.com, Reader-Response, and the Changing Fortunes of Christian Fiction in America," *Book History* 5 (2002), 209–236.

Halberstam, Judith. "Mackdaddy, Superfly, Rapper: Gender, Race, and Masculinity in the Drag King Scene." *Social Text,* no. 52/53 (fall/winter 1997), 104–132.

Hall, David D. *Worlds of Wonder, Days of Judgment: Popular Religion in Early New England.* New York: Knopf, 1989.

———, ed. *Lived Religion in America: Toward a History of Practice.* Princeton, N.J.: Princeton University Press, 1997.

Hall, D. E., ed. *Muscular Christianity: Embodying the Victorian Age.* New York: Cambridge University Press, 1994.

Hall, John R., Philip Schuyler, and Sylvaine Trinh. *Apocalypse Observed: Religious Movements, Social Order, and Violence in North America, Europe, and Japan.* London: Routledge, 1999.

Hall, Stuart. "Encoding/Decoding." In *Culture, Media, Language,* edited by Stuart Hall, Dorothy Hobson, Andrew Lowe, and Paul Willis. London: Hutchinson and Co., 1980.

———. "Notes on Deconstructing the Popular." In *People's History and Socialist Theory,* edited by R. Samuel. London: Routledge and Kegan Paul, 1981.

———. "Signification, Representation, Ideology: Althusser and the Post-structuralist Debates." *Critical Studies in Mass Communication* 2.2 (1985): 91–114.

Hanson, Paul, ed. *Visionaries and Their Apocalypses.* Philadelphia: Fortress, 1983.

Harding, Susan. "Convicted by the Holy Spirit: The Rhetoric of Fundamental Baptist Conversion." *American Ethnologist* 14 (1987): 167–181.

———. "Representing Fundamentalism: The Problem of the Repugnant Cultural Other." *Social Research* 58 (1991–1992): 373–393.

———. "Imagining the Last Days: The Politics of Apocalyptic Language." In *Accounting for Fundamentalisms: The Dynamic Character of Movements,* edited by M. E. Marty and R. Scott Appleby. Chicago: University of Chicago Press, 1994.

———. *The Book of Jerry Falwell: Fundamentalist Language and Politics.* Princeton, N.J.: Princeton University Press, 2000.

Hawley, J. S., ed. *Fundamentalism and Gender.* London: Oxford University Press, 1994.

Hayward, Jennifer. *Consuming Pleasures.* Lexington: University of Kentucky Press, 1997.

Hellholm, David. "The Problem of Apocalyptic Genre and the Apocalypse of John." *Semeia* 36 (1986): 13–64.

Hill, Craig C. *In God's Time: The Bible and the Future.* Grand Rapids, Mich.: Eerdmans, 2002.

Himrod, David K. "The Syncretism of Technology and Protestantism: An American 'Popular Religion.'" *Explor* 7 (fall 1984): 49–60.

Hochschild, Arlie Russell. *The Managed Heart: Commercialization of Human Feeling.* Berkeley: University of California Press, 1983.

Hollinger, Dennis. *Individualism and Social Ethics: An Evangelical Syncretism.* Lanham, Md.: University Press of America, 1983.

Horrocks, R. *Male Myths and Icons: Masculinity in Popular Culture.* New York: St. Martin's, 1995.

Hunter, James Davidson. *American Evangelicalism: Conservative Religion and the Quandary of Modernity.* New Brunswick, N.J.: Rutgers University Press, 1983.

———. *Evangelicalism: The Coming Generation.* Chicago: University of Chicago Press, 1987.

———. *Culture Wars: The Struggle to Define America.* New York: Basic, 1991.

Jameson, Fredric. "Reification and Utopia in Mass Culture." *Social Text,* no. 1 (1979): 130–149.

———. "On 'Cultural Studies.'" *Social Text,* no. 34 (1993): 17–52.

———. "Antinomies of Postmodernity." In *The Cultural Turn: Selected Writings on the Postmodern, 1983–1998.* London: Verso, 1998.

Kaplan, Cora. *Sea Changes: Essays on Culture and Feminism.* London: Verso, 1986.

Kayser, Wolfgang. *The Grotesque in Art and Literature.* Translated by Ulrich Weisstein. New York: Columbia University Press, 1981.

Keller, Catherine. *Apocalypse Now and Then: A Feminist Guide to the End of the World.* Boston: Beacon, 1996.

Kelley, Mary. "Taking Stands: American Studies at Century's End, Presidential Address to the American Studies Association, October 29, 1999." *American Quarterly* 52.1 (March 2000): 1–22.

Kermode, Frank. *The Sense of an Ending: Studies in the Theory of Fiction.* London: Oxford University Press, 1968.

Kimmel, M. S. *Manhood in America: A Cultural History.* New York: Free Press, 1996.

Kintz, Linda. *Between Jesus and the Market: The Emotions That Matter in Right-Wing America.* Durham, N.C.: Duke University Press, 1997.

Kintz, Linda, and Julia Lesage, eds. *Media, Culture, and the Religious Right.* Minneapolis: University of Minnesota Press, 1998.

Kirsop, Wallace. "The State of the Discipline: Booksellers and Their Customers: Some Reflections of Recent Research." *Book History* 1.1 (1998): 283–303.

Kort, Wesley. *"Take, Read": Scripture, Textuality, and Cultural Practice.* University Park: Pennsylvania State University Press, 1996.

Leclercq, Jean. *The Love of Learning and the Desire for God: A Study of Monastic Culture.* Translated by Catharine Misrahi. New York: Fordham University Press, 1961.

Lefebrve, Henri. *Everyday Life in the Modern World.* Translated by Sacha Rabinovitch. New Brunswick, N.J.: Transaction, 1984.

Linkon, Sherry Lee. "Reading Lind Mania: Print Culture and the Construction of Nineteenth-Century Audiences." *Book History* 1.1 (1998): 94–106.

Lipsitz, George. *The Possessive Investment in Whiteness: How White People Profit from Identity Politics.* Philadelphia: Temple University Press, 1999.

Lofland, John, and Lyn Lofland. *Analyzing Social Settings: A Guide to Qualitative Observation and Analysis.* New York: Wadsworth, 1995.

Long, Elizabeth. "Women, Reading, and Cultural Authority: Some Implications of the Audience Perspective in Cultural Studies." *American Quarterly* 38.4 (1986): 591–612.

———. "Textual Interpretation as Collective Action." In *The Ethnography of Reading,* edited by Jonathon Boyarin. Berkeley: University of California Press, 1993.

Long, Elizabeth, and Janice Radway. "The Book as Mass Commodity: The Audience Perspective." *Book Research Quarterly* 3.1 (1987): 9–30.

Lopez, Donald S., Jr. "Belief." In *Critical Terms for Religious Studies,* edited by Mark C. Taylor. Chicago: University of Chicago Press, 1998.

Lowe, Lisa, and David Lloyd, eds. *The Politics of Culture in the Shadow of Capitalism.* Durham, N.C.: Duke University Press, 1997.

Lubiano, Wahneema. "Black Nationalism and Black Common Sense." In *The House That Race Built,* edited by Wahneema Lubiano. New York: Random House, 1997.

Lyotard, Jean Francois. *The Postmodern Condition: A Report on Knowledge.* Translated by Geoff Bennington and Brian Massumi. Minneapolis: University of Minnesota Press, 1984.

Machor, James, ed. *Readers in History: Nineteenth-Century American Literature and the Contexts of Response.* Baltimore: Johns Hopkins University Press, 1992.

Manguel, Alberto. *A History of Reading.* Toronto: Knopf, 1996.

Marcus, George E., and Michael M. J. Fischer. *Anthropology as Cultural Critique: An Experimental Moment in the Human Sciences.* Chicago: University of Illinois Press, 1986.

Marsden, George. *Fundamentalism and American Culture.* Oxford: Oxford University Press, 1980.

———. *Reforming Fundamentalism: Fuller Seminary and the New Evangelicalism.* Grand Rapids, Mich.: Eerdmans, 1987.

———. *Understanding Fundamentalism and Evangelicalism.* Grand Rapids, Mich.: Eerdmans, 1991.

Marty, Martin E. *The Glory and the Power: The Fundamentalist Challenge to the Modern World.* Boston: Beacon, 1992.

Marty, Martin E., and R. Scott Appleby, eds. *Accounting for Fundamentalisms: The Dynamic Character of Movements.* Chicago: University of Chicago Press, 1994.

Marx, Karl. *Capital.* Vol. 1. Translated by Ben Fowkes. New York: Random House, 1977.

Marx, Leo. *The Machine in the Garden: Technology and the Pastoral Ideal in America.* New York: Oxford University Press, 1964.

McClymond, Michael J. "Footnotes to the Future: The Evolution of Apocalyptic in the *Scofield Reference Bible,* 1909–1967." Paper presented at the annual meeting of the American Academy of Religion, Boston, November 1999.

McDannell, Colleen. *The Christian Home in Victorian America, 1840–1900.* Bloomington: Indiana University Press, 1986.

————. "Creating the Christian Home: Home Schooling in Contemporary America." In *American Sacred Spaces*, edited by David Chidester and Edward Linenthal. Bloomington: Indiana University Press, 1995.

————. *Material Christianity: Religion and Popular Culture in America*. New Haven, Conn.: Yale University Press, 1995.

————. "Beyond Dr. Dobson: Women, Girls, and Focus on the Family." In *Women and Twentieth-Century Protestantism*, edited by Margaret Lamberth Bendroth and Virginia Lieson Brererton. Urbana: University of Illinois Press, 2002.

McGinn, Bernard. *Apocalypticism in the Western Tradition*. Hampshire, England: Variorum, 1994.

McLoughlin, W. G., ed. *The American Evangelicals, 1800–1900*. New York: Harper and Row, 1968.

McRobbie, Angela. "Post-Marxism and Cultural Studies." In *Cultural Studies*, edited by Lawrence Grossberg, Cary Nelson, and Paula Treichler. New York: Routledge, 1991.

Messer-Davidow, Ellen. "The Right Moves: Conservatism and Higher Education." In *Literature, Language, and Politics*, edited by Betty Jean Craige. Athens: University of Georgia Press, 1988.

Messner, M. *The Politics of Masculinity: Men in Movements*. Thousand Oaks, Calif.: Sage, 1997.

Michaels, Walter Benn. *Our America: Nativism, Modernism, and Pluralism*. Durham, N.C.: Duke University Press, 1995.

Miller, Albert G. "The Construction of a Black Fundamentalist Worldview: The Role of Bible Schools." In *African Americans and the Bible*, edited by Vincent L. Wimbush. New York: Continuum, 2000.

Miller, Donald. *Reinventing American Protestantism: Christianity in the New Millenium*. Berkeley: University of California Press, 1997.

Montgomery, Maxine. "The Fire This Time: Apocalypse and the African American Novel Tradition." In *African Americans and the Bible*, edited by Vincent L. Wimbush. New York: Continuum, 2000.

Moore, R. Laurence. "Insiders and Outsiders in American Historical Narrative and American History." *American Historical Review* 87 (1982): 390–412.

————. *Religious Outsiders and the Making of Americans*. New York: Oxford University Press, 1986.

————. *Selling God: American Religion in the Marketplace of Culture*. New York: Oxford University Press, 1994.

Morley, David, and Charlotte Brunsdon. *The Nationwide Television Studies*. London: Routledge, 1999.

Morris, Meaghan. "Banality in Cultural Studies." *Discourse* 10.2 (spring–summer 1988), 3–29.

Morrison, Toni. *Playing in the Dark: Whiteness and the Literary Imagination*. Cambridge, Mass.: Harvard University Press, 1992.

————. "Home." In *The House That Race Built*, edited by Wahneema Lubiano. New York: Random House, 1998.

Morrison, Toni, and Claudia Brodsky Lacour, eds. *Birth of a Nation'hood: Gaze, Script, and Spectacle in the O. J. Simpson Case*. New York: Pantheon, 1997.

Mosse, George L. *Nationalism and Sexuality: Middle-Class Morality and Sexual Norms in Modern Europe.* Madison: University of Wisconsin Press, 1985.

Mott, Frank Luther. *Golden Multitudes.* New York: Macmillan, 1947.

Moylan, Michele, and Lane Stiles, eds. *Reading Books: Essays on the Material Text and Literature in America.* Amherst: University of Massachusetts Press, 1996.

Nell, Victor. *Lost in a Book: The Psychology of Reading for Pleasure.* New Haven, Conn.: Yale University Press, 1988.

Niebuhr, H. Richard. *Christ and Culture.* New York: Harper & Row, 1951.

Nightengale, Virginia. *Studying Audiences: The Shock of the Real.* London: Routledge, 1996.

O'Leary, Stephen D. *Arguing the Apocalypse: A Theory of Millennial Rhetoric.* New York: Oxford University Press, 1994.

Quinby, Lee. *Anti-apocalypse: Exercises in Genealogical Criticism.* Minneapolis: University of Minnesota Press, 1994.

Palmer, Jerry. *Thrillers: Genesis and Structure of a Popular Genre.* New York: St. Martin's, 1979.

Poulantzas, Nicos. *State, Power, and Socialism.* London: Verso, 1978.

Probyn, Elspeth. *Outside Belongings.* New York: Routledge, 1996.

Radway, Janice A. "Reading Is Not Eating: Mass-Produced Literature and the Theoretical, Methodological, and Political Consequences of Metaphor." *Book Research Quarterly* 2.3 (1986): 7–29.

———. *Reading the Romance: Women, Patriarchy, and Popular Literature.* Chapel Hill: University of North Carolina Press, 1991.

———. "Reception Study: Ethnography and the Problem of Dispersed Audiences and Nomadic Subjects." *Cultural Studies* 2.3 (1988): 359–376.

———. *A Feeling for Books: The Book-of-the-Month Club, Literary Taste, and Middle-Class Desire.* Chapel Hill: University of North Carolina Press, 1997.

Resnick, Daniel P., and Lauren B. Resnick. "Varieties of Literacy." In *Social History and Issues in Human Consciousness: Some Interdisciplinary Connections,* edited by Andrew Barnes and Peter Stearns. New York: New York University Press, 1989.

Reynolds, David S. *Faith and Fiction: The Emergence of Religious Literature in America.* Cambridge, Mass.: Harvard University Press, 1981.

Robbins, Thomas, and Susan J. Palmer, eds. *Millennium, Messiahs, and Mayhem: Contemporary Apocalyptic Movements.* London: Routledge, 1997.

Robinson, Douglas. *American Apocalypses: The Image of the End of the World in American Literature.* Baltimore: Johns Hopkins University Press, 1985.

Roof, Wade Clark. *Spiritual Marketplace: Baby Boomers and the Remaking of American Religion.* Princeton, N.J.: Princeton University Press, 1999.

Rosaldo, Renato. *Culture and Truth: The Remaking of Social Analysis.* Boston: Beacon, 1989.

Rotundo, E. A. *American Manhood: Transformations in Masculinity from the Revolution to the Modern Era.* New York: Basic, 1993.

Ryan, Mary. *The Cradle of the Middle Class: The Family in Oneida County, New York, 1790–1865.* Cambridge: Cambridge University Press, 1981.

Sandeen, Ernest. *The Roots of Fundamentalism: British and American Millenarianism, 1800–1930.* Chicago: University of Chicago Press, 1970.

Schultze, Quentin J., ed. *American Evangelicals and the Mass Media.* Grand Rapids, Mich.: Academie, 1990.

Sedgwick, Eve, ed. Introduction to *Novel Gazing: Queer Readings in Fiction.* Durham, N.C.: Duke University Press, 1997.

Shibley, Mark A. *Resurgent Evangelicalism in the United States: Mapping Cultural Change Since 1970.* Columbia: University of South Carolina Press, 1996.

Smith, Christian. *American Evangelicalism: Embattled and Thriving.* Chicago: University of Chicago Press, 1998.

———. *Christian America? What Evangelicals Really Want.* Berkeley: University of California Press, 2000.

Smith, G. S. "The Men and Religion Forward Movement of 1911–1912: New Perspectives on Evangelical Social Concern and the Relationship between Christianity and Progressivism." *Westminster Theological Journal* 49 (1987): 91–118.

Stacey, Judith. "Can There Be a Feminist Ethnography?" *Women's Studies International Forum* 11.1 (1988): 21–27.

———. *Brave New Families: Stories of Domestic Upheaval in Late-Twentieth-Century America.* New York: Basic, 1991.

Stacey, Judith, and Susan Elizabeth Gerard. " 'We Are Not Doormats': The Influence of Feminism of Contemporary Evangelicals in the United States." In *Uncertain Terms: Negotiating Gender in American Culture,* edited by Faye Ginsburg and Anna Lowenhaupt Tsing. Boston: Beacon, 1990.

Stedman, Barbara. "The Word Become Fiction: Textual Voices from the Evangelical Subculture." Ph.D. diss., Ball State University, 1994.

Stoller, Paul. "Rationality." In *Critical Terms for Religious Study,* edited by Mark C. Taylor. Chicago: University of Chicago Press, 1998.

Stone, Jon R. *On the Boundaries of American Evangelicalism: The Postwar Evangelical Coalition.* New York: St. Martin's, 1997.

Strozier, Charles B. *Apocalypse: On the Psychology of Fundamentalism in America.* Boston: Beacon, 1994.

Strozier, Charles B., and Michael Flynn, eds. *The Year 2000: Essays on the End.* New York: New York University Press, 1997.

Taves, Ann. *Fits, Trances, and Visions: Experiencing Religion and Explaining Experience from Wesley to James.* Princeton, N.J.: Princeton University Press, 1999.

Taylor, Mark C., ed. *Critical Terms for Religious Studies.* Chicago: University of Chicago Press, 1998.

Tebbel, John. *History of Book Publishing in the United States,* 4 vols. New York: R. R. Bowker, 1972–1981.

Tompkins, Jane. *Sensational Designs: The Cultural Work of American Fiction, 1790–1860.* New York: Oxford University Press, 1985.

Van Leeuwen, M. S. "Servanthood or Soft Patriarchy? A Christian Feminist Looks at the Promise Keepers Movement." *Journal of Men's Studies* 5 (1997): 233–259.

Vaughn, Alden T., and Edward W. Clark, eds. *Puritans among the Indians: Accounts of*

Captivity and Redemption, 1676–1724. Cambridge, Mass.: Harvard University Press, 1981.

Viswanathan, Gauri. *Outside of the Fold: Conversion, Modernity, and Belief*. Princeton, N.J.: Princeton University Press, 1998.

Wacker, Grant. *Heaven Below: Early Pentecostals and American Culture*. Cambridge, Mass.: Harvard University Press, 2001.

Watt, David Harrington. *A Transforming Faith: Explorations of Twentieth-Century American Evangelicalism*. New Brunswick, N.J.: Rutgers University Press, 1991.

Weber, Eugene. *Apocalypses: Prophecies, Cults, and Millennial Beliefs through the Ages*. Cambridge, Mass.: Harvard University Press, 1999.

Weber, Timothy P. *Living in the Shadow of the Second Coming: American Premillennialism*. New York: Oxford University Press, 1979.

Welter, Barbara. *Dimity Convictions: The American Woman in the Nineteenth Century*. Columbus: University of Ohio Press, 1976.

Williams, Raymond. *Marxism and Literature*. Oxford: Oxford University Press, 1977.

Williams, Rhys, ed. *Promise Keepers and the New Masculinity*. Lexington, Ky.: Lexington, 2001.

Willis, Paul. *Learning to Labor: How Working-Class Kids Get Working-Class Jobs*. New York: Columbia University Press, 1977.

Wilson, John. *Public Religion in American Culture*. Philadelphia: Temple University Press, 1979.

Wimbush, Vincent L., ed. *African Americans and the Bible: Sacred Texts and Social Textures*. New York: Continuum, 2000.

Wojcik, Daniel. *The End of the World as We Know It: Faith, Fatalism, and Apocalypse*. New York: New York University Press, 1997.

Wolf, Margery. *A Thrice-Told Tale: Feminism, Postmodernism, and Ethnographic Responsibility*. Stanford, Calif.: Stanford University Press, 1992.

Wray, Matthew. "White Trash Religion." In *White Trash: Race and Class in America*, edited by Matthew Wray and Annalee Newitz. New York: Routledge, 1997.

Wuthnow, Robert. *The Restructuring of American Religion: Society and Faith since World War II*. Princeton, N.J.: Princeton University Press, 1988.

———. "The Cultural Turn: Stories, Logics, and the Quest for Identity in American Religion." In *Contemporary American Religion: An Ethnographic Reader*, edited by Penny Edgell Becker and Nancy L. Eisland. Walnut Creek, Calif.: Alta Mira, 1997.

Young, Iris Marion. *Justice and the Politics of Difference*. Princeton, N.J.: Princeton University Press, 1990.

Zamora, Lois Parkinson, ed. *The Apocalyptic Vision in America: Interdisciplinary Essays on Myth and Culture*. Bowling Green, Ohio: Bowling Green University Popular Press, 1982.

Index

Made in the USA
Coppell, TX
29 August 2021